The Future of
Corporate Globalization

The Future of
CORPORATE GLOBALIZATION

*From the Extended Order to the
Global Village*

Jeremiah J. Sullivan

Q

QUORUM BOOKS
Westport, Connecticut • London

Library of Congress Cataloging-in-Publication Data

Sullivan, Jeremiah J., 1940–
    The future of corporate globalization : from the extended order to the global
village / by Jeremiah J. Sullivan.
       p. cm
    Includes bibliographical references and index.
    ISBN 1–56720–516–X (alk. paper)
    1. International business enterprises. 2. Globalization—Economic aspects.
    3. Globalization—Social aspects. 4. Globalization—Political aspects. 5. International
economic relations. I. Title.
  HD2755.5.S857   2002
    338.8′8—dc21   2001048122

British Library Cataloguing in Publication Data is available.

Library of Congress Catalog Card Number: 2001048122
ISBN: 1–56720–516–X

First published in 2002

Quorum Books, 88 Post Road West, Westport, CT 06881
An imprint of Greenwood Publishing Group, Inc.
www.quorumbooks.com

Printed in the United States of America

The paper used in this book complies with the
Permanent Paper Standard issued by the National
Information Standards Organization (Z39.48–1984).

10 9 8 7 6 5 4 3 2 1

"Veniet tempus quo posteri nostri tam aperta nos nescisse mirentur."

[The day will yet come when posterity will be amazed that we remained ignorant of things that will seem to them so plain.]

—Lucius Annaeus Seneca, *Questiones Naturales*

CONTENTS

INTRODUCTION

"Can failure give birth to progress?" That was the theme debated in a Paris philosophy café in 1999 a few days after the World Trade Organization's (WTO) ministerial meeting collapsed under the weight of discord inside the Seattle Convention Center and the rioting outside. Trying to put a positive spin on things, WTO supporters noted that the 1982 ministerial meeting of the General Agreement on Tariffs and Trade (GATT) had failed to launch a new round of trade liberalization, but a round was indeed launched at the Uruguay meeting four years later. Similarly, Uruguay Round meetings in 1988 in Montreal and in 1990 in Brussels had failed to conclude an agreement. Yet a few years later an agreement was reached, and the WTO emerged to manage a newly energized move towards free flows of goods, services, capital, and information. Perhaps the 1999 failure was just the usual prelude to success.

I was out on the streets during the Battle of Seattle, and what I saw convinced me that this time failure was failure. None of the other GATT and WTO meetings had provoked such an uproar, and none had been graced by the visit of a U.S. president, Bill Clinton, bent on supporting the demonstrators outside rather than the ministers inside. What they wanted was what he said he wanted: a world less driven by economic exchange and more concerned with values, rights, and norms. Some demonstrators called for an end to globalization, which they saw as the relentless push into the world of giant, power-mad multinational corporations (MNCs). Others, union members mostly, wanted justice for workers everywhere and secure jobs for themselves in the United States. Environmentalists—most of them happy-go-lucky types but a few either enraged or in tears—were conspicuous, not just for the turtle costumes some of them wore but, for me at least, for the electronic gadgetry dangling from shoulders or hanging from necks. I saw hundreds of people with cell phones, video cameras, still cameras, and bullhorns. Many people were constantly on the phone. "Yeah, the pigs gassed us this morning. It was great. We'll probably get arrested this afternoon," said one young man, connected as never before to supporters worldwide. For the first time in history a martyr could take charge of documenting his sacrifice and in a sense thus create his destiny. It didn't matter that martyrdom would consist of a dose of mild pepper spray. (When Seattle police ran out of pepper spray, they asked for a loan from an affluent suburban force. "Sorry," they were allegedly told, "we only use oregano.") What mattered was that one could seemingly have it all: the splendid, heroic isolation of the one who stands up and stands out, as well as the comforting sense that one was rooted and embedded in a new global community whose support was every minute in evidence.

The Battle of Seattle raised issues for me which provide the themes of this book: the growing disenchantment with an economic way of thinking that both legitimizes and drives the globalization of business by multinationals and the slow but palpable coalescing of beliefs about order, sovereignty, justice, and morality into a new, world-encompassing communitarian paradigm. I believe that the economic model works for the most part in fostering better living standards and increased well-being, and that globalization makes the process go faster and spread out. What Seattle taught me was that lots of other people believe in a different model of well-being and see it as increasingly endangered. Some of these are attacking the old model or calling for its modification. Others seek radical changes, often in terms of such things as sustainable orderly development; the maintenance of national sovereignty and cultural identity; the replacement of economic exchange with justice-based alternatives emerging out of democratic debate; and the move away from a crude utilitarianism to a virtue ethics in business life.

At the beginning of the 1980s world foreign direct investment totaled about $40 billion. By 2000 the total was hovering around $1 trillion, most of it involving mergers and acquisitions. What this means is that businesses over the last twenty years or so have decided to develop production and marketing systems on a worldwide scale, and they are doing it by teaming up with or buying out other businesses. None of this could have happened without dramatic reductions in the barriers to the free flow of capital, goods, services, managerial talent, and information. These reductions were driven by policy changes, technological developments, and, above all, a shift in attitudes as the peoples of the world began to learn more about each other and became more tolerant and even curious about outsiders.

Globalization of business involves the rapid increase in cross-border trade and investment and the development by multinational corporations of integrated, rationalized worldwide operations. I refer to the economic ideas, theories, and ideologies guiding this process as the *extended order* (using Friedrich Hayek's terminology). I call the set of ideas proposed to augment or even replace the extended order the *Global Village* (a term first used by Marshall McLuhan). During the 21st century, multinational corporations will be challenged to change their ways of thinking about markets, property, workers, and customers as the world of capitalism and homo economicus (a 19th century phrase popularized by John Maynard Keynes' father) comes under attack from those energized by differing visions. What those challenges involve and what they may require of corporations over the century make up the issues discussed in the following chapters.

Economics is in part the study of how goods are produced and distributed in ways that maximize individual and societal well-being. However, right from the beginnings of the modern era, some economists have focused on the existence and causes of non-well-being—poverty. At the start of the 20th century, poverty was defined as a condition in which a household's earnings were not sufficient to cover food, rent, and other costs incurred to maintain physical existence. This was the definition throughout the century. By 2000, an expanded definition had emerged. Besides a lack of basic necessities, poverty now was being seen also as vulnerability and voicelessness in the world. To be poor was to lack purchasing power, security, and an ability to have some control over one's destiny. Implicitly, then, well-being was being redefined. The truly well-off enjoy good incomes; a stable, orderly existence; and meaningful personal autonomy. They can buy what they need in a society free of economic crises, and they can express their identity to the world in ways that ensure their needs and beliefs will be attended to. Led by the World Bank, which was responding to critics of the received economic wisdom, a new economic model is emerging in which what is maximized is social order, individual identity, and national sovereignty as well as household income. In a sense this movement constitutes a return to premodern and even ancient ideas of the good life as an ordered, coherent existence rather than one where the ability to satisfy transient, disorderly, and incoherent desires grew and grew.

An expanded well-being model of this kind is difficult to reconcile with globalization, which fosters increased purchasing power at the same time as trade and capital flow expansions may evoke dislocations and a feeling in individuals that they are in thrall to great powers and vast systems over which they have no control. For example, let's say a poor country suddenly is able to increase exports to the developed world as certain trade barriers come down. As earnings pile up, incomes rise and people start buying consumer goods that formerly they could not afford. However, the road and rail systems become clogged as more and more goods travel to and from the country's ports, which themselves soon become clogged. Air and water pollution increases, as does corruption as businessmen bribe officials for

access to transport hubs. Banks, flush with loan applications from both local and foreign investors, raise interest rates, which shuts out small farmers
from crop financing. These farmers abandon their lands and head for the
cities, where they have heard that job opportunities are increasing. All of
these strains and movements put pressure on authorities, who begin to exhibit ill-considered aggressive or perhaps nonresponsive behavior. The
people become distrustful and conspiratorial as they seek ways to hang on
to their expanded purchasing abilities. Soon cries are heard that the society
is becoming unjust, disorderly, immoral, and is losing control of its destiny.
When economists respond that economic growth eventually will reduce
poverty, improve health, fund education, and build needed infrastructure,
not everyone is willing to wait. Some will want to shut out the foreign traders and investors, while others will say that participation in the global economy should only occur if the needs for justice, order, virtue, and
sovereignty are met.

The anti-globalization and controlled globalization advocates in each
country are beginning to talk to each other and, with the support of
nongovernmental organizations (NGOs) and a variety of street demonstrators and student activists, to develop a rhetoric that is both hostile to the
reigning economic paradigm and, however haltingly and disorganized,
evocative of a new paradigm. In the new global paradigm, the Global Village, multinational corporations will be asked to see markets as places
where non-arm's-length exchanges occur among parties sharing common
commitments to order, justice, identity, autonomy, and virtue. A hint of
what may be coming emerged in 2000 when Coca-Cola announced its intention to become a "valued citizen" in the societies in which it does business. Although mostly focused on building political goodwill for
bottom-line reasons, the company made it clear that it was at least toying
with the idea of meliorism through norm-driven rather than interest-driven behavior. For example, it planned on making its vast distribution networks available to the movement of medical aid without
compensation. How far Coca-Cola and other companies could or would go
along Global Village lines was dependent on how serious the challenges
became. It is my premise here that those challenges are indeed going to be
quite serious and that multinational enterprises will be compelled to respond to them during the 21st century. If the Global Village model becomes
dominant during the century, we can expect the following impacts on corporations:

1. Corporate governance groups will be expanded to include NGO representatives
   and employees.
2. Goals of efficiency and profitability will be augmented by goals of justice, stability, virtue, and national identity.

3. Customer linkages will move away from arm's-length exchanges in markets towards obligation-enriched trust relationships in quasi-market conditions.

4. Global corporate strategies will become more risk-averse than they are now.

5. Employee relations will expand the model of work as a labor market exchange to include the idea of work as a meaningful, sense-making process of experiencing.

6. The craft of managing will be professionalized as managers become more like public servants than agents.

Whether or not these things will happen, why they may happen, and how they may happen are the subjects of this book.

CHAPTER 1

THE CHALLENGES OF GLOBALIZATION

When you get down, deep down, into the world of global business, it does-n't look like a Harvard Business School case. Consider Leung Tsor, the now-retired head of a recycling company that collected steel and alumi-num in the United States, exported the materials to Hong Kong, and sent them on to factories in southern China. There the materials were sorted, graded, processed, and compressed into cubic shapes. The cubes were loaded into trucks, driven to the port in Hong Kong, and exported to cus-tomers in Japan. This complex process mostly went along smoothly, except, that is, for encounters with criminal gangs along the road to Hong Kong.

Sometimes . . . they would throw a dead body on the road at night. When the driver stopped after hitting the body, they would say that he had killed the person and would demand money for not reporting to the police.

Mr. Leung's drivers had to carry large amounts of cash on each trip to deal with this expense.[1]

Now consider a man who wants to be known only as Mr. H. After Viet-nam opened up in the 1990s, he saw an investment opportunity focused on the expected increase in tourism as American veterans returned to view former battlegrounds. He opened five hamburger restaurants in Ho Chi Minh City. After profits disappeared because employees pilfered food and money, Mr. H. closed the restaurants and opened a beer distributorship. That folded after competitors hired handicapped veterans of Vietnam's war with Cambodia to harass customers. His final effort involved building a hotel. While he negotiated with officials on the amounts of bribes needed for various licenses, inflation made the prices of building materials soar, making the project uneconomic. Mr. H. gave up and returned to the United States. As the Vietnamese say, he had tried to "ride a crippled tiger" and failed.

Next, put yourself in the shoes of Zhang Jialing, Chairman and President of China Qingqi Group, a motorcycle manufacturer in Jinan, China. Mr. Zhang, who bears an uncanny resemblance to Mao Zedong, is saddled with 12,000 employees, most of whom he doesn't need. In 1997 he had a great idea. He would borrow money from the banks, change it into dollars, and invest in motorcycle production in Pakistan, where labor costs were lower and fewer employees were needed. He would export low-priced cycles to rapidly developing Southeast Asia and use the hard currency earnings to upgrade his factories in China to make them globally competitive. When he sought government permission, however, he was turned down and had to go back to what he had done for years: obtain loans that would never be paid back to pay workers who did no work. I have not spoken to Mr. Zhang since 1997, but he was right about the low-end motorcycle market in Southeast Asia. By 2001 it was booming. Perhaps he has somehow figured out how to go global, but one doubts it.

Finally, ask yourself how you would cope if you were one of the British managers working for Nakhodka Telecom (NT). Nakhodka Telecom, in the Russian Far Eastern cities of Nakhodka and Vladivostok, operates a digital overlay network with direct connection via the AsiaSat telecommunications satellite to Hong Kong. It provides a fully independent wireless system for its customers separate from the poorly functioning local telephone system. Ownership of NT is divided as follows:

- Cable and Wireless, a large British telecommunications company, 50 percent
- Comincom, a Moscow-based company formerly associated with the KGB, 20 percent
- Nakhodka Free Economic Zone, 14 percent
- Far East Shipping Co. (FESCO), 12 percent
- Individuals, 4 percent

In fact, as one of the British managers put it, "We have 50 percent participation, 100 percent capital commitment, and no control." Although various security pledges were given, the Russian side had gained control of the $9.5 million worth of equipment contributed by Cable and Wireless. In addition, the British firm had loaned NT a substantial sum, and it was up to the Russians whether or not the loan would be repaid.

Multinationals are not nearly as powerful as their critics say they are, and the experiences of Cable and Wireless' employees are illustrative.

- When the venture was formed a prominent resident of Nakhodka recommended a local bank, of which he happened to be the chairman. NT used the bank for several years, until its confidence in the institution grew. Finally it deposited $400,000, its largest deposit ever. The bank closed at once, bankrupt. Only a portion of the $400,000 was recovered.

- The British managers believed that NT was being used as a screen to cover various activities. They suspected that the Russians were bringing in more than electronic equipment in the containers that NT received from abroad. Moreover, when import licenses were needed, the Russians tended to offer bribes or to engage in complicated side deals with local officials.

- Many of the Russians hired by NT stayed only long enough to learn the business and to identify profitable niche markets that NT was not yet serving. They then quit and set up their own companies. In these conditions no one took any interest in growing the company.

As if difficult partners were not enough, NT was also at the mercy of government regulations. One of these regulations required banks not to dispense funds if the company was showing a loss! Apparently this rule was designed to force companies to show a profit so that the government could collect a profits tax. Often a company having trouble making a profit would forgo salaries for employees for one or two months. It then would show a profit and be able to receive funds to pay employees. This was the reason Russian workers frequently went several months without pay. NT had positive cash flow but showed a loss after deducting interest payments and depreciation. To get funds from its bank (presumably its new bank), it had to do some creative accounting to show a profit.

Even with the conditions described, NT had the potential to make money. Indeed the financial manager noted, "Give us control and we could be profitable in six months." With control the Britishers would cut the workforce of deadwood, getting rid of the hangers-on; work towards entering the lucrative cable market; and above all, begin making sales calls on businesses—the Russian salespeople did not make visits, deeming it beneath them.

Dreams about a profitable future helped the expatriates cope with the miserable conditions in Nakhodka, a former fishing port at one terminus of the Trans-Siberian Railway. One of the expatriates had had to be evacuated after he had been observed banging his head against a wall and "gibbering." The others endured food shortages in winter, no hot showers or baths ever, power cuts, and wretched housing arranged by one of the partners to help persuade the British to go home. At times the water supply would disappear, requiring expatriates to line up with local residents to fill their pots from water trucks. They were lonely—only six expatriates lived in the city and their families were back in Britain—and welcomed visitors. But few came.

The people who actually do the globalizing must cope with criminals, incompetent governments, and corrupt local partners. Sometimes, like the poor expatriate at Nakhodka Telecom, they go mad. It isn't a pretty picture, and it belies the rhetoric one hears about the relentless expansion of corporate power throughout the world. Businesses are crossing borders more than they ever have before, and both big and small companies are doing it. It's true that industrialized-country multinationals dominate, but none of them has the clout to work its will on the far-from-helpless peoples they encounter. All of this is by way of saying that globalization is throwing up challenges to the organizations and the people responsible for it. And it isn't just the day-to-day operations that are messy and full of uncertain dangers. The ideological and theoretical bases supporting the expansion of the reigning economic paradigm, which I call the *extended order*, are being called into question, and the elements of a new model are emerging and perhaps coalescing. In this book I call it the *Global Village* paradigm. The paradigm is not as dangerous as dead bodies in the road or as sad as crippled veterans screaming at customers on the sidewalk. It will not drive businesspeople insane as assignments to the Russian Far East might. It could be the best thing that ever happened to capitalism—or the worst. All we know is that the changes we call globalization are provoking questions, summonings to account, and even demands that everything halt and justify itself before proceeding. Globalization challenges are in the air, and in the 21st century they will become deafeningly loud and perhaps quite destabilizing.

THE NEW NEW WORLD ORDER

My great-grandmother lived through the Irish starvation of the late 1840s, and when she was very old she told a young boy in the village how she survived. Just before his death, he told me. She and the other children would sneak into the fields at night and cut the veins of rich farmers' cows, drinking the blood as it fell into their cupped hands. Famines and food shortages occurred frequently during the 19th century and even in the 20th, and the discipline of economics was called "dismal" because so many of its practitioners claimed that such miseries were inevitable. This kind of gloom no longer pervades the profession. In 2000 Professor D. Gale Johnson of the University of Chicago announced:

People today have more adequate nutrition than ever before and acquire that nutrition at the lowest cost in all human history. . . . The twentieth century can be remembered as the century in which hunger could have been eliminated and, to a significant extent, has been.[2]

Talk of this kind infuriates some people, who focus on the future rather than the past and compare where we are with where we ought to be rather than where we were. No amount of amelioration will satisfy them until some ideal point has been reached—and reached in a way that is just, orderly, moral, and sensitive to principles of individual autonomy, national sovereignty, and cultural identity. No matter how much economists, businessmen, and friendly politicians crow about the successes of the reigning economic order—and they have a right to crow—it is becoming clear that that order is being challenged and that disparate, hostile forces are beginning to coalesce into a new paradigm. The challenge and the likely nature of the new paradigm form the content of the following chapters.

In September 2000 protestors at the combined International Monetary Fund (IMF) and World Bank meetings in Prague shouted "No new world order!" as they burned a U.S. flag before the conference hall and trashed a McDonald's. Inside, Czech President Vaclav Havel called for "a restructuring of the entire system of values that forms the basis of civilization today." The new world order was seen as new only in the sense that the U.S.-style model of capitalism—free products markets, free flows of capital, unregulated labor markets, and respect for property rights—was seen as extending itself globally in the wake of U.S. post–Cold War hegemony. A kind of Global American was thought to be emerging, and people like President Havel didn't like it. Some of these people wanted to revive national identity while others wanted a Global Citizen to emerge. A few felt that the 21st century could accommodate both in a Global Village where individuals were embedded in the local yet integrated within the global.

Although Balkan wars and the pronouncements of Asian paternalists had convinced the public and many leaders that nationalism was on the rise, it in fact had diminished greatly since the 19th century. Vibrant nationalism thrives on an us-them dichotomy supported by entrenched stereotypes. Here are the major stereotypes of a hundred years ago. How many can you identify?

- John Bull
- Brother Jonathan
- Cousin Michel
- Colin Tampon
- Nic Frog
- Mossoo

In order, these refer to an Englishman, an American, a German, a Swiss, a Dutchman, and a Frenchman.[3] Few of us today have the vivid images of such stereotypes before us when we encounter foreigners. We do employ a few vague generalities (Japanese are group-oriented, Germans are efficient), but our commitment to them is weak. As Europe has integrated, Americans have traveled more, and Japanese have gaped at television images of Westerners, a sense of a common humanity has started to emerge. And with this sense has emerged the idea of the global citizen.

It isn't a new idea. In 1765, reflecting 18th-century enlightenment thinking, Oliver Goldsmith announced the threat to global citizenship:

We are now become so much Englishmen, Frenchmen, Dutchmen, Spaniards, or Germans, that we are no longer citizens of the world.... We no longer consider ourselves as the general inhabitants of the globe, or members of the grand society which comprehends the whole human kind.[4]

In 2000, Annie-Christine Habbard of the Paris-based International Federation of Human Rights echoed Goldsmith. "Ours is a new planetary citizenship, reflecting the fact that decisions have migrated from state level," she said.[5] Her employer was one of 350 citizens' groups and nongovernmental organizations (NGOs) taking part in the IMF-World Bank meeting in Prague. Many of those represented ardently nationalist perspectives, but, in their rhetoric at least, they were willing to talk about global citizenship just as Goldsmith did 235 years earlier. The global citizen still would be embedded in her local culture and care about such things as individual autonomy within a national identity, but she also would see herself as integrated in an organic, earthly whole linked by common concerns over justice, stability, and morality. Some NGOs and demonstrators in Seattle in 1999, Prague in 2000, and Genoa in 2001 wanted one thing while others were possessed of different visions, leading most observers to conclude that the forces arrayed against globalization or seeking a different kind of globalization were hopelessly fragmented and at odds with one another. This was true enough as far as it went, but my experiences on the gas-soaked streets of Seattle convinced me that thoughtful protestors were quite prepared to coalesce around criticism of the "new" economic order, and they shared sentiments regarding justice and other values, as well as an emerging sense that a global communitarianism was possible in a new new world order.

GLOBALIZATION EXPANSION AND INTEGRATION

Globalization is best thought of as two things: the *expansion of trade and investment* across borders and *increased linkages* so that a company's or a country's economic actions affect and are affected by economic, political, social, and cultural events in other societies. We had lots of expansion in the 19th century but not much linkage, so the current globalization, which is just getting started, is truly a new thing.[6] It is being driven by improvements in technology, communications, and transportation; by liberalization of national trade policies since World War II; by a stabilization of inflation rates at low levels (stable, low inflation reduces uncertainties and allows for global risk assessments and risk-taking by companies); by privatization, as governments sell off business assets, often to foreigners; and by deregulation in many countries that have encouraged market-based efficiencies. The impacts of globalization are many, but the most important is competition. In industries in the United States and elsewhere, entry and exit rates have increased, labor markets have heated up (a postwar labor market for middle managers in Japan hardly existed until the 1990s, for example), more new products are being developed and introduced than ever before, and the market for ownership (mergers and acquisitions) is vibrant.

All of this competition is pushing domestic and multinational corporations—who, being most visible, bear the brunt of criticism—into strategic responses that sometimes evoke hostility so that attacks on multinationals end up being attacks on globalization, and vice versa. If multinationals outsource labor-intensive production to a poor country and lay off home-country workers, they are accused of being unjust and fostering social disorder. If they form international strategic alliances to exchange technology for marketing knowledge, they are accused of threatening their country's "economic security." If they set up operations abroad and hire people straight off the farms, they are accused of fragmenting national culture. The list of accusations goes on but the process is clear. As late-20th-century technological and policy changes have pushed business across borders and linked operations and markets as never before, huge increases in competition are driving corporations to take steps that are rational, efficient, innovative, and clearly productive of national well-being. At the same time, if one so chooses, many of these steps and the globalization driving them can be perceived as unfair, destabilizing, insensitive to moral concerns, and threatening to sovereignty, identity, and autonomy.

WHICH CAPITALISM: GLOBALIZATION OR GLOBALISATION?

In the 1960s European opponents of the Vietnam War took to spelling *America* as *Amerika* to suggest a Kafkaesque alternative image to the last-best-hope-of-mankind rhetoric of U.S. admirers. Today we are seeing some Europeans proclaiming *globalisation* as the spread of a capitalism contrasting sharply with the *globalization* led by the United States. Where the Americans focus on individual liberty and the creative powers of competition and self-interest, the Europeans advocate collective action, cooperation, and social rather than selfish values. Both sides agree on the importance of market-based exchange and property rights, but the Europeans argue that transaction costs would rise to unbearable levels in a capitalist system without social norms evoking trust and hindering opportunism. Europeans say that global capitalism cannot develop unless their version of it prevails, a version in which a company is a community rather than a collection of interests; an industry is a collaborative effort rather than a set of competing firms; customers have non-arm's-length relationships with sellers; banks finance operations and ask for growth rather than stockholders asking for profitability; things like culture and nature are thought of as endogenous rather than exogenous; and the prime goal of society is producing quality jobs rather than quality goods.[7]

Because capitalist globalisation of the European sort is less flexible and more inefficient than globalization American-style, its advocates tend to be less accommodating than their easygoing American cousins. The Europeans see the 21st century as a battleground in which their socioeconomic system must win out or die. Americans, in contrast, have worried not about the global struggle over varieties of capitalism—all varieties are welcome and may the best man win—but instead have anguished in the last fifty years over whether or not capitalism would survive totalitarian and command economy threats. When these collapsed with the end of the Cold War, Americans entered a threat vacuum. They are not yet ready to see globalization versus globalisation as the coming struggle. From their perspective, there is no reason they should, and the U.S. responses to the old world's ravings about the evil of the "Anglo-Saxon model" and the saintliness of the "third way" often are indifference or bemused bewilderment. When Americans do manage to get offended, they simply and silently point to the high European Union (EU) unemployment rate and go on about their global business. A better reaction would be to recognize that the Europeans and their potential supporters in Asia are quite emotional about these things. They are going to get louder and louder in this century in attacking the globalization model and advocating a different way. The Americans should be asking themselves three questions. Will the European and Asian globalisation advocates come together in joint opposition to globalization? Will these opponents somehow find common ground with the haters of any kind of global paradigm? And, if they do, what will their agenda look like and what will it mean? The people who regularly trash McDonald's stores in Seattle, Paris, and Prague don't seem to have much in common, yet there they are in their black scarves and turtle costumes.

On a more fundamental level, globalization (the spelling used in this book reflects both convention and authorial ideology) in the 21st century will be driven by answers to two other questions. What is well-being? When should it be enjoyed? Early economists and political thinkers defined wealth—presumably the source of well-being—as the accumulation of gold and commodities in the present. Later on, 19th- and 20th-century writers emphasized wealth as production capacity and focused on its ability to yield future increases in goods and services.[8] This contrasting of wealth and well-being in the present versus in the future has reemerged today, although in a different form. Also contrasted today are different ideas of what wealth-produced well-being is. The American or Anglo-Saxon model, which I call the extended order, focuses on the accumulation of wealth as a factor of production of future goods and services, with well-being associated with increased individual control over the satisfaction of material needs and wants. The European or Third Way model, the precursor of the emerging Global Village, emphasizes wealth accumulation and production factors in terms of present well-being, defined broadly as coherent, communal existence in a just, ordered, moral world. The extended order's citizen is happy because she expects her purposes to be attained. The Global Villager is happy because her present existence is value-driven and meaningful. The debate over globalization verses globalisation, then, really is a controversy over the economic paradigm that should guide us for the rest of this century. As it currently is unfolding, globalization means expansion, linkages, competition, specialization, efficiency, and higher incomes. However, forces are coalescing that will redefine it as community, coherence, connectedness, values, and enhanced stability. In one model, corporations are the agents of turbulent change. In the other, they are the servants of village-like stability. They really cannot be both, but they may have to try.

THE ARGUMENT: FOR

Globalization as cross-border economic expansion and integration has two kinds of supporters, those who like its development along current lines and those who want it modified and managed. Opponents of globalization, such as Patrick Buchanan in the United States, want to throw up trade and investment barriers and to drain corporations of the power to integrate. All groups tend to make up long lists of advantages or disadvantages, and it all gets very complicated and confusing. In 2000, a Japanese newspaper asked 217 Tokyo managers if globalization affected their lives and futures. Over 52 percent answered "don't know."[9] Supporters argue that globalization improves peoples' lives. Critics and opponents say it threatens national identity, fosters disorder, demolishes the moral fabric of a society, and violates principles of justice.

Does globalization foster increased well-being? The answer is probably yes, but in a roundabout sort of way. What really tends to push up the standard of living in a society is reductions in the cost of production. These raise profitability levels, which in turn attract increased investment, which evokes economic growth, rising incomes, and increased well-being.[10] Cross-border activities contribute to this process in several ways. As a country's exports increase, its big firms may develop cost-reducing economies of scale, and export earnings may be used to purchase machinery fostering further efficiencies. The ensuing economic growth may attract foreign investors, who bring better technology into the country and train local people in its use. These and similar learning processes will bring out further unit-cost decreases.[11] However, none of this is inevitable. Increased exporting may not lead to economies of scale, or if it does, the pressure on infrastructure (ports, roads, and rail lines) may lead to offsetting transportation cost increases. If export earnings do increase, they may be taxed away by a government led by corrupt bureaucrats eager to get their hands on the money so that they can spirit it away to Swiss bank accounts. Or companies themselves may use their earnings in frivolous ways. If foreigners come in, they may compete for skilled labor and bank loans, thus raising the costs of both. Or they may upset delicate social networks, leading to instability and costly unrest. Even more troubling is that element of globalization based on integration. A major and important foreign investor in a country may, in response to events in other countries, suddenly pull back and even leave the local market. For example, in 2000 Ford, probably because of a cost-increasing tire scandal in the United States, withdrew as the buyer of giant but bankrupt Daewoo in South Korea, thus putting that country's recovery from the Asian Crisis at risk.

In the current economic model, increased well-being is the result of productivity increases which are the result of innovation, especially innovation that pushes unit costs down. But why should innovation suddenly increase in a society? The model offers one overwhelming answer: increased competition born of globalization. As trade and investment flows increase and multinational corporations enter markets in greater numbers, competitive forces are unleashed that drive prices down and compel businesses to find ways to lower costs. Moreover, in addition to competition in product markets, capital markets competition forces technological progress. As domestic firms see the flow of savings—the source of their investment funds—begin to cross a nation's borders in search of higher returns, they desperately innovate to drive costs down and profitability up.[12] Increased efficiency and productivity foster low inflation and capital inflows rather than outflows, thus setting off a growth cycle and better living standards.

This globalization-competition-innovation-productivity improvements-and-well-being increases model sounds good, but it is too soon to tell if it legitimizes globalization. One problem is that enormous innovation occurred in the first part of the 20th century, during which globalization mostly was going backwards. The IMF admits that "the cause of such an acceleration in technical progress remains largely a mystery."[13] If it could not have been globalization, then what was it? The IMF suggests several answers, including laws defending an innovator's property rights, well-functioning domestic markets that increase the potential gains from innovation and productivity growth, good education systems to train engineers, and high-quality communication systems so the innovators and engineers can learn from each other.[14] Basically, this approach says that throwing open the borders and integrating into the world economy might be helpful, but what really drives better living is better institutions within a nation. If globalization is to be really useful, it will not be through fostering greater competition but instead through institution-building as people exposed to the world learn how to develop better legal, economic, education, and other systems.

THE ARGUMENT: AGAINST

The positive effects of globalization, then, may be real though not necessarily benign if they are also associated with increases in ruthless competition. And lots of things can go wrong, so that positive impacts are not inevitable. However, if globalization encourages learning and institution-building, then it can evoke development which is both sweet and useful—*dulce et utile*. American globalizers tend to focus on increased competition, while European and some Asian supporters stress institutional development. Of course, both routes to well-being can exist at the same time. It is just a matter of emphasis. Opponents, in contrast, see both competition and institutional change as disorderly, unjust, immoral, and threatening to sovereignty. They want either a halt to globalization or a different, much constrained globalization.

We can define a nation as a social rather than a political artifact rooted in tribal and cultural ways of making sense of the world, or we can see it as a state built, we hope, on a structure of laws and democratic processes. The first is a closed society, according to Karl Popper in *The Open Society and Its Enemies* (written during the high tide of National Socialism in 1942–1943), whose existence depends on barriers defending an us-them mentality. The second is an open society, a "cosmopolitan" entity.[15] Closed society defenders hate globalization, seeing it as a threat to national identity.

As the powers of sovereign states wither, those of multinational corporations wax. As national cultures become little more than consumer preferences, so companies become ever more cosmopolitan in their corporate cultures.[16]

According to John Gray in *False Dawn* (1998), globalization really is "de-localization," the uprooting of local cultures as the nation's peoples become immersed in and dependent on world market processes that take no account of history and social relations. The result is a loss of identity and national autonomy.

In response to this kind of talk, some open-society globalizers like Thomas Friedman point out that

individuals become empowered, even super-empowered. That is, their ability to gather information themselves, earn a living and assert their will directly—as individuals—greatly increases thanks to globalization.[17]

Anti-globalists are not liberals, focused on the individual as the prime unit of society. For them an individual existence, no matter how much under the control of the will, is meaningless unless it is embedded in a coherent network of cultural and social connections. What is the point of globalization giving a person power, they say, if at the same time it renders his life absurd.

John Gray argues that as de-localization progresses and sovereignty fades, a "disordered, anarchic capitalism" floods across a country's borders in the person of multinational corporations. These corporations produce, along with goods, social dislocation and political instability as industries and livelihoods wax and wane and currency values soar and plummet. Jobs become insecure and, perhaps, class warfare breaks out. This is the position of Patrick Buchanan in *The Great Betrayal* (1998). On the one side are the beneficiaries of globalization, the "bankers, lawyers, diplomats, investors, lobbyists, academics, journalists, executives, professionals, and high-tech entrepreneurs." On the other are the resentful losers. "White-collar and blue-collar, they work for someone else, many with hands, tools, and machines in factories soon to be hoisted onto the chopping block of some corporate downsizer in some distant city or foreign country."[18] Both Gray and Buchanan portray a nation as a land of static people, unable or unwilling to move from goods to service production, from one city to another, from one cultural value to another, or from one identity to another. With this kind of delicacy as the guiding protocol of its makeup, one wonders how the human race has survived as long as it has. Nevertheless, critics are right in pointing out that globalization affects sovereignty and stability. Indeed, World Bank economists have concluded that the country crises in Mexico (1995), East Asia (1997), Brazil (1998), and Russia (1998) were in part brought on by "such external factors as terms of trade shocks, volatile capital flows, and contagion in international capital markets."[19] The extended order, it seems, is not always orderly.

Besides threatening identity and stability, globalization is accused of violating principles of justice, especially if one defines justice in terms of equality. For example, a number of critics have claimed that increased capital mobility will allow investors to seek out countries with the lowest corporate taxes, thus forcing other governments eager to hold on to capital to lower theirs. The result will be immiseration as authorities lose the funding to meet full employment and welfare goals. There is a glimmer of truth seeping out from this assertion in that European investors have been flooding into the United States, in part because of its lower taxes, and Germany is beginning to reduce taxes in response. But to claim that this process has "made the central policies of European social democracy unworkable," as John Gray does, is something of a stretch.[20] However, if one justice argument falters, others are ready to take its place. Globalization will be accused of fostering the unjust, undemocratic "patriarchy" (a favorite term of street protestors) of multinational corporations, whose own governance systems unjustly deprive workers and the people—as represented by NGOs—of a say. Until these corporations can be reined in, justice advocates call for a halt to their worldwide expansion and integration.

Finally, global markets allegedly pressure people into a consumerism that demolishes virtues such as "saving, civic pride, respectability, and family values," among others. These norms become "profitless museum pieces. They are bits of bric-a-brac dusted off for public display from time to time by the Right-wing media, but having few uses in an economy founded on ephemera."[21] In sum, then, globalization's enemies march to the tune of several different drummers. Some fear de-localization and yearn for the closed-society paradigm. Others see a coming instability and even class warfare if the globalizing process continues. The cause of justice may be betrayed as multinational corporate powers increase, and perhaps moral value will give way to cash value.

PARADIGM CONFLICT IN THE 21ST CENTURY

Hard-core critics of globalization often are oblivious to its benefits because they reject the extended order economic paradigm on which it rests. While they do not yet have an alternative model to replace it, communism and various versions of national socialism having failed, they know that it will emphasize identity, justice, order, and virtue rather than utility, purposefulness, risk, interests, and gain. Consider what they are rejecting. Since 1950 gross domestic product (GDP) per capita increased 3.1 times in the developed and 2.9 times in the developing world, with the ghastly exception of sub-Saharan Africa, where virtually no change in well-being occurred. Life expectancy in the developing countries in 1950 averaged forty-one years. Now it is sixty-two—not as high as the seventy-four years of the developed nations, but a big improvement nonetheless. Similarly, developing country adult literacy rates went from 40 percent in 1950 to 70 percent in 1998.[22] These gains probably are associated with the liberalization of and increases in cross-border trade and investment during the last few decades of the 20th century. This is in accord with a globalization scenario in which people eking out a bare subsistence living as agricultural workers suddenly get a chance to earn a wage by producing export goods in a factory financed by foreign investors and to spend their earnings on imported products of great benefit to their well-being. Other people, seeing this increased purchasing power, start local businesses and create more jobs and spending. Government tax revenues rise and schools are built. Soon people become more productive and their wages increase even more. A spiraling upward ensues, until incomes in most trading nations equalize. General health begins to improve and people live longer.

For critics and those moving towards an alternative paradigm, it doesn't matter whether or not the above scenario is true. For them globalization "dissolves all customary relationships, tears the fabric of kinship and corrodes the web of human togetherness."[23] This is from Jeremy Seabrook, who writes about the seamy side of life in developing nations. In his view an improvement in life expectancy brought about by increased trade and investment will merely increase the time people must spend as miserable wage slaves in service to multinational corporations. People like Mr. Seabrook, and there are lots of them, criticize the economic model for not being value-oriented and communitarian. Remarkably, a number of economists agree. Cultural values, norms, rules of thumb, and kin-like relationships can be just as influential on individual decision-making as naked self-interest. Workers tend to treat their level of pay as both a symbolic affirmation of their worth in the organizational community as well as an element in an arm's-length labor market exchange. Egalitarian societies are no less productive than those less communal. And the organization of small production and distribution communities may be just as important as the play of supply and demand within large, impersonal markets.[24] Research of this sort calls some of the key elements of microeconomic philosophy into question and invites debates on new approaches.

In its influential *World Development Report* (2000), the World Bank saw the light—or wrapped itself in new kinds of fog, according to some—and proclaimed that the course of economic development should involve not just movements to increase income and security but also community-building and empowerment, so that the poor of the globe become price-makers like the giant multinationals rather than passive and increasingly desperate price-takers. More radical thinkers than World Bank economists see this empowerment as rooted in the weakening of corporations. They ask us to imagine in the 21st century

new corporate charters (created by the initiative process) that might, for example, forbid corporations to leave a community, to buy other corporations, to take tax deductions for advertising campaigns, to harm others without paying a criminal price, or to pay salaries to top managers that are widely disproportionate to those paid to line workers.[25]

According to Jerry Mander, the activists in this new, empowered global community will be "environmentalists, human rights groups, workers' unions, small businesses, consumer groups, small farmers, and the new economic thinkers." Mostly these people have a bewildering variety of agendas, but if they coalesce in a new or altered economic paradigm around the values of communal identity, justice, order, and virtue, they could indeed become quite powerful. In this book I am calling the emerging model the Global Village, but in current discussions one hears talk about "diversity capitalism" and the "stakeholder model." Some of the things all models have in common are the belief that trust rather than contract should dominate economic relations; markets can and should work differently in different places; social capital is more important than financial capital; technological development should be an effect rather than a cause of institutional structures and political process; a stable, moral life is a better indicator of well-being than a materially rich life; justice is as much equality as it is fair treatment; committed conservation should dominate efficient allocation; and nothing is, can be, or should be done at arm's length.

MULTINATIONAL CORPORATIONS AND GLOBAL BUSINESS

If globalization guided by the extended order model continues along current lines, trade and investment will expand, integrated global operations will emerge, competition and innovation will increase, productivity leaps will occur, and incomes will rise. But along with expansion and integration engineered by huge multinational corporations will come turbulence; perceived threats to autonomy, identity, and sovereignty; a sense of growing inequality as some people benefit before others; outcries against "crony capitalism"; anxiety over declining resources and environmental degradation; and complaints that a virtue ethics is being replaced by a crude utilitarian calculus. In Mexico, multinationals are accused of fostering U.S. hegemony. In Canada, Canadian culture is at risk. Some Japanese worry about foreigners threatening racial security, while in France cuisine and *gloire* are endangered by corporate Yankees. Outsiders might be overly critical of the *bumiputra* state in Malaysia or rigid "family values" in Singapore. In India and China, history is seen as potentially repeating itself as 21st-century European commercial forces seek footholds the way they did in the 18th and 19th centuries.

Here are the world's biggest publicly held companies as of August 15, 2000, in terms of:

	Market Value	1999 Revenues	1999 Profit
1.	General Electric	Exxon Mobil	General Electric
2.	Intel	Wal-Mart Stores	Citigroup
3.	Cisco Systems	Royal Dutch/Shell	Microsoft
4.	Microsoft	Toyota Motor	Royal Dutch/Shell
5.	Exxon Mobil	General Electric	SBC Communications[26]

Only one, GE, appears on all three lists. Intel and Cisco are highly valued even though revenues and profits are relatively modest, and Citigroup has huge profits but not a top-ranked market value. Data like these suggest that even the experts on Wall Street and in London have trouble figuring out what to make of the giant multinational corporations, and if they have trouble, imagine how the man in the street and the turtle costume-clad street demonstrator react. Some people see the multinationals as immensely powerful and inhuman in their practices, while a case can be made that most of them really are rather weak and credulous responders to whatever pressures happen to be pervasive at any one time.

The term "multinational" actually encompasses four types of firms doing cross-border business. International companies focus on domestic sales and exporting. Global corporations produce highly standardized products (Levi Strauss jeans or television sets, for example) for global markets within highly complex, rationalized, worldwide manufacturing operations. Transnational companies do this too, but they also try to localize products in terms of quality, price, and marketing. Genuine multinationals (MNCs), by far the biggest group, are highly decentralized, with semiautonomous country operations reporting back to a headquarters staff made up of financial analysts and accountants. In 1920 U.S. Steel's multinational operations were supervised from a New York office with room for the boss, his secretary, and four or five assistants (I've seen it). A multinational headquarters today sometimes is in what some call derisively "the big glass house," where it employs thousands of people. Most of these do not do much, as is revealed every few years when massive downsizings occur with no appreciable effect on operations. However, most MNCs are so decentralized that the chances of anyone knowing the answer to the question "Do you have a Bangkok office?" are slim—unless the Thai country manager fails to repatriate some profits every so often. Nevertheless, even with all this bumbling, the multinationals add value to the world and will continue to do so in the 21st century.

What worries critics are the transnational and global corporations, such as General Electric, Ford, and General Motors, who really are big and powerful. They are few in number, a fact that ought to reduce the current sense of menace some have about them, but use of the label "multinational" in referring to them evokes the impression that thousands of alleged villains are on the global march, when only a few score are. Critics mostly are not being careless or disingenuous here, since the globals really are influential (although in my view not especially villainous) and the multinationals could be globals and transnationals in the making. In fact, globalization, for good or ill, can be defined as the shift of multinationals (decentralized cross-border exporters and producers) into multinationals (encompassing all types, especially a much larger group of transnationals and globals). For convenience, I will use "multinationals," but the complexity of the concept should not be downplayed. When extended order defenders talk about multinationals functioning in highly competitive markets that are getting more competitive, they are speaking about the majority of cross-border companies. When critics talk about all-powerful multinationals fostering instability and threatening sovereignty, they are referring to a current few, and a potentially future many, corporations.

Multinationals are driven by expectations based on observed emotions, fads, trends, and prices.[27] Thus they are servants to the perceptions and feelings of customers, suppliers, regulators, journalists, and competitors, as well as to their own tendency towards risky actions based on upbeat assessments, or what John Maynard Keynes called "animal spirits." This is what was known in the 1920s as the "oil-for-the-lamps-of-China" syndrome. There were then about 800 million Chinese, and each of them had a small oil lamp that was filled once a day with four ounces of oil. That's 3.2 billion ounces daily. Since China had very little oil and no refining capacity, it would have to import any oil it desired. In the past people simply went to bed at sunset, but, according to 1920s modernists, they would want to stay up and read or listen to the radio. They would want the oil, and American corporations would stand ready to deliver it. We're all going to be rich! Update "oil for the lamps of China" to the 1990s, and you get Coca-Cola, Eastman Kodak, and General Motors, all of which have poured over a billion dollars each into the Peoples Republic of China.

It is easy to see these investments as faddish, ill thought out, and burdened by "something-will-turn-up" optimism. But it is just as easy to see them the way critics do, as carefully developed plans to build power bases within societies ripe for exploitation and degradation. The optimism model, in my view, is a major part of the globalization process. As competition forces corporate executives to become change agents, they convince themselves that the future will be better than the present. They forge on, and then they are compelled to make something of the changes that they have effected. Coca-Cola already is starting to make money in China after a decade of failure, and General Motors may yet figure out how to sell Buicks in Shanghai. Nevertheless, critics and emerging Global Villagers have a right to worry and complain. After all, corporations like to think of themselves as being run by relentless opportunity-seekers, exquisitely tuned in to every possibility in every corner of an imaginary globe especially squared for simulation purposes. This image of impersonal, profit-and-power-driven human calculating machines is picked up on by anxious outsiders and used to support their worries about globalization. The result, as we will see in the following chapters, is that the critique of globalization is both an attack on the reigning economic paradigm, which includes hostility to multinationals as active purveyors of the model across borders, and a so-far disorganized set of proposed alternatives revolving around ideas about sovereignty and identity, justice, stability, and virtue.[28]

The globalization process, then, involves the expansion and integration of business across borders in a way that in some respects is new and only just beginning. It is associated with dramatic increases in competition, equally dramatic increases in material well-being, and a good deal of turbulence. The big and small corporations carrying out the process, the multinationals, are having a tough time of it; and most have nowhere near the power critics award them. The economic ideology that guides the thinking of corporate executives is under severe attack, and a new model is beginning to emerge. The Global Village model's supporters are coalescing around (1) a disdain for the extended order's focus on exchange driven by desires, the pleasure principle, reasoned calculation, and property rights; and (2) a belief that values rather than interests should (or should be made to) guide market or market-like behavior. The idea of a world citizen is being revived after 250 years of rejection by nationalism; she is a Global Villager integrated into a world community yet rooted in local culture and identity. What she allegedly wants is to live a coherent, meaningful existence in a just, ordered, moral world. The challenges facing 21st century multinationals will involve a calling into question of the reigning capitalist paradigm and the gradual formation of a new paradigm centered on ideas of identity, sovereignty, autonomy, justice, order, and virtue. These challenges are set out in the following chapters.

NOTES

1. The stories told in this section are from my book, *Exploring International Business Environments* (Needham Heights, MA: Pearson Publishing, 1999) and from my own interviews.

2. D. Gale Johnson, "Population, Food, and Knowledge," *American Economic Review*, 2000, 90(1), 1.

3. According to E. Cobham Brewer, *The Dictionary of Phrase and Fable* (New York: Avenel Books, 1978). Originally published in 1870 in Great Britain, Brewer's book is an inestimable resource. For example, according to Brewer, in 1721 Britain levied a fine of five pounds on any woman found wearing a calico dress to discourage the purchase of foreign-made calico. Failure to pay resulted in confinement in a debtor's prison, tantamount to a death sentence. We can only imagine the encounters that must have occurred on London's streets as gangs employed by British cloth manufacturers tried to drag off female violators to a magistrate. Eventually authorities realized that the tariff, which was mostly used as a source of government revenue, was a less destabilizing way to protect national interests (which of course did not include the well-being of women).

4. Oliver Goldsmith, "National Prejudices," *Essays*, 1765. Reprinted in H. Peterson, ed., *50 Great Essays* (New York: Pocket Books, 1954), p. 97. As we will see in the last chapter, Goldsmith hated global trade because it destabilized local communities. But he believed that one could be both an English village dweller *and* a global citizen. This position will be revived in the 21st century.

5. Quoted in the *New York Times*, September 24, 2000, Section 4, 1.

6. See M.V. Makhija, K. Kim, and S.D. Williamson, "Measuring Globalization of Industries Using a National Industry Approach: Evidence Across Five Countries and Over Time," *Journal of International Business Studies*, 1997, 28 (9), 679–710. According to their data, increases in expansion and linkages both are occurring in most manufacturing industries. See also Herman Schwartz, *States versus Markets, the Emergence of a Global Economy* (New York: St. Martin's Press, 2000).

7. For discussions on the different versions of capitalism, see Richard Whitley, *Divergent Capitalisms*. (Oxford: Oxford University Press, 1999) and Richard Bronk, *Progress and the Invisible Hand* (Boston: Little, Brown, 1998). The "Anglo-Saxon" model is critiqued and found wanting in Ronald Dore, *Stock Market Capitalism, Welfare Capitalism, Japan and Germany versus the Anglo-Saxons* (Oxford:

Oxford University Press, 2000). The "third way" model is the theme of Adair Turner, *Just Capital: The Liberal Economy* (London: Macmillan, 2001) and Anthony Giddens, *The Global Third Way Debate* (London: Polity, 2001).

8. See Mark Perlman and Charles R. McCann, Jr., *The Pillars of Economic Understanding, Ideas and Traditions* (Ann Arbor: University of Michigan Press, 1998), especially p. 191. This excellent book describes the major paradigms ("patristic approaches") of economic thought.

9. Minoru Naito, "Japan greets changes with cautious optimism," *Nikkei Weekly*, 24 July 2000, 3. Of those with an opinion, most thought globalization was a positive thing, especially in giving consumers lower prices and more choices.

10. Arnold C. Harberger, "A Vision of the Growth Process," *American Economic Review*, 1998, 88 (1), 1–33. Harberger emphasizes increases in productivity, profitability, and investment as all required for growth.

11. The importance of economics of scale and learning in fostering productivity increases and growth is described in Eric Bartelsman and Mark Doms, "Understanding Productivity: Lessons from Longitudinal Microdata," *Journal of Economic Literature*, 2000, 38 (3), 569–594.

12. See the discussion of capital mobility's impacts in the IMF's *World Economic Outlook*, May 2000 (Washington, DC: IMF, 2000), 168 ff. Along with the positive effects of capital flows, the IMF recognizes the instability capital flows can cause.

13. Ibid., 153.

14. Ibid., 153 ff. Also see Robert J. Barro and Xavier Sala-i-Martin, *Economic Growth* (Cambridge, MA: MIT Press, 1999) and Hernando de Soto, *The Mystery of Capital* (New York: Basic Books, 2000).

15. Popper refers to the "cosmopolitanism" of the open society in *The Open Society and Its Enemies, Hegel and Marx* (Princeton: Princeton University Press, 1971), 49.

16. John Gray, *False Dawn, The Delusions of Global Capitalism* (New York: The New Press, 1998), p. 67. Mr. Gray claims that he is not against globalization, only the American-led version of it. His remarks make it clear, however, that he is hostile to the global expansion and integration of markets and businesses.

17. Thomas L. Friedman, "A Russian Dinosaur," *New York Times*, 5 September 2000, A 31.

18. Patrick J. Buchanan, *The Great Betrayal* (New York: Little, Brown and Company, 1998), 6–7.

19. World Bank, *World Development Report 2000 / 2001, Attacking Poverty* (New York: Oxford University Press, 2000), 162. With this book, the World Bank seems to have begun a retreat from wholehearted support for globalization.

20. See Gray, *False Dawn*, 89.

21. Ibid., 38.

22. The World Bank each year collects and publishes hundreds of pages of data on these topics, and economists regularly summarize them. The economists' enemies ignore the mostly positive trends and focus on the negative, if indeed they bother consulting data at all. See Richard A. Easterlin, "The Worldwide Standard of Living Since 1800," *Journal of Economic Perspectives*, 2000, 14 (1), 7–26. In the same issue, Paul Krugman defends the U.S.-style extended order in "Can America Stay on Top?" (169–175). If other nations adopt the reigning paradigm, he says,

they eventually will have U.S.-level incomes. This equalization will be good for both the world and Americans.

23. Jeremy Seabrook, "Nasty, brutish, and long," *Financial Times*, 14 April 2000, 17.

24. See Samuel Bowles, "Endogenous Preferences: The Cultural Consequences of Markets and Other Economic Institutions," *Journal of Economic Literature*, 1998, 36 (1), 75–111; Joseph Henrich, "Does Culture Matter in Economic Behavior? Ultimatum Game Bargaining Among the Machiguenga of the Peruvian Amazon," *American Economic Review*, 2000, 90 (4), 973–979; Richard Freeman, "Single-peaked v. Diversified Capitalism: The Relation Between Economic Institutions and Outcomes," Working Paper 7556, 2000, National Bureau of Economic Research; Truman F. Bewley, *Why Wages Don't Fall During a Recession* (Cambridge: Harvard University Press, 2000); Daniel Kahneman and Amos Tversky, eds., *Choices, Values and Frames* (Cambridge: Cambridge University Press, 2000); Harold Lydall, *A Critique of Orthodox Economics: An Alternative Model* (New York: St. Martin's Press, 1998).

25. Jerry Mander, "Facing the Rising Tide." In Jerry Mander, ed., *The Case Against the Global Economy* (San Francisco: Sierra Club Books, 1996), 16.

26. Data are from the World Business Rankings in the *Wall Street Journal*, 25 September 2000, R 24.

27. Ideas about expectations and trends driving corporate decisions in dynamic rather than static markets are becoming influential among economists, according to Robert M. Solow, *Monopolistic Competition and Macroeconomic Theory* (Cambridge: Cambridge University Press, 1998). In contrast, some economists worry that huge corporations, beholden to no one, may emerge in some industries prone to winner-take-all markets (where first movers enjoying economics of scale and near-zero variable unit costs expand until they become monopolies). See Carl Shapiro and Hal R. Varian, *Information Rules: A Strategic Guide to the Network Economy* (Boston: Harvard Business School Press, 1999). The latter group, no matter how small and shifting, terrifies critics of the extended order.

28. According to Britain's Ethical Investment Research Service (EIRIS), attacks on multinationals cover twenty-six topics, from Alcohol, Animals, and Arms to Tobacco, Waste Disposal, and Water Pollution. The full list is available from EIRIS at ethics@eiris.win-uk.net.

BIBLIOGRAPHY

Barro, Robert J., and Xavier Sala-i-Martin. *Economic Growth*. Cambridge, MA: MIT Press, 1999.

Bartelsman, Eric, and Mark Doms. "Understanding Productivity: Lessons from Longitudinal Microdata." *Journal of Economic Literature* 2000, 38(3), 569–594.

Bewley, Truman F. *Why Wages Don't Fall During a Recession*. Cambridge, MA: Harvard University Press, 2000.

Bowles, Samuel. "Endogenous Preferences: The Cultural Consequences of Markets and Other Economic Institutions." *Journal of Economic Literature*, 1998, 36(1), 75–111.

Brewer, E. Cobham. *The Dictionary of Phrase and Fable*. New York: Avenal Books, 1978.

Bronk, Richard. *Progress and the Invisible Hand*. Boston: Little, Brown, 1998.

Buchanan, Patrick J. *The Great Betrayal*. New York: Little, Brown, 1998.

De Soto, Hernando. *The Mystery of Capital*. New York: Basic Books, 2000.

Dore, Ronald. *Stock Market Capitalism, Welfare Capitalism, Japan and Germany versus the Anglo Saxons*. Oxford: Oxford University Press, 2000.

Easterlin, Richard A. "The Worldwide Standard of Living Since 1800." *Journal of Economic Perspectives*, 2000, 14(1), 7–26.

Freeman, Richard. "Single-peaked v. Diversified Capitalism: The Relation Between Economic Institutions and Outcomes." National Bureau of Economic Research Working Paper 7556, 2000.

Friedman, Thomas L. "A Russian Dinosaur." *New York Times*, 5 September 2000, A31.

Giddens, Anthony, ed. *The Global Third Way Debate*. London: Polity, 2001.

Goldsmith, Oliver. "National Prejudices." *Essays*. 1765. Reprinted in H. Peterson, ed., *50 Great Essays*. New York: Pocket Books, 1954.

Gray, John. *False Dawn, The Delusions of Global Capitalism*. New York: New Press, 1998.

Harberger, Arnold C. "A Vision of the Growth Process." *American Economic Review*, 1998, 88(1), 1–33.

Henrich, Joseph. "Does Culture Matter in Economic Behavior? Ultimatum Game Bargaining Among the Machiguenga of the Peruvian Amazon." *American Economic Review*, 2000, 90(4), 973–979.

International Monetary Fund. *World Economic Outlook 2000*. Washington, DC: IMF, 2000.

Johnson, D. Gale. "Population, Food, and Knowledge." *American Economic Review*, 2000, 90(1), 1–13.

Kahneman, Daniel, and Amos Tversky, eds. *Choices, Values and Frames*. Cambridge: Cambridge University Press, 2000.

Krugman, Paul. "Can America Stay on Top?" *Journal of Economic Perspectives*, 2000, 14(1), 169–175.

Makhija, M.V., K. Kim, and S.D. Williamson. "Measuring Globalization of Industries Using a National Industries Approach: Evidence Across Five Countries and Over Time." *Journal of International Business Studies*, 1997, 28(9), 679–710.

Mander, Jerry, ed. *The Case Against the Global Economy*. San Francisco: Sierra Club Books, 1996.

Naito, Minoru. "Japan greets changes with cautious optimism." *Nikkei Weekly*, 24 July 2000, 3.

Perlman, Mark, and Charles R. McCann, Jr. *The Pillars of Economic Understanding, Ideas and Traditions*. Ann Arbor: University of Michigan Press, 1998.

Popper, Karl. *The Open Society and Its Enemies, Hegel and Marx*. Princeton: Princeton University Press, 1971.

Schwartz, Herman, *States versus Markets, The Emergence of a Global Economy*. New York: St. Martin's Press, 2000.

Seabrook, Jeremy. "Nasty, brutish, and long." *Financial Times*, 14 April 2000, 17.

Shapiro, Carl, and Hal R. Varian. *Information Rules: A Strategic Guide to the Network Economy*. Boston: Harvard Business School Press, 1999.

Solow, Robert M. *Monopolistic Competition and Macroeconomic Theory*. Cambridge: Cambridge University Press, 1998.

Sullivan, Jeremiah. *Exploring International Business Environments*. Needham Heights, MA: Pearson Publishing, 1999.

Turner, Adair. *Just Capital: The Liberal Economy*. London: Macmillan, 2001.

Whitley, Richard. *Divergent Capitalisms*. New York: Oxford University Press, 1999.

World Bank. *World Development Report 2000/2001, Attacking Poverty*. New York: Oxford University Press, 2000.

CHAPTER 2

POINTING THE WAY:
1900 TO 2100

Where are we going? What dramas will we witness and be a part of? One could answer questions like these by consulting social science theories, but they have little to say about the long run of 100 years. Experts are available, but often they contradict each other or are blatantly self-serving. Why not consult the older generation? I asked my mother, born in 1908, what was the most dramatic event in her life. She thought for a moment, then said,

It was when the Fourteenth Regiment from Brooklyn came home from the war [in 1919]. All the men from the neighborhood were in the regiment, and they all marched through Brooklyn to their armory. We were in the crowd on the sidewalk and we looked and looked for my brother Don, but he wasn't there. My mother was shocked and didn't know who to ask. Later we heard he was left behind to guard Germans.

Sheer terror and, happily for most Americans, relief from terror were hallmarks of the 20th century. No wonder it was sometimes called the "age of anxiety." By consulting the feelings and stories of individuals, we get a grounded sense of what mattered and what will matter. Twenty-first-century globalized Americans will want relief from anxiety, authenticity rather than anonymity, and a sense of the coherence of things rather than fragmentation. How do we know that? Because the storytellers and thinkers of 1900 and thereabouts have told us so.

ILLUSION, BETRAYAL, AND DISORDER

In 1900, the average person had less than one-fifth of the purchasing power of the average person in 2002, due in part to goods prices five times greater than today's in real terms and food costs about two or three times greater.[1] Most thoughtful people knew that conditions had improved from a century earlier and were likely to improve a century hence, yet in no way did they see human destiny as assured, enveloped in a protective layer of progress as it hurtled through the coming decades. Where once the fundamental issues of sin, free will, fate, and death had been understandable, if not quite explainable, in terms of a recognized and recognizable Christianity, new philosophies and ideologies had emerged to call the old order into question. Dispassionate forces were said to exist and to direct the universal workings, historical processes, and even human biology. Ideas of the individual as possessor of himself or herself and therefore ultimately autonomous—ideas over which 600,000 Americans had fought and died a few decades earlier—seemed delusional, and a theme of life as a series of illusions and betrayals emerged. By 2000, the theme was stronger than ever, amply supported by a hundred years of humanity's seeming helplessness to control or even comprehend processes of carnage and chaos. The same sense of dispassionate forces also supported a movement that had emerged a hundred years earlier: the tendency to stop seeing individuals as such and to identify them as group members. Skin color, income, and gender always had counted as attributes of individuals, but by 1900 they had insinuated themselves into the very nature of selfhood. To the up-to-date scientific mind of the day and its supporters, this approach to typing people made sense. Typing allowed forests to be seen where trees had been, the better to understand and cope with nature's forces. Moreover, support for the scientific approach came from the business sector as it mobilized itself to create and serve mass consumer markets which could be managed only by manipulation of groups, segments, and categories. This theme of the person as a category also has survived.

The 20th century began with U.S. society attempting to cope with the failures of Civil War Reconstruction and the ensuing re-subjugation of blacks, ongoing westward expansion, new rights sought by individuals asserting group membership as labor or women, and urban disarray as waves of immigrants desperately tried to cope with their lot in the face of a new urban middle class both supportive of and in turn worried by change. In these conditions of turmoil, a series of conflicts and problems emerged which still energize our discourse and will continue to do so. The immense value of technology and its misuse had been introduced as a concern by Mary Shelley in *Frankenstein* (1817), and the continued popularity of that work at both the beginning and the end of the twentieth century suggested that discussion of machines and machine processes would continue. Associated with the machine problem was the debate over urban versus rural values. Cities were and are seen by some people as places where technology fosters excess, dissolution, disease, and ultimately chaos; while allegedly pristine rural settings encourage sustainability, a faith in and connectedness with nature, and a reliance on the commonplace rather than the urban sensational as the organizing theory of social life.

It was the perceived failure of the Civil War to create an ordered, secure world that influenced American writers to take up the themes of illusion and betrayal. These themes were especially notable in the work of Stephen Crane. In *The Red Badge of Courage* (1895), Henry Fleming, the young soldier comfortable in his mythic understanding of war, encounters a tattered soldier during his first battle who asks, "Where you hit?" In Crane's deeply symbolic rendering, this is equivalent to asking, "Where is your sense of reality?" Henry is beset by what he later calls his "brass and bombast" after receiving a minor wound. This theme of the wounded man, later prevalent in Ernest Hemingway and other writers, suggests a degeneration into reality from illusion and a regeneration into virtuous existence, often signified by courage, from mere animal existence. The American social agenda requires character of its citizens, but character and the commitment accompanying it come at the price of facing up to the nation's deep flaws. Few Americans were willing to follow the paths of Henry Fleming or Jake Barnes in *The Sun Also Rises* (1926), but the degeneration-regeneration theme was immensely provocative in the ways it was rejected.

Chaos is at the heart of *Miss Lonelyhearts* (1933), Nathanael West's bleak exploration of illusions as the placebos taken to mask the pain of societal disorder. As a young reporter reads and responds to letters to Miss Lonelyhearts, he feels that the great mass of Americans do not have the character, code, or theology needed to organize their existence in a time of great distress. Instead they fall into the illusory belief that advice from newspapers or movie stars somehow can help them cope with their worlds. Researchers have since identified this phenomenon as the "halo effect" in which perceived prominence and distinction in one endeavor spills over into other perceptions. Thus Miss Lonelyhearts' readers see someone powerfully able to communicate with millions and conclude that they are morally powerful. Scores of television evangelists have amassed huge followings based on this illusory correlation, and for the rest of the century various entertainers found that their opinions on moral and political issues were carefully attended to. Frank Sinatra, for example, once was interviewed by *Playboy* as a political pundit. Ronald Reagan based his political career on his success as an entertainer.

West's point was that sooner or later the public's faith in media creatures would be seen for what it is—a stopgap illusion of little merit and some danger. At that point the American public would have to go back to working out acceptable ethical codes, building character in the young, and establishing an enriched spiritual life—all of the things that structure and shape life in ways that order it into meaningfulness. The 21st century would be one of titanic struggle among media whose guru offspring would become more and more intrusive in the home as the Internet joined the radio, television, and telephone, and a public yearning for an enriched social order. One path the public could take would be from desire to frustration, from frustration to addled discontent, and from discontent to frenzied search for order that never comes. This nightmarish scenario would spell disarray for U.S. institutions, including business. It is not hard to imagine a world in which people suddenly start to see worms in hamburgers, or signs of the devil in products, or evil sayings in advertising jingles, since these things have already come to pass on occasion. Now magnify them and add on dark fears that corporations are poisoning people in genetically modified foods, that the very air we breathe and the water we drink are polluted beyond saving by big business, that mysterious global organizations have taken control of society, and that foreigners are taking jobs away from Americans. The disorders of market exchange would come under attack as the public demanded easing of alleged burdens.

The 20th century, then, began with a sense among thinking people that the old fundamental order was dying and the idea of individual autonomy was somehow an illusion. The noble sacrifices of the Civil War had been betrayed as some Americans sank back into servitude and others took on existence as either subjects of an emerging science or as consumer categories in the new world of big business. Anxiety rose over the growing influence of machines on daily life and their powerful pull of people out of imagined rural Edens into equally imagined urban disorder. Calls arose for the citizens of the great land to cast off their illusions, face up to betrayal and disorder, and rebuild their society and themselves. False faith in war myths would not help, nor would reliance on the ersatz models of the mass media. These themes continued to resonate throughout the century, are still powerful today, and will be the source of much concern in the future. American corporations will be the recipients of insistent demands that they market to people as individuals rather than as segments, use technology in ways that foster rather than threaten autonomy and humanity's bond with nature, and take great care in using the communication power of mass media, lest they evoke increasing social disorder along with profits.

EMERGENCE OF THE "ISMS"

Out of the thought of the 19th century, a series of paradigms emerged as guides to understanding, explaining, predicting, and, it was hoped, controlling social, economic, and individual existence. Rooted in Darwinian debates over heredity and environment, the faith in science of Auguste Comte, as well as the influential writings of John Stuart Mill, Herbert Spencer, Thomas Henry Huxley, and Ernst Haeckel, determinism, materialism, and empiricism became influential, first in the work of philosophers, then social critics, and finally in the way the growing powers of the emerging middle class were apprehended and applied.[2] Inspired by the work of

Isaac Newton, early 19th-century thinkers like Pierre Laplace had argued that past conditions determined current states, while current states determined future states. Here the "divided stream" of *determinism* emerged and stimulated debate and social policy throughout the rest of the 19th and right to the end of the 20th century and beyond. Pessimists focused on the past and identified environmental and racial conditions which, with law-bound regularity, had engendered current conditions that could not have been avoided and cannot be ameliorated. The pessimist stream, armed with IQ test apparatus and—in the work of Cyril Burt and others—an almost manic desire to convince the public of the gloomy truth of the model, flowed on into the future.[3] The optimist stream, focused on controlling the present to bring forth a glorious future, also became characterized by strong emotional and ideological commitments. The age of the planner, the expert, and the social engineer emerged.[4]

The second "ism," *materialism*, had had a curious history. Popularized in the seventeenth century by Thomas Hobbes and others debating Descartes's philosophy of mind, materialism embodied the argument that everything is physical, including the mind. This approach to explaining values and judgements as the offspring of brain activities rather than a mind rooted in a soul and a spiritual existence set off intellectual, scholarly, and scientific debates which have not faded and are likely to continue. More important, however, was the effect on Christian religious belief, which by 1900 had become among the Protestant middle class a form of shared sentiment and among the lower class an excuse for emotional discharge. Neither class was prepared under these circumstances to undertake a rigorous defense of the soul, and a tendency emerged to label reality as that which could be observed as physical. The prominence of things occurred, urged on by the makers of things, who sought mass markets in the great nation that had finally pushed the frontier into the Pacific Ocean. An equally vigorous market emerged as some makers of entertainment services—books, movies, and later radio and television—sought to persuade the public that abstractions associated with the mind-soul, such as love, would and should triumph over things. No matter which way the debate over materialism turned out in the 20th century, then, business sought to win.

Empiricism was another theory in philosophy that emerged from dark academic recesses to enjoy the spotlight shone on it by 1900. Empiricism generally holds that experience has primacy in human knowledge and justified belief.[5] John Locke, whose ideas on individualism had so influenced American political values at various times, argued that mental concepts—the classifications one employs in thinking and feeling—must be rooted in experience rather than embedded in inherited human nature. Determinists of the optimist stream took this idea and began to assert a model in which educators and planners controlled experiences of the current populace so as to control future social structures in a manner that promised unending progress in the United States. Two things were lost in this movement. First, the idea of the individual as the prime unit of society gave way to society itself as the focus of care and attention. Individuals began to be seen as passive receptacles of experience manipulation in service to public good. Second, the idea of the present as a lengthy period of time in which existence occurs receded in favor of a sense that the perceived future ought to be the main concern. Current experience lost its status as an end in itself, and Americans were asked to redefine it as but a means or a tool to pry loose some future end. The attacks on both the individual and the present provoked frequent social crises during the twentieth century as beatniks, hippies, Generation X-ers, and various groups of the disaffiliated asserted the primacy of the person in the here and now. These upheavals will continue in the 21st century, since no resolution is possible in a society that values both a material progress born of postponed gratification, vigorous education, and expert planning, as well as a vision of the individual as by right and duty free to grasp whatever advantages offer themselves in the present. The attack on the market system discussed in later chapters illustrates this conflict as it will work itself out in the coming decades.

The dominance of the "isms" in American intellectual life and societal agendas was received by the people with grave misgivings. Optimistic determinists sought control over all aspects of life, while pessimistic determinists wanted to lock individuals in closets labeled "race" and "intelligence" and then throw away the keys. Materialists scoffed at believers in a spiritual existence and were gleefully joined by mass merchandisers eager to ride the tidal wave of things. Perhaps most threatening of all, progressives, reformers, and social scientists in thrall to empiricism emphasized the primacy of the future, with the present only the place where strings were to be pulled to make the new society strut onstage. Businessmen were faced with a dilemma. They wanted to sell things to the public now, but prevailing wisdom suggested that future gains associated with purchases should be emphasized, rather than present enjoyment. Thus was born modern microeconomic and marketing theories defining goods as bundles of attributes yielding some future gain, with the future anywhere from a few minutes to a few years away.

As 2000 approached, cultural critics were not surprised that themes of disillusion, illusion, betrayal, and distrust still characterized American society, at least at the margins. Americans were a happy people in 2000, but changes occur at the margin, and a serious economic downturn, a pointless war, or a stock-market collapse could evoke the gloom that the "isms" brought with them in their romp through the 20th century. Christopher Lasch, in *The True and Only Heaven* (1991), urged Americans to look again at their spirited and spiritual ancestors and to reverse the decline in "community." For him this meant a return to the idea of work as a process of craftsmanship, a recognition that consumerism and "material comforts will extinguish a more demanding ideal of the good life," and a renewed movement towards syndicalism and guild socialism in which market exchanges are replaced by justice as the rationale for matching supply and demand.[6]

WHY WAS AND IS BUSINESS TOLERATED?

Big Business emerged at a time when what has been called America's "cosmic optimism" was wavering, yet it eventually was this optimism that fostered tolerance for the corporations and their ways and continues to legitimize business activities to this day. Inherited from the Enlightenment and modified by the sophisticated gloss of Benjamin Franklin and other Founding Fathers, cosmic optimism saw the universe as supporting both order and disorder, reason and unreason, generosity and selfishness, integration and disintegration, hope and despair, and love and hate. Order and reason would predominate in a well-governed society supporting "natural man" and what Adam Smith had called "natural liberty." These abstractions were seen to operate in a democratic nation of relatively equal, free individuals pursuing agrarian lives outside of cities in "natural" settings. Nothing had shaken this view during most of the 19th century. When recognition occurred that many individuals were not free and equal under the law, colossal efforts were made in 1861–1865 to put things right. However, when it became clear that Jim Crow laws and practices had undone the earlier successes, confidence in the cosmic optimism model was shaken. It was further eroded as seemingly unnatural foreigners flooded into the country and settled in rapidly expanding unnatural cities. The greatest blow of all came with the rise of Big Business and what appeared to be impending chaos brought on by speculation, corruption, monopoly, brutal treatment of labor, sweatshops, and ghastly mines and factories. These were seen as too much to pay for what was until 1900 only a modest increase in the standard of living.

To the American middle class of 1900 it seemed as if disorder, disintegration, and despair were candidates for dominance in the 20th century. Given what eventually occurred in Europe, the people were correct to have worried. But nothing of this sort came to pass in the United States, and cosmic optimism survived. It grew in strength as the century went on and the economic benefits of the business system became manifest. What saved U.S. society for optimism and progress was, first, a belief that as long as the business system valued and rewarded thrift, prudence, diligence, and honesty—which in general it did—occasional excesses would either be tolerated or weakened in their effect through regulation. Second, Americans adopted a form of Christian Socialism emphasizing brotherhood and leadership by the prosperous. From Andrew Carnegie's gospel of wealth through John D. Rockefeller to Bill Gates, this ameliorating force has continued powerful. Third, entrepreneurs and inventors were admired, and their work was amply rewarded. Fourth, the power of laborers as voters was not thwarted, and labor's success in unionization, social security, and workplace safety efforts fostered a reduction in the violence of labor actions which had grown in the 1880–1900 period. In a sense, these emphases on virtue, benevolence, creativity, and democracy were simply evidence that the old model had not gone under but instead had flourished. What saved America's cosmic optimism in the face of a threat from Big Business and other forces was even more cosmic optimism. And cosmic optimism then saved business.

In *Memoirs of an American Citizen* (1905), Robert Herrick presented a study of a corporate executive who looks back on his business life as he is about to leave it for a career in politics. Edward Van Harrington has always measured himself in terms of his ability to succeed in the Darwinian struggle that Herrick characterizes as American business. Van Harrington is a man whose allegiances have been to causes and people who could serve his interests and to nothing else, but as he reviews his career he is troubled by a sense of incompleteness in the face of a felt moral laxity. Herrick's novel illustrates the theme of business success at the expense of moral strength as a kind of tragedy of the human spirit. The theme is more fully developed in Henrick's earlier work, *The Common Lot* (1904), in which Jackson Hart, an architect, fails in his ideals and throws in his lot with an unscrupulous contractor. Eventually his wife leaves him, one of his buildings burns up, and his life collapses around him. His spiritual rebirth begins when he accepts the "common lot" of a fifty-dollar-per-week draftsman and begins to find in the natural world about him hints of a higher power.

Jackson Hart is made to follow the Puritan path of acknowledging sin, feeling guilt, and finding the will to be reborn, something that Van Harrington fails to do. In these books and others, Robert Herrick and novelists of the period explored the Puritan ethos and its impact on economic life. Basically, they argued for what has been called the "Puritan Compromise": acquiescence in the capitalist system as long as the means employed by businessmen exhibited the old virtues of thrift, industry, reliability, temperance, and simplicity. Violators of the Compromise, like Jackson Hart, needed regeneration and were expected to be driven by their nature to seek it. What troubled Herrick and other critics were the Edward Van Harringtons, who showed a seemingly untroubled reverence for piling up wealth, creating useless creature comforts, and ignoring the cultural and social problems of the day. We can see here the source of two paths business life took throughout the century. On one path were those who covered their getting and spending in a veneer of respect for the Puritan virtues. This blatant hypocrisy later on gave way to the corporate responsibility movement in which business executives put their strenuous efforts to work for both their own and the greater good. While hypocrisy lurked just beneath the glossy surface of some annual reports, it was clear that the Puritan Compromise of 1900 was still evocative in 2000 and had been expanded to include good works as well as good character as legitimizing factors for the capitalist system. But voices were beginning to be heard asking the obvious question: If society's goals are good character and good works, why do we need capitalism?

ALTERNATIVES TO CAPITALISM

Even cosmic optimism could not thwart a small coterie of thinkers and politicians from rejecting the market model and proposing a variety of statist solutions to the problems posed by capitalism. The most important utopian work focused on late-19th-century society was Edward Bellamy's *Looking Backward* (1888). Enshrined in a mélange of bad writing were Bellamy's ideas on power, equality, and efficiency. He preached a doctrine in which the wise economy of human effort carried out in an egalitarian society by a democratically chosen body of social engineers would lead to the control of nature to humankind's benefit.[7] Influenced by 18th-century ideologies of man's inherent perfectibility, Herbert Spencer's visions of social evolutionary progress, and the development of technology, Bellamy hated the prevailing capitalist system. He saw it as wasting resources in needless competition, mistaken investments, and periodical gluts. Similar concerns were voiced by Henry D. Lloyd in *Wealth Against Commonwealth* (1894), an exposé of the gulf between laissez-faire theory and actual practice, and Lester Frank Ward, whose *Outlines of Sociology* (1898) advocated an expanded role of government as an active economic and social planner. The themes of waste and a need for planning also energized Thorstein Veblen's work, which described society as a conflict between the few but powerful predatory robber barons and the weak, industrious many. Modern business, in Veblen's bitter prose, threatened the institutional structures of society with its rationalized defense of wastefulness.[8] Finally, the implicit cry for a new order through attacks on existing arrangements characterized Ambrose Bierce's *Fantastic Fables* (1891), a collection of short, cynical allegories lambasting greed, hypocrisy, and ignorance as legitimized by government ("the hauls of legislation"), Christians, corporations, and the judiciary.

While Bellamy's visions and Veblen's critiques set the stage for radical social transformations in the 20th century and were widely read, they lacked the kind of specific agenda that could effect change. In a series of novels, speeches, and political movements, a Minnesota populist, Ignatius Donnelly, presented a program that looks now very much like a prototype for the modern liberalism of the Democratic Party, in which government regulation and subsidies would help Americans attain the freedom and dignity advocated by Thomas Jefferson.[9] In *Caesar's Column: A Story of the*

Twentieth Century (1890), Donnelly described a social and economic system in which laws put a ceiling on wealth, with all income over that going to the state. Gold and silver would be replaced by paper money, allowing government to more easily manage the money supply so that a small annual inflation would spur business investment and consumption. The book has been all but ignored, however, since Donnelly's anti-Semitism and hatred of immigrants ensured a quick burial for *Caesar's Column*.

All in all, the utopians never mounted a credible attack on the business system. However, the theme of capitalism's wastefulness reemerged late in the 20th century in the environmental and conservation movements, which often targeted corporations as purveyors of destruction and poorly conceived ventures. Moreover, critics argued that what had legitimized the business system for all those years—association with virtuous behavior, benevolence, creativity, and democracy—did not apply to huge corporations, which were faceless, merciless, not very innovative, and highly authoritarian in their functioning. Massive public-relations campaigns were mounted by big businesses to convince the public that its cosmic optimism was not threatened, since corporations were made up of people who contributed to United Way, invented "neat" (Bill Gates's phrase) products, and used society's resources efficiently.[10] Although mostly these assertions were true, it was apparent that new utopias were likely to be presented to the public in the 21st century.

HUMANITY RED IN TOOTH AND CLAW

If capitalism and big business were wasteful in the eyes of some social critics and utopians in 1900, literary leaders and their followers were terrified by a powerful and alarming vision of nature. In *The Open Boat*, Stephan Crane referred to a "high cold star one winter's night" as a symbol of nature's utter indifference in a mechanistic Newtonian universe inhabited by chillingly savage Darwinian creatures. To counter the horror of existence in such an environment, American meliorists such as W.D. Howells preached a doctrine of solidarity and brotherhood—what Howells called "complicity"—in U.S. society. By the end of the 20th century, however, nature had become organic, benign, and threatened by a humankind that now had become either indifferent or savage. This astonishing reversal in social perception constituted the reemergence of the transcendentalist model of nature as God made manifest, brought about partly by the Disney Corporation and partly by Rachel Carson. But if by 2000 humans were the enemy, where did that leave solidarity and brotherhood?[11] The problem was dealt with by those who took an interest in such things by dividing humanity into two camps. In one were the corporations, big government, and business followers of market exchange processes. This camp had to be resisted by committed defenders of indigenous peoples, people of color, "victims," and women—all presumably somehow of and in nature. What was it that held the defenders of nature together and attracted at least some of the defendees to their camp? T.S. Eliot in *The Wasteland* (1922) had portrayed the world as sick, violated, infertile, and dried out and in his essays had called for a return to tradition, or the presentness of the past, as a unifying force capable of energizing betterment. No one of any camp paid attention. More influential was Robinson Jeffers, who in *Roan Stallion* (1925) dwelt on the theme of "inhumanism" in which some "obscure human fidelity" endlessly drew mankind back from choosing the world of spirit, nature, and fecundity symbolized by the stallion. "Who gets your fidelity," asked the emerging Global Village camp of 2000 to the world community, "nature (including the humans allegedly natural) or humanity?" That such a question could even be formulated suggested trouble in the new century.

WHAT IS AN INDIVIDUAL?

The flip side of the grouping and segmenting movements common in the century was a fuzzy sense of just what it meant to say that one is an individual. While some sidestepped the problem and focused on the masses, classes, races, or genders, others dug deeper into personhood, often in contradictory ways.

The literature of the early period showed a confused vision of the individual which paralleled a similar confusion in society. In the novels of Henry James, especially *Portrait of a Lady* (1881) and *The Golden Bowl* (1904), individuals of distinction and worth are presented as masters of will and consciousness that determine action. In contrast, Stephen Crane's major characters are shown in *The Red Badge of Courage* to react to instinctive emotion beyond will and consciousness. When Hollywood got around to filming James's and Crane's works later in the century, it could not handle either author's vision. James's autonomous women often were seen to be driven by some feminist agenda, while Crane's driven Henry Fleming took on the character of the autonomous hero who chooses greatness over cowardice. These reversals illustrated a muddled movement in the century to resolve the issue of autonomy: the extent to which one's motivations, deliberations, intentions, judgements, and choices are under one's control. Women often were portrayed in film and literature in the 1980–2000 period as choosing to be driven by love, feminism, or a desire for power, while men were shown choosing to be exemplary in cowboy, war, and science fiction epics. The idea that a person can be autonomous yet in thrall to an ideology, a passion, or the behavioral requirements embedded in a series of war and frontier myths may have served as a middle ground between the visions of Henry James and Stephen Crane, but it had a hollow ring to it.

The ring was especially hollow if one went back and read Walt Whitman's *Democratic Vistas* (1871). Whitman sought to define the individual's role for the coming 20th century. In his perspective, the idea of democracy is paramount, and democracy must transcend institutional agendas and self-interest. The fruition of democracy is yet to come, but come it will, built on the current edifice of money-grubbing but potent capitalism as balanced and softened by the American individual, who is true to his or her own central idea and purpose, which is the assertion of his or her will. Although similar to the "hero" of Thomas Carlyle and Ralph Waldo Emerson, both of whom described a model of the great man looking very much like a modern dictator, Whitman's "great person" will be an everyman American who stands up for his beliefs.[12] The echo of Whitman suffuses the 1930s films of Frank Capra, which starred Henry Fonda and James Stewart. Stewart in real life did stand up for his beliefs and became a much-decorated World War II hero, honored for his courage and leadership as a bomber pilot with the U.S. Eighth Air Force. Had Stewart chosen to submerge himself in the mythic flows of red-blooded manhood, as Hollywood would have it? Had he simply been a cog driven by forces beyond his ken, as Stephen Crane saw it? Had he triumphantly exhibited Jamesian will and consciousness in dealing with societal stress? Or was he Walt Whitman's great American person?

When James Stewart—and many other heroes—were asked what they did and what drove them, the answer was invariably the same: "I just did my job." Implied here was a new 20th-century concept of the person as "he who performs tasks with skill and efficiency." We can see it in Crane's *The Open Boat*, in which individuals cover up their sense of helplessness in an indifferent universe with the exhibition of a satisfying expertise. Ernest Hemingway also explored this cover-up theme, as did Arthur Miller in the character of Willy Loman in *Death of a Salesman* (1949). These and other authors show their characters layering over the fear of the unknown with the familiarity of technique and salvaging elements of the shattered illusion of the natural man in concert with nature in the new illusion of task mastery and business skill. Serious artists generally have shown that technique and skill are not enough, but in the upbeat world of modern organizational life, "human capital" became the rallying cry for personal and economic salvation by 2000.[13] All that one allegedly needed for personhood and authentic individual existence was a set of learned behaviors that led to socially valued outcomes. "Is that all there is?" sang Peggy Lee, anticipating a question that was likely to be raised in the 21st century. James Stewart fended off prying interviewers by implying that mastery and team spirit made living meaningful, but that was only because he would have been laughed at if he had said, "I am an American, I stand for something, and by God I will be heard." The assertion of Whitmanesque autonomy was likely to be a factor in 2055 just as it had been in 1855, when *Leaves of Grass* appeared, or in 1943, when James Stewart climbed into the cockpit of his B-17.

THE BACKWARD TREK

The change from the secure, confident American bellowing out Whitman's "barbaric yawp" as he loped across the prairies towards manifest destiny to the whiny, existentially challenged urbanite stuck on the Grand Central Parkway bemoaning his fate exhibited a colossal failure of nerve, which by 2000 was no longer tolerable. The backward trek towards coherence in a benevolent cosmos had begun. Some took the planner's route of progressivism and called for government agendas focused on amelioration and inclusion. Some became activists and worked through nongovernmental organizations. Still others called for a new commitment to the old certainties about God's, man's, and nature's unity or to processes of market exchange working themselves out to the betterment of all. The first two groups constituted the left and right wings of the Democratic Party while the last two occupied the left and right wings of the Republican Party. All, however, were united in their faith in movement rather than stasis, democratic processes rather than statist authority, discourse rather than assertion, and inclusion rather than exclusion. Nevertheless, adherents of the market model were decided outliers in that all the other groups placed people of goodwill at the center of social action, while they placed an abstraction, the market, at the center with people of self-interested will at the margin. It was clear that this state of affairs would not continue long into the 21st century. As John Maynard Keynes had tried to save the market in the 1930s, someone would have to do the same in the 2030s. But if the old Keynes saw salvation in government actions to energize consumption functions, the new Keynes faced a daunting task. He or she would need to place caring individuals back at the center. No longer would anyone be forced to submit to the mercy of the market. Even if inefficiencies and their costs would have to be endured, mercy and justice as exercised by authentic individuals would take a central position.

THE NEW INDIVIDUAL

In 1906 children could not take out *The Adventures of Huckleberry Finn* from the Brooklyn Public Library. What they and their parents could and did take out were sentimental novels such as *Mrs. Wiggs of the Cabbage Patch* and *Rebecca of Sunnybrook Farm*, religious works such as *In His Steps* and *The Little Shepherd of Kingdom Come*, and adventures like *The Prisoner of Zenda* and *Graustark*—this last gave a name to the uniforms of White House guards in Richard Nixon's era, "Graustarkian." Popular art and literature preached the status quo, self-control, a distrust of the body, past tradition and future progress, and order as the basis for society. By 2000, the status quo was mocked or feared, self-expression ruled over self-control, bodily activities such as sex were coming to be seen as virtuous, the past was the stuff of entertainment rather than education, and the future was a terrifying

unknown burdened by perceived threats in the environment and institutions that allegedly thwarted freedom. Some high school students of my acquaintance began growing food in their parents' backyards because they
envisioned supermarkets as depositories for genetically modified organisms posing as peas and corn. It was not unheard of for couples to live together for a decade without enduring the freedom-restricting bonds of
marriage. Advocates of a steady march towards human betterment were
scorned or labeled as cynical manipulators.

The more the material well-being of Americans increased, the more
Americans were willing to tolerate cinematic and literary images of society
as dull, sterile, and insensitive. The more settled the society became, the
more the belief emerged that only in violence can man show himself to be
better than the world allows him to be. Movies like *Pulp Fiction* (1994) and
the novels of Mickey Spillane in the 1950s oozed feelings of doom and the
sense that the bottom was about to drop out of everything, yet the heroes of
these works, without roots, without faith, and without hope, nevertheless
exhibited moral goodness.[14] What was left, then, in the wreckage of the
20th century was the American. Amidst the supposed ruins of institutions,
the horrors of environmental collapse, and the menace of globalism, the individual still reigned. Pulled one way by a desire for freedom and another
way by a yearning for community, his moral integrity held him and his society together. Americans paid their taxes at the end of the century, did not
riot at football games, and worked longer hours than anyone. Their world
was prosperous and orderly, even though they didn't want to believe it,
and their future was bright, although they refused to admit it. What troubled them was their alleged waning faith in religion, marriage, family, education, and business, the great institutions of society, even though these
were functioning and seemed likely to continue doing so. What would happen in the new century when Americans decided to reinvent their institutions? Since they were unwilling to perfect themselves and the perfection of
nature had turned out to be an environmental nightmare in the 20th century, the only things left to perfect were the institutions. New ideas of marriage, education, religion, and family would be needed. Crucial to the
agenda, however, would be the perfection of the market mechanism. No
one in either of America's first two centuries had been able to link market
exchange to the individual morality of the free citizen. The 21st-century
Americans were poised to try.

The new individual would be similar to Edgar Allan Poe's detective,
Auguste Dupin, in *The Murders in the Rue Morgue* (1841). He illustrates the
dictum that "the ingenious are always fanciful, and the truly imaginative
never otherwise than analytic," a statement which today could easily have
come from the pages of a *Harvard Business Review* article on entrepreneurs
and innovators. The far-seeing man of reason also appears in *A Descent Into
the Maelstrom*, in which the narrator loses his fear as he stands in awe of a

menacing but wondrous nature.[15] His loss of fear energizes his reason, which he uses to save himself. Without fancy and imagination, then, reasonable men and women will not create the Internet or conquer cancer. Ralph Waldo Emerson takes up similar themes in his essay *Nature* (1836), in which the human faculty of "moral sentiment" fosters the ability to see order in chaos, unity in diversity, and solutions in quandaries. This faith in the fully equipped individual led Henry David Thoreau to say, "Let him step to the music which he hears, however measured or far away." What does such a man have to fear? Herman Melville considered this question in the character of Captain Ahab in *Moby Dick* (1851), in which he showed that deep down in the murky depths of the human unconscious there lurked a sense of man as apart from and in mortal combat with nature. Just as the white whale occasionally rose from the depths, so this human savagery sometimes surfaced. When it does, the vessel we all sail on, the United States—called *Pequod* in the novel—is in danger. Whereas Poe's and Emerson's American stands in awe of nature's mysteries and is liberated to succeed, the Ahabs of the society disintegrate in the face of the inscrutable and its secrets. The explanation of human woe, Melville implied, cannot be wrested from the heavens, and Americans must not try. The bumper sticker on the back of the *Pequod* should be: "Seek whale oil, not salvation, and all will be well." Yet the redeeming qualities of economic life and market exchange will increasingly come under attack as the 21st century progresses and the new individual takes charge. Left behind, perhaps, would be homo economicus, the rational man so beloved of economists and their corporate supporters in the 20th century.

HOMO ECONOMICUS

The first appearance of the economists' rational man in American literature probably occurred with Theodore Dreiser's creation of Carrie Meeber in *Sister Carrie* (1900). Carrie has "an unsophisticated and natural mind" unburdened of class interest, religious belief, and faith in social codes. She is a simple seeker of self-interest in the form of fame, power, love, beauty, and wealth—attributes which in an expanded form constitute the panhuman set of desires, according to Gary Becker, a well-known University of Chicago economist, in *The Economic Approach to Human Behavior* (1971). Like Becker's protohuman, Carrie is a maximizer of pleasure. She appears in the novel living with her sister in a narrow, empty, dull, poor, and stagnant environment. But beyond is the city of Chicago, the object of desire and the living force to be mastered if Carrie's maximization of pleasure is to occur. *Sister Carrie* portrays the urban landscape as kinetic pleasure to be consumed by those with enough will and energy. Whereas Walt Whitman had seen New York City as the place where democratizing processes would lead humankind towards spiritual unity, Dreiser shows Chicago to be a giant ice-cream cone to be licked clean and chewed up. This tension between competing urban visions has continued to this day.

Before consuming, homo economicus must survive, and Carrie is a master of making her desires work themselves out within the social conventions of the day without in fact allowing herself to subscribe to them. Just as norms and values have no place in economic models, so Carrie sees these as some economists do: constraints to be dealt with or endured. Facades and hypocrisy are tools available to the rational maximizer, and they allow Carrie to make norms work for rather than against her. Dreiser implies that none of this is wrong, since when humans follow their instincts and use reason, they cannot commit evil. Sin is the violation of codes to which one subscribes, and if the economic animal subscribes to no codes, he or she cannot sin. The mere observance of codes for survival's sake and for gain, at which Carrie becomes an expert, does not constitute belief and cannot thus be sinful. Absolved in this way, homo economicus is free to pursue self-interest. Although Carrie Meeber is not held up as a model of the microeconomic human to students by modern economics professors—either because they never have read Dreiser or don't have the guts to stand by their beliefs—she ought to be.

In the economic world of pure pursuit of self-interest unmodified by the feeble protests of Adam Smith that men do or ought to have "sympathy" towards each other, what then keeps society from turning savage?[16] Dreiser offers money. Whereas economists see money as a store of value and a medium of exchange, Dreiser sees it as the only force implicitly motivating social order.[17] Those with lots of money (and the wealth it commands) want to hold onto it, and they concoct moral conventions and social rituals that render society placid. The poor, who desire money, believe that adherence to conventions and rituals will open the door to more money to them. It is money that keeps Chicago relatively tame, and it is money that makes life endurable even for the desperately poor, who yet have hope for gain.

The idea of money motivating a bogus social order that keeps economic man in line is not just a literary theme. In a somewhat different form it appears in the preoccupations of two famous economists, John Neville Keynes and his better-known son, Maynard. It was the father who introduced the term "homo economicus" in a textbook popular at the turn of the century, and it was Maynard who wrestled with the problem of how the variability of the creature's "animal spirits" and "spontaneous optimism" could be tamed to society's benefit. Maynard fixed on money as the key element in the discussion:

Money in its significant attributes is, above all, a subtle desire for linking the present to the future, and we cannot even begin to discuss the effect of changing expectations on current activities except on monetary terms.[18]

It was the desire to pile up money—Sister Carrie's desire—that bothered John Maynard Keynes. Savings beyond some base amount were for him a kind of betrayal of the economic system, and he sought an expanded role for government to keep the system functioning. Dreiser suggests that hoarding money or the desire to do so fosters social order at the cost of hypocrisy and that the resulting meretricious society is not a world well lived in. Keynes argued that the same phenomenon fostered economic stagnation and decline and that the resulting immiseration produced a world also not well lived in. From both aesthetic and economic factions active in the early 20th century, then, money was seen as a potential source of disruption. Later, when industrialized countries' governments began to use inflation as a policy tool with disastrous results, money again became a problem. But it was really the same problem as earlier. Homo economicus wanted money, and either directly or through government action he was bent on getting it. The fact that hoarding it often fostered social dysfunction, economic stagnation, or falls in purchasing power—depending on the time period—did not seem to bother most people. Money was one of the major themes of the century, but no real resolution of the problems raised was possible until late in the century when computers and the Internet emerged. With them came a flood of ideas for replacing money with information as the store of value and knowledge as the medium of exchange. The idea emerged that hoarding money is a pointless activity. It was not pointless for unskilled but aggressive people like Dreiser's Carrie Meeber or Keynes's businessmen. Animal-like, they survived and prospered by following their instincts. However, the new middle classes at century's end recognized that, while some money always would be needed, piling up knowledge and information was better at producing well-being and social distinction. Moreover, whereas a money world fostered a social order associated with conventions, a knowledge world evoked an order allied with expanded choices. Whereas conventions provided coherence and stability for the early money-hoarders, expanded choices based on knowledge provided a coherence of sorts for information-hoarders. The question was: How orderly would such a world be?

THE RATIONAL MAN FALTERS

Carrie Meeber as a triumphal although flawed homo economicus can be contrasted with George Babbitt in Sinclair Lewis's *Babbitt* (1922) as a kind of faltering rational man. The two characters together set the tone of American attitudes towards economic life for the rest of the century. Together they provide some answers to the questions always in the American mind, "What does it take to make it? How much will it cost?" Sister Carrie takes on whatever roles society offers if they advance her interests, and she succeeds. The cost is a sense of rootlessness and drift—the novel ends with her sitting in her rocker aimlessly swaying back and forth, an ironic reference to Whitman's more optimistic poem, "Out of the Cradle Endlessly Rocking." George Babbitt tries desperately to play one role, the hail-fellow-well-met man of business, and achieves his material interests at the expense of his character. The bleak visions of Dreiser and Lewis, in which homo economicus' life ends up either successful but meaningless or devoid of virtue, were highly influential in forming attitudes towards business in the ensuing decades, and Hollywood films invariably treated business life as grasping and sordid. Gordon Gekko in *Wall Street* (1984) was little more than a resurrected Carrie Meeber bent on success and dismissive of or uninterested in the costs. However, by the end of the century, Americans had begun to redefine the nature of economic life, perhaps in reaction to the gloom cast over it by the century's literature and cinema. The concept of success broadened to include more than outcomes that enhanced material well-being. As we will see, economic achievement began to include participation in satisfying work processes as environments wherein one could exercise skill, craft, and professional commitment. Americans were becoming focused on their pursuits of new, expanded modes of authentic, autonomous existence, and pressures were building on the corporations and enterprises of the nation to adjust.

Just what was the problem with George Babbitt anyway? In Lewis's rendition he was prosperous, possessed of a fine family, and living in a town brimful of life and promise. But Babbitt had committed the unpardonable sin in America; he had cast off the individuality that was the source of his interests in order to achieve those interests. Success, then, could never fully register in the deep cash box—what William James called the "cash nexus"—of a self that no longer was there to tote up accounts. The values Babbitt exhibited were those of his class, assumed without thought or consideration. Quantity counts more than quality. To love is to possess. Things are to be displayed, not used. The illusion of courage and daring is more important than courage and daring (a few days spent listening to big talk and "business-is-war" metaphors from Wall Street traders and deal-makers in the modern era will show that Lewis's list of business class values has some staying power). Thinking is not doing, and work without physical activity is downtime. What yields money is ethical (since speed laws hinder profit-making, Babbitt ignores them in his auto and is content). These and other values fostered a rigidity in Babbitt and his fellows which diminished their ability to adapt. Decades later, businessmen began to worry about this problem, and endless management books on flexibility and effective time management began to appear.[19]

Babbitt's class took a different approach and sought to remake the world to suit its habits and rituals. What was different was condemned, and the book is full of wary hostility to "socialists," "artists," and "Europe." Indeed, change itself is terrifying, and conversation in Babbitt's world invariably is affirming rather than probing or discursive. The only thing that changes and is still an acceptable dinner-table topic is the weather. One can still find this kind of talk in suburban American settings, but thankfully the practice is fading. America is about change, and most Americans now embrace it. Only those who already have it made—tenured professors, entrenched public servants, rich retirees, and so forth—still exhibit Babbittry.

By the end of the novel, the self-destroying emptiness and rigidities of his life begin to weigh down on Babbitt. He briefly becomes a rebel without a cause, finding some solace in the arms of the wonderfully named Tanis Judique and in alcoholic excess. But when the Good Citizen's League offers an escape back to soulless security, he eagerly accepts it, especially when they back up their offer with threats. The only upbeat note of the novel occurs as George notices a spirit of rebellion in his son, Ted, who may just be able to move back to that spirit of determined individualism and adaptability that Lewis sees as the only worthy complement to the paradise in which Americans live. It probably is not ironic that George's and Ted's home town is called Zenith. The businesspeople of America are going to have to live up to the zenith they have inherited from their agrarian ancestors, and a broadened homo economicus possessed of a self, flexibility, and mobility can take on the job.

WHAT ARE WE BEING TOLD?

Is history bunk, as Henry Ford once claimed? In a sense it is, since a purely rational calculation over whether or not to undertake a future endeavor should concern itself only with future costs and benefits. Past costs, suffering, hopes betrayed, illusions shattered, and values crushed allegedly are of no account. Moreover, Americans are a forward-looking, not a backward-looking people, and to consult history is not necessarily to listen to the breezes blowing in from the future. In one of his songs, Chuck Berry called for education based on "American history and practical math," but neither of these is much in evidence as the 21st century gets under way. Nevertheless, the era of 1900 is telling us something useful if we are ready to listen.

- *Our views of nature have shifted dramatically, and the consequences of the shift have yet to work themselves out.* From an alarming vision of man apart from and endangered by an indifferent nature, we now see nature as endangered by one element of humanity—that associated with commerce, trade, and agricultural and goods production—and defended by another element. That element, variously labeled as indigenous, gendered, victims, or poor, currently is marginal and fragmented. With better organization and a unifying theme evoking nature, it could become quite powerful.

- *Religion has faded as a force to be reckoned with, but that is likely to change.* In the 20th century religious practices served as outlets for emotions or as the sharing of watered-down sentiments. However, a return to religion as a source of faith, coherence, and meaning is likely, especially if we begin to abandon modern definitions of reason and re-evoke older, pre-Enlightenment models. Our idea of reason, which justifies, legitimizes, and excuses us and our actions, is that behavior which is purposeful and resulting from calculations of benefits and costs is rational. The Greeks did not conceptualize reason in this way, nor do most cultures. For these people, an act or a person is rational that coheres, that fits into the universal scheme of things. Reason here requires a sense of the spiritual and metaphysical, in other words religion. As religion returns to American life, it will make demands on economic life that it could not make in the previous century.

- *The American as a willing, autonomous, assertive, moral self will make a comeback.* The movements to look at a person and see either a group or a market segment do not have much staying power. Both are rooted in the social sciences, whose influence is waning because of their failures to develop important explanatory and predictive theories. Economics is the only body of theory with explanatory power, but it mostly fails as a source of useful predictions. The other sciences, especially psychology, have little to say about human nature and how it responds to and acts upon the world. In later chapters I will expand on the reemergence of panhuman nature, which after all is the best way to approach studies of humanity in an age of globalism. Here all that needs to be said is that people are beginning to reassert themselves as individuals. Partly this is due to implied promises from Internet gurus that marketing to every taste soon will replace selling to market segments, but more important is the growing sense that homo economicus is too narrow and inflexible a concept for a society whose members generated the Declaration of Independence and the Gettysburg Address. The comeback of the self will have profound effects on the worlds of work and consumption.

- *Work will be redefined as a process involving community, creativity, and happiness.* Currently work is characterized in economic theory and the extended order as an individual doing something which she would not do unless compensated to do it. It is the opposite, in its impact, of pleasure and leisure. While elements of this model always have and always will be associated with work, calls also will increase for work that evokes virtuous behaviors such as loyalty, courage, diligence, seriousness, and innovation. These are what the Puritan Compromise required of capitalism, and they will still be required in the coming decades.

The artists and thinkers of our past, then, are telling us that our economic system will have to adapt to the 21st century just as it adapted to the 20th century. Part of that adaptation will require a return to 19th-century American values and paradigms. The transcendentalists' sense of unity among man, society, and nature will return in the Global Village model, as will the Jeffersonian and Lincolnian evocation of the individual as the prime unit of society. To be reasonable will be to fit into a meaningful whole rather than to maximize one's utility, and to be employed will be to exist in a community of individuals with a sense that they are connected to something beyond themselves. The idea of the American will reemerge, but not the American jingoist of the past. As the great wave of immigrants in the late 20th century assimilates and intermarries, connected, globally sensitive Americans will develop. Nevertheless, they will maintain the sense that the nation is something quite special and its citizens extraordinary.

NOTES

1. See *The Economist*, 31 December 1999, various pages. Industrial prices hardly varied from 1860 to 1900 and wholesale prices were about the same in 1900 as they were in 1860. Thus the 0.6 percent annual rise in agricultural wages constituted a 20–30 percent gain in purchasing power for farm workers. In the 1960–2000 period, most U.S. workers improved their purchasing power about 60 percent.

2. See Richard Hofstadter, *Social Darwinism in American Thought: 1860–1915* (Philadelphia: University of Pennsylvania Press, 1944); Merle Curti, *The Growth of American Thought* (New York: Harper, 1951); and Philip P. Wiener, *Evolution and the Founders of Pragmatism* (Cambridge: Harvard University Press, 1949). Ernst Haeckel argued that mankind had evolved from, but still contained, elements of a primitive state. The idea of savagery thus became prominent.

3. For a summary, see Stephen Jay Gould, *The Mismeasure of Man* (New York: Norton, 1996).

4. See Eric F. Goldman, *Rendezvous with Destiny: A History of Modern American Reform* (New York: Knopf, 1952).

5. N.P. Wolterstorff, "Empiricism." In Robert Audi, ed., *The Cambridge Dictionary of Philosophy* (Cambridge: Cambridge University Press, 1995), 224.

6. Christopher Lasch, *The True and Only Heaven, Progress and its Critics* (New York: Norton, 1991), 16.

7. See Donald E. Pitzer, *America's Communal Utopias* (Chapel Hill: University of North Carolina Press, 1997) for a discussion of real attempts to create utopias from the free-love community of the Oneida perfectionists to the modern utopias of California and elsewhere.

8. Recent work on Veblen is discussed in John Patrick Diggins, *Thorstein Veblen: Theorist of the Leisure Class* (Princeton: Princeton University Press, 1999). Veblen was one of the first thinkers to note that social and institutional structures had a great deal to do with the way capitalism and market systems functioned. As institutions changed or were made to change, economic relations also would change.

9. See Martin Ridge, *Ignatius Donnelly: Portrait of a Politician* (Saint Paul: Minnesota Historical Society Press, 1991). Donnelly appears to have gotten some of his ideas from John Law, the early 18th-century economist and financial speculator.

10. See Roland Marchand, *The Rise of Public Relations and Corporate Imagery in American Big Business* (Berkeley: University of California Press, 1998). Marchand shows how U.S. corporations have worked hard to show that they possess corporate "souls" and are not dangerous threats to American values. As an anonymous Amazon.com reviewer noted, executives of big business have sought to "wrap their enterprises in the imagery of intimacy and neighborliness."

11. The modern "religion of ecology" and its moralizing is attacked by Steven E. Landsburg in *The Armchair Economist* (New York: Free Press, 1993). Landsburg

paints a picture of radical environmentalists as not nature lovers but humanity haters.

12. See Thomas Carlyle, *On Heroes, Hero-Worship, and the Heroic in History* (Berkeley: University of California Press, 1992). Carlyle's ideas, first presented in the 1840s, inspired Ralph Waldo Emerson's *Representative Men* (Cambridge: Belknap Press of Harvard, 1996). Both men emphasized individual personality as crucial to historical change. They were thinking of Napoleon, among others, but their ideas offered some inspiration for Italian and German fascists in the 20th century.

13. See Gary Becker, *Human Capital: A Theoretical and Empirical Analysis, with Special Reference to Education* (Chicago: University of Chicago Press, 1993). Management discussions are found in Thomas O. Davenport, *Human Capital: What It Is and Why People Invest It* (San Francisco: Jossey-Bass, 1999). Most writers treat workers as calculating owners of skills who seek to maximize returns on those skills. Whitman's individual is more of a value-driven political creature who asserts rather than negotiates and demands rather than sells.

14. See Leo Charney, *Empty Moments: Cinema, Modernity, and Drift* (Durham: Duke University Press, 1998) and Max Allen Collins and James L. Taylor, *One Lonely Knight: Mickey Spillane's Mike Hammer* (Bowling Green: Bowling Green University Press, 1984).

15. Edgar Allan Poe, *The Collected Tales and Poems of Edgar Allan Poe* (New York: Random House, 1992).

16. Smith's *The Theory of Moral Sentiments* argues that individuals can sense and share in the emotions of others. This empathy keeps us all from cheating or slaughtering each other. Emotion and shared sentiments have never really caught on as governing forces in society, except in 1960s communes and television melodramas at Christmas. They have, however, energized modern religious communities.

17. See Jack Weatherford, *The History of Money: From Sandstone to Cyberspace* (New York: Crown Publishing Co., 1998).

18. John Maynard Keynes, *The General Theory of Employment, Interest, and Money* (San Diego: Harcourt Brace, 1964), 294. Keynes's ideas on government manipulation of economies seem to have set off a deluge of post–World War II inflationary policies. At different times Keynes had called for credit controls by government to deal with this problem. He seemed to want to remove the individual from the economic system on occasion in his writings, replacing her with a coterie of elites with vast powers over allocation of resources. However, in the Great Depression many fine thinkers desperately advocated extreme remedies.

19. The list is endless. For a sample of the genre, see Loren B. Belker, *The First-Time Manager* (New York: AMACON, 1997). My favorite story concerns the Texas A & M professor who taught a seminar in time management to inmates of a nearby penitentiary. All the books have a central implicit premise: change is horrible, but we can manage the transition. Babbitt managed it by hoping it would go away, modern managers by pretending they could control it. The first would have to endure despair, the second the fruits of delusion.

BIBLIOGRAPHY

Becker, Gary. *Human Capital: A Theoretical and Empirical Analysis, with Special Reference to Education*. Chicago: University of Chicago Press, 1993.

Belker, Loren B. *The First-Time Manager*. New York: AMACON, 1997.

Carlyle, Thomas. *On Heroes, Hero-Worship, and the Heroic in History*. Berkeley: University of California Press, 1992.

Charney, Leo. *Empty Moments: Cinema, Modernity, and Drift*. Durham: Duke University Press, 1998.

Collins, Max Allen, and James L. Taylor. *One Lonely Knight: Mickey Spillane's Mike Hammer*. Bowling Green: Bowling Green University Press, 1984.

Curti, Merle. *The Growth of American Thought*. New York: Harper, 1951.

Davenport, Thomas O. *Human Capital: What It Is and Why People Invest in It*. San Francisco: Jossey-Bass, 1999.

Diggins, John Patrick. *Thorstein Veblen: Theorist of the Leisure Class*. Princeton: Princeton University Press, 1999.

Goldman, Eric F. *Rendezvous with Destiny: A History of Modern American Reform*. New York: Knopf, 1952.

Gould, Stephen Jay. *The Mismeasure of Man*. New York: Norton, 1996.

Hofstadter, Richard. *Social Darwinism in American Thought: 1860–1915*. Philadelphia: University of Pennsylvania Press, 1944.

Keynes, John Maynard. *The General Theory of Employment, Interest, and Money*. San Diego: Harcourt Brace, 1964.

Landsburg, Steven E. *The Armchair Economist*. New York: Free Press, 1993.

Lasch, Christopher. *The True and Only Heaven, Progress and Its Critics*. New York: Norton, 1991.

Marchand, Roland. *The Rise of Public Relations and Corporate Imagery in American Big Business*. Berkeley: University of California Press, 1998.

Pitzer, Donald E. *America's Communal Utopias*. Chapel Hill: University of North Carolina Press, 1997.

Ridge, Martin. *Ignatius Donnelly: Portrait of a Politician*. Saint Paul: Minnesota Historical Society Press, 1991.

Weatherford, Jack. *The History of Money: From Sandstone to Cyberspace*. New York: Crown Publishing Co., 1998.

Wiener, Philip P. *Evolution and the Founders of Pragmatism*. Cambridge: Harvard University Press, 1949.

Wolterstorff, N.P. "Empiricism." In Robert Audi, ed., *The Cambridge Dictionary of Philosophy*. Cambridge: Cambridge University Press, 1995.

CHAPTER 3

THE MARKET MODEL FALTERS

If ever a television quiz show for intellectuals appeared, a good question to keep contestants from making off with a million dollars of the producers' money would be, "Who said the following?"

We destroy the beauty of the countryside because the unappropriated splendors of nature have no economic value. We are capable of shutting off the sun and the stars because they do not pay a dividend. . . . Once we allow ourselves to be disobedient to the test of an accountant's profit, we have begun to change our civilization.[1]

The utterer of these Global Village-like words does not seem to be a big fan of capitalism and the profit motive. Yet it was John Maynard Keynes, the 20th century's most prominent economist. Here's another question: "Who said, 'Liberty may be incompatible with, and better than, too much efficiency'?" [2] It was Isaiah Berlin, one of the century's great champions of individual freedom and tolerance. With friends like these, the market model is in no need of enemies.

At the beginning of the 21st century, an observant banker sounded a note of caution over proclamations that with the death of communism, capitalism was triumphant. "The intellectual faith we now have in markets provides hope for the future," said Lawrence Lindsey, currently a lead advisor to President Bush, "but also holds a risk. Markets are not perfect, even though they beat any alternative form of economic decision making."[3] Lindsey noted that market mechanisms matched risk and reward so that those who dared greatly would either suffer greatly or reap great rewards. Consider how Keynes and Berlin would have reacted. "You want the present to be servant of the future," they might have collectively responded.

"But in the mayhem of risk taking today for some future reward, we are quite capable of destroying what makes life worthwhile now and in the future. What kind of devil's bargain is that?" Yet these men spent their lives defending the market model and despised Marxism and government bureaucracies. Clearly, the market model is in trouble. It stands as a colossus in comparison with statist models of production and distribution, but attacks by environmentalists, believers in justice rather than exchange as the basis for transfers, guild socialists in nongovernmental organizations (Ralph Nader probably fits in here), and others are constantly chipping away at the base. In this chapter, I will examine the crisis over market exchange which is coming in this century.

THE EXCHANGE MODEL

How do people who need or desire something get it in a world where not everyone can have everything? They can take it by force or use political power to legitimize their commandeering of it. They can persuade someone to give it to them, using rhetoric that involves reason, an appeal for charity, or perhaps implied violence if transfer does not take place. They can fall back on rules, norms, or values which require transfer or claim that habit or custom entitles them to the thing desired. They even can make it, mine it, harvest it, or catch it themselves. Economists and defenders of the market exchange model tend to argue that none of these approaches to production and transfer of scarce resources will foster well-being as well as "voluntary exchange [that] involves trading bundles of commodities or obligations to the mutual advantage of all parties to the transaction."[4] Barter, then, is the key to human betterment, with money as a medium of exchange making good things happen even faster through the pricing mechanism. Crucial to the model also are enforceable contracts and private property, since without them uncertainties, misunderstandings, and distrust would slow most things down and stop many transactions and information flows, needed so that market participants can learn where the best deals are. Most important, individuals are assumed to be purposeful and to seek transactions that best achieve their goals. Such behavior is considered "rational," a word that used to refer to acts in accord with or fostering universal order and coherence. Now the word, in America at least, means calculating behavior that maximizes one's desired outcomes. We can see here the first note of worry about the market model creeping in. If its advocates were so certain of its benefits, why did they need to take a legitimacy-inducing word like "rational" and redefine it for their uses? Indeed, why did economists feel a compelling need to begin awarding themselves a kind of Nobel Prize in the latter half of the last century? Even the priests in the temple, it seems, need to buck themselves up on occasion.

The big problem economists face is answering the question, "What is it in the market model that allocates resources so well to society's benefit?" Certainly competition is most important, since it forces prices down to the lowest possible level and makes more goods more affordable. But in addition, procedural rules for trading may be necessary with some rules or norms better than others. The period between agreeing to a deal and getting compensated also may be a factor, and while individuals discount delayed gains from trade, no one really ever knows if the discount rate used is the right one in the sense of best serving societal welfare. Another problem is information. How much is too little or too much? Related to this is the actual time it takes to trade. Consider the manager in Rosabeth Moss Kanter's organization, examined later in this chapter. If she spends all her time in the labor market within the organization negotiating compensation, when will she have time to produce anything of value or to search out information of use to her in her preparations to trade her labor for money?

In my view, and the views of most people who think about these things, none of these uncertainties and questionings detracts from the manifest benefits to humans of the market model, yet the model is somewhat mysterious in its origins—is it inherent in human nature or is it learned and culture-bound—and in its workings. And the puffed-up rhetoric of economists makes one wonder just how confident market defenders are in their advocacy. In fact, they have reason to worry behind the scenes.

HAYEK BURNS THE VILLAGE TO SAVE IT

Friedrich Hayek was a fine thinker and a great economist, but he had a talent for generating "uh-oh" responses. Nowhere is this more clear than in *The Fatal Conceit*, in which he attacks vain bureaucrats who claim to see the future more clearly than markets do and ends up convincing the reader that our faith in markets easily could disappear over the course of a few decades. Hayek implicitly asks the question, What is it that people are responding to when they work?[5] In other words, what is driving labor market activity? Three possible answers are:

- Genetic imperatives involving self-interest and instrumentalism resulting from natural selection (this is Gary Becker's view, discussed below).

- Stimuli created by enlightened governments applying reason to the management of society and the mobilization of workers (this is the fatal conceit of socialist governments).

- An evolved tradition of rules of conduct—the "extended order"—which legitimizes and evokes creative, entrepreneurial, and motivated barter and exchange behavior. (In his earlier writings Hayek also uses the term "spontaneous order.")

Hayek dismisses the fatal conceit as the vanity of elites and self-evidently destructive. As for genetic imperatives, he argues that the dominant human propensities are solidarity and altruism rather than instrumental self-interest. Left to itself, the great mass of humanity has stagnated in a communal tribalism in which work is a response to deep-rooted needs to belong and to contribute to one's group. This is the nonmarket exchange vision of work argued for by American sociologists such as Robert Bellah in *Habits of the Heart* (1985) and Christopher Lasch in *The True and Only Heaven* (1991), and by numberless ex-hippies from the 1960s. When they claim that their vision is the primary vision of humans as workers, Hayek would agree. But he then argues that some humans can and have learned a new vision of work which mutes the natural, communal vision. In modern industrial societies, the genetically inspired tribal vision may foster functioning in small work groups and perhaps even in larger organizations, but the success of those organizations depends much more on worker responses to the traditions and values of the extended order.

The extended order consists of "end-independent abstract rules and values of conduct."[6] Some of these are: each individual is the owner of himself and herself, and where there is no private property there is no justice. These rules and others like them lead to concepts of "self-interest" and "exchange relations" which in turn generate work of great productivity. Hayek makes it clear that the economic model of work as an exchange relation in a labor market is not very descriptive of Western industrial life. More explanatory is his view that interests and instrumental-like behavior are but intermediary steps. What really is happening is that sets of learned rules and values cause people to see themselves as having interests and purposes that require bartering in labor markets. The rules make work happen through interests, but interests and exchanges alone do not lead to the kind of work that made the West rich. Modern Western labor, then, is supposedly rooted in a set of traditions and rules that call for "the burdens of disciplined work, responsibility, risk-taking, saving, honesty, the honoring of promises. . . ."[7] Pure self-interest as the sole driving vision behind work would not have developed these canons, which have been so important. Rather these canons came first, and they mobilized self-interest. They developed because they were observed to work better than those guiding other people not of the West, and their use value ensured their survival. Of early humankind, Hayek wrote, "Neither his reason nor his innate 'natural goodness' leads man this way, only the bitter necessity of submitting to rules he does not like in order to maintain himself against competing groups that had already begun to expand because they stumbled upon such rules earlier."[8]

The extended order provides a vision which serves society but often is resisted by some of the intelligentsia, who see labor as the output of social planning's stimuli. Of these, Hayek said, "That better educated people should be more reluctant to submit to some unintelligible direction [of the extended order]—such as the market . . .—thus has the result . . . that they tend to resist just what . . . would increase their usefulness to their fellows."[9] Some left-wing intellectuals, proponents of guild socialism, reject the extended order's valuing of competition, private property, and markets because these values interfere with the human propensity towards group solidarity. Hayek once again agrees, but he emphasizes that only labor which responds to the learned values of the extended order has led to dramatic gains in welfare.

In arguing on behalf of the market model, Hayek ends up seriously undermining it. Instead of barter being driven by self-interest served by rational calculation, he describes a modern industrial society in which workers, managers, and consumers respond to a learned set of values and rules which teach them to act as if individual self-interest were the be-all and end-all of living when in fact the real human nature-driven end is a communal, village-like existence of solidarity among one's fellows. Market exchange behavior, in Hayek's view, is unnatural, irrational (in the classic sense of not fostering human coherence), and fabulously successful at improving human well-being. Or, if you prefer, barter is a form of submission to disliked rules out of bitter necessity rather than to a felt urge to "truck and barter," as Adam Smith claimed. The learned set of values and rules is enshrined in a set of traditions encouraging a sense of self-interest, instrumental calculating, honesty in dealings, thrift to foster efficiency and investment, and responsibility to fulfill obligations. What's more, a market society never can be certain that the artifice of the extended order will continue, so it must constantly educate its citizenry to hold proper beliefs. In the United States, Junior Achievement clubs in high school inculcate the extended order's values. Managerial training often involves a rhetoric of advocacy for the market. Merit in some organizations is based not just on performance but on attitude. A "bad" attitude may be associated with criticism of market mechanisms, private property, etc. Honors are granted by business clubs such as Kiwanis and the Rotary to upholders of the order. All of this is required to persuade the mass of people not to drift back into natural but inefficient communalism. Hayek would approve, since increases in the standard of living cannot continue without a constant stream of shoring operations to prop up faith in the order.

Hayek's goal was to intellectually emasculate the socialist paradigm, which envisions societal well-being as the result of clever manipulations and commands by a bureaucratized elite. He did this and almost as a by-product helped to establish the extended order as the economic model for the late 20th century in the United States. In achieving the goal, however, he argued that well-being is the result of adherence to a set of grotesque traditions that must be constantly advocated by a different set of elites. The market all but disappears in his model, and nothing precludes a radical change in ways of learning the tradition of the extended order in the

21st century. Indeed, alternative visions are all around us, and as we will see, they are being attended to.

MARKET BEHAVIOR AS ANIMAL SPIRITS

Hayek was not the only great economist to implicitly question the foundations on which his discipline was based. Here is John Maynard Keynes again on why classical economic theory had become so dominant in the 20th century:

That it reached conclusions quite different from what the ordinary uninstructed person would expect added, I suppose, to its intellectual prestige. That its teaching, translated into practice, was austere and often unpalatable, lent it virtue. That it was adapted to carry a vast and consistent logical superstructure, gave it beauty. That it could explain much social injustice and apparent cruelty as an inevitable incident in the scheme of progress, and the attempt to change such things as likely on the whole to do more harm than good, commended it to authority. That it afforded a measure of justification to the free activities of the individual capitalist, attracted it to the support of the dominant social force behind authority.[10]

Nowhere does Keynes say that the market model of self-interested barterers engaging in supply-and-demand activities subject to budget constraints and all the other characteristics of the classical model actually describes the way the world really is. Most economists would agree with Keynes up to a point and say that a highly stylized model can offer rich explanatory power, and economics is mostly an explanatory social science. Keynes, however, wanted economics to have predictive power, and he believed that economists would have to move away from pleasing but sterile formalisms and accept that there was more to markets than rational, calculating behavior. Only by including that "more" in its model could economics become useful to society.

In the justly famous Chapter 12 of his *General Theory*, Keynes paints a picture of what ought to be seen as the purest-of-the-pure economic animals, the capitalist. In former times, he says, businesses were places where friends came together and "embarked on business as a way of life, not really relying on a precise calculation of prospective profit."[11] Businesspeople were motivated by "constructive impulses" and the "temptation to take a chance." Self-interest recedes here, replaced as the driver of capitalism by a spirit of optimism and a passionate intensity motivating businessmen in their calling towards "a spontaneous urge to action rather than inaction." Successful pursuers of the business way of life possess "animal spirits." Of course they are self-interested and calculating, but as often as not they fall back on "whim or sentiment or chance." Keynes argued that economic theory must come to see the capitalist as more than a calculating machine maximizing utility. He or she also is an inhabitant of a way of life that attracts emotional people capable of quite dramatic behavior. The old economics, focused on *demand*, must give way to a new, broader economics stressing *effective demand*. Keynes's whole theoretical edifice rests on this differentiation, and while his work has not stood up very well over time, his rich characterization of the business calling still is influential.

A life in the markets as a life of emotion and perhaps a calling: this was not the stuff of Economics 101 in the 20th century, but it is likely to be prominent in this century's teaching. Below I want to comment on the idea of a calling, and then I will discuss emotions and "quasi-rational" behavior.

THE IMPORTANCE OF A CALLING

In 1849 a Southern plantation owner, as part of an ongoing debate about how to get the most work out of slaves, observed, "Experience has long since taught masters that every attempt to force a slave beyond the limits that he fixes as a sufficient amount of labor to render his master, instead of extorting more work, only tends to make him unprofitable, unmanageable, a vexation and a curse."[12] It is not surprising to learn that this "sufficient" labor was usually quite a bit less than that of which a slave was capable.[13] What is surprising is the inability of slaveholders to get more work out of their slaves, either through coercion or incentives. We will never know what actually went on in this darkened period of American history, but it seems as if slaves early on developed a sense of what the identity of slave entailed and worked in response to the identity. Variations in that level of work probably occurred as part of economic exchanges with masters or because of threats and punishment, but the base level was a response to what amounts to a "calling."[14] In *The Slave Community* John Blassingame notes that black slaves in the American South and European white slaves in North Africa both exhibited this kind of behavior, so there is nothing particularly racial or ethnic in it. People just develop a sense of what work behavior is required as appropriate for a given profession, status, class, etc. Jews in concentration camps and Soviet slave laborers also have behaved in a similar manner. This tendency helps explain why so few overseers, drivers, or guards have been needed over the last five hundred years to mobilize the efforts of what must have been about 50 million people. In a setting from which there is no escape, an individual eventually finds his or her calling and responds to it. The response will not vary much as long as conditions remain stable.

If we extend the idea of a calling from nonmarket to labor and capital market environments, we come to Max Weber, who noticed the same idea of calling as an important influence on the work of English Protestants from the seventeenth century onwards. Work as calling is more than simple role play. It is "the fulfillment of the obligations imposed upon the individual by his position in the world."[15] One senses one's duty in one's job, which is ordained by the nature of things, and responds accordingly with work. Although Weber picked up this idea from events in early modern England, it has a long history in the Great Chain of Being philosophy, which had influenced social and religious thinking since the beginning of the Christian era. In this view humans have been placed by God on a hierarchy of existence (the chain) somewhere between animals below and angels above. A fixed number of unchanging levels exists with no gaps and no possibility of levels being added or subtracted (since God does not change his or her mind or make errors). On the human scale people are ranked according to their status. In practice, the work they do becomes their calling and identifies their unchanging existence on the chain.

Weber, however, did not see work as calling to be the natural state of affairs among humanity. In fact, he observed, "At all periods of history, wherever it was possible, there has been ruthless acquisition." In the same passage he referred to " the universal reign of absolute unscrupulousness in the pursuit of selfish interests" and "the instinct of acquisition."[16] In other words, like it or not humans have an inherently economic approach to everything and, without constraints, they act in accord with it. The Great Chain idea and the laws based on it (requiring workers to wear certain clothing to identify their status or calling, forbidding job changes or migration) acted as a constraint and kept Europe poor until the English Protestants figured out how to use the ideas of the Great Chain and work as calling to accumulate capital, a dramatic innovation which in part has led to the current wealth of the industrial world.

For Weber, then, humans are generally disposed to truck and barter in highly self-interested ways, but that alone is not what made the West rich. Rather it also was a series of clever reinterpretations of the idea of a calling driving one's behavior in labor and capital markets. Capital acquisition (referred to by economists as the market for ownership) has fostered ever-increasing well-being in the West not because of better and more broadly functioning markets, although these certainly count, but primarily because calling activities became associated with businessmen piling up surpluses as savings which then were available for investment. A similar process, according to Weber, occurred in labor markets from the 17th century onwards. Labor was said to exist for God's glory and was thus a moral act. To act morally, in Calvinist theology, was a sign of being one of God's elect, while unemployment merited scorn. The more one worked in one's calling, the more moral one was. In 1600, annual work hours in Europe were 1,980; by 1850, at the height of the Protestant work ethic's influence, they were 3,650, almost twice 2000's amount.[17] It was labor savings added to capitalists' surpluses that ensured the availability of funds for investment in wealth-enhancing economic activities. Weber's individual is rational, calculating, exchange-oriented, and self-interested, but what ensured Western well-being from 1600 onwards was a learned value that emphasized work and managerial and ownership behavior as a response to a calling involving saving, either directly as part of one's duty or as a by-product of increased effort. Keynes hated this savings as ethical model and toyed with the idea that animal spirits and emotions really drove progress. Hayek disagreed with both of them and proclaimed that humans are affiliative, non-bartering creatures who grow wealthy only when they learn values associated with calculation and self-absorbed, individual, goal-directed behavior. None of these thinkers was willing to bet on the market model alone as the major ingredient in the recipe for societal success. Oh, it was necessary all right, but other things really kept the economic engine running. The market model of Economics 101 merely kept it from stalling.

EMOTIONS AND THE DECLINE OF RATIONAL MAN

Homo economicus—or rational man—engages in "the instrumentally efficient pursuit of given ends."[18] Some economists envision this behavior as mostly maximizing, while others introduce constraints such as information search costs and talk about "satisficing," but market theory holds that the individual and individuals in the aggregate are mostly rational most of the time. Note how incomplete the model is. It says nothing about the quality of ends, nor does it specify how homo economicus normatively deals with risk and uncertainty.[19] Moreover, a growing body of research towards the end of the last century made it clear that context, task, and task importance count in determining when individuals act rationally. Mostly homo economicus shines when tasks can be structured and analyzed, when they are important to the individual, and when information needed to make a choice or state a preference is framed in appropriate ways.[20] If information is presented so that individuals are primed to think in terms of values such as fairness and equity, their preferences may not be in accord with their interests. Naturally some economists simply make the preference for a value into an interest so that all behavior becomes rational. This kind of theorizing is called "imperial economics," and while it is wonderfully interesting when applied to such things as choosing a mate or deciding on one's religion, imperial economists tend to take themselves a bit too seriously. Most reasonable discussions of rationality admit that values and ends are different things. Values, and the emotions and quasi-rational decision tools that go along with them, are in the realm of causes and explanations, while ends are in the domain of outcomes, surprises, and the exercise of the will. Human behavior is associated with both prior influences, which social scientists, aping physics, like to call "causes" and with future goals.

As we saw in Chapter 2, most Americans do not like to see themselves characterized as bubbles tossed about on causal waves. This is good for economists, who emphasize goal-directed life as the only life that makes sense. However, Americans also are a people who moved away from

19th-century spiritual and political values in the 20th century but now are moving back to them in the 21st. This is not good for economists and the philosophical bases of the market model. People who truck and barter with a deep concern for the well-being and autonomy of the other party are not acting in accord with the model. They are not engaging in "arm's-length" exchanges, and people who embrace are not easily understood by economists (except for the imperial sort, of course).[21]

An emotion is a noncognitive experience of anger, fear, joy, and the like, according to Jon Elster, who has summarized research on emotions and economics in *Alchemies of the Mind* (1999). Emotions are not part of the knowledge/belief/need/desire rational man paradigm; rather they partake of "visceral arousal," although they usually have an intention associated with them. Thus hunger is a state of arousal caused by lack of food. The vicarious experience of joy at the thought of eating generates a purpose to eat. The anger experienced at the thought of a betrayal by a client generates a purpose to somehow punish the client in future dealings, even at the cost of lost income. How can an economic transaction of this kind be considered rational and explainable by the standard model? And if this transaction and the billions of similar emotion-driven transactions which occur every day do not fit the model, perhaps the model is not as useful as was once thought.

Elster holds that emotions are capable of "subverting the rationality of action, of belief formation, and of information acquisition."[22] For example, emotions can influence an individual not to consider easily available, consequential information that is known to exist. Economists try to save the model by arguing that emotions are simply a source of preferences, which then guide purposes towards ends in a calculating manner. But there is no getting away from the reality that emotions associated with affiliation—as Hayek noted—drive lots of business transactions in many societies. One does not talk of purposes and calculations in describing the complex *keiretsu* networks among Japanese suppliers, manufacturers, and distributors. Or among the family-focused *chaebol* firms of South Korea. Although these arrangements are now seen to be economically inefficient and not long for the world of the 21st century, the knowledge has not hindered American market critics from proposing Asian models as replacements for British and American paradigms.[23] When we talk about emotions, we really are not in the homo economicus environment any longer. While some economists may analyze the costs or benefits of emotions in transactions, humans rarely see their own emotions this way. Consider this: Each of us would gladly act to reduce living costs but few would act to banish the ability to ever experience pain. We might casually say we would, but in the sense of giving up an element of our nature, abandonment is highly unlikely (see more on this in the "bomb-in-the-brain" discussion later in this chapter).

The animal spirits of Keynesian entrepreneurs and investors as well as the visceral feelings of community and joy in group belongingness of Hayek's poor benighted humanity are both akin to the emotions analyzed by Jon Elster, and all three note that the market model and the classical paradigm do not deal adequately with or do not include the emotions. What is to be done? Hopefully, 21st-century theorists will expand the model in ways that make it more realistic. If this work does not occur, the public will relegate economic thinking to the backwaters of popularity where anthropology, political economy, and political science unfortunately now reside. But with their less formal and more inclusive ways of thinking about human behavior, they may be the hot academic departments of the future.

THE MARKET AS CONVERSATION

A noted economist, Donald McCloskey, argues that markets be thought of as ongoing conversations that are more than simply barter exchanges.[24] "A price is a remark in an ongoing conversation," he notes, and the information it contains passes among persons in their various roles of producer, distributor, retailer, buyer, and user. The hum and buzz of the conversations, which includes added-on information about emotions, habits, rules of thumb guiding action, callings, and, yes, interests, persuade the parties to see themselves, others, and the world in ever-changing ways, some of which evoke actions called demand and supply. To study this great complexity, one needs to simplify, but the simplifications of the rational man and the market model may be inappropriate. According to McCloskey, the market as a conversation metaphor expands our ways of understanding economic life without in fact giving up the classical paradigm. The emotions and grandiose dreams of the entrepreneur—Keynes's man of animal spirits—now are seen to foster a stream of rhetoric as he persuades himself and his backers to go forward, his banker to lend him money, his employees to do what is needed, and his clients to purchase. Supply and demand still guide economic actions, but our understanding of the process grows, and with a sense of the process comes a sense of how it can be improved.

Without this enriched paradigm, how will defenders of the market model cope with the guild socialists who will reappear in this century from the early decades of the 20th? These people will call for justice rather than barter to govern the exchange of goods and will argue that consumers should pay and producers receive what is fair, with "fair" to be determined by participatory democracy rooted in endless consumer and producer committees. Classical economists will say that such behavior is inefficient. McCloskey's heirs hopefully will point out that the rhetoric of price discovery and discussion is preferable to the bureaucratic proclamations of government officials stating the price of a good as determined by a thousand committee reports (the next chapter discusses the new guild socialists and the alternatives to the market model they will propose).

The conversation metaphor also allows us to grasp the importance of trust in economic transactions. Parties must persuade each other of their trustworthiness if exchange is to occur. The condition of goods must be as the seller proclaims them to be, and the payment must occur when the buyer announces it will occur. Trust is the willingness of one party to depend on the statements and behavior of another, and it only can be established through conversations and inquiry or through symbols and rituals which signal trustworthiness. Thus when an individual seeking a job wears the right clothes, sits the right way at an interview, and uses speech common to the industry, she is implicitly communicating that in this particular labor market she can be trusted. Here is another example. In an American restaurant, waiters are trained to use a ritualized dialogue with the patron which steers him towards higher spending and faster eating than he would do without the ritual encounter. A clever economist once noted that if the patron recognized how untrustworthy the ritual is, he somehow could avoid the ritual, and his chances of reducing costs and increasing eating time would go up. The economist proposed the following: When the waiter approaches, the patron should jump up and proclaim, "Hi. My name is Bob and I'll be your customer!" The waiter would be so flustered that he would fail to employ the ritual and would engage in a transaction conversation of greater advantage to the customer. Only economists who think "out of the box" can come up with such wonderful ideas, and it is these ideas that will legitimize the market model when it comes under attack.

THE NUTTINESS OF DISCOURSE IN THE MARKET MODEL

To see what happens when classical models of labor markets are used to guide the communication of managers as they pursue their careers, we can examine the ideas of Rosabeth Moss Kanter, Harvard Business School management guru, about "the new managerial work." According to Kanter, traditional power bases are eroding in American organizations with the blurring of such hierarchical demarcations as task, title, and department.[25] Driven by competitive pressure, flexible strategies and structures are emerging: increased horizontal peer communication, greater use of outside purchasing of formerly internal services, strategic alliances, and supplier-customer "partnerships." With all of this complexity, old ideas of "boss," "job," and "career path" have fallen by the wayside. Rewards are increasingly tied to performance rather than to role or seniority. The manager and employee are now internal entrepreneurs, ever on the alert for an opportunity to seize, a deal to make, or a failure to avoid. The new American work model signals a reliance solely on the market model. In this perspective the organization becomes a large marketplace in which employees endlessly bargain with each other in millions of constantly shifting exchange relationships. Here is a possible scenario:

Manager A: If you assign me two MBAs to work on product design, I will push back the date you are to deliver your completed product plan to me.

Manager B: If I do that, I will need quicker access to the CAD system on the mainframe.

Manager A: I think I can get that for you. I'll offer the system head a share of my budget allocation next year.

Manager B: But if his department starts looking really good because of low costs, he'll have to maintain those low costs after your one-time deal expires. He'll reduce resources supplied to me to control costs. I better negotiate a long term contract with him now before you approach him.

Manager A: Good. I'll give you a week. Then I'll negotiate with him.

All of these exchanges supposedly add efficiency, flexibility, and creativity to American organizations. Cynics might say that all that will occur is the substitution of bureaucratic wheel-spinning with bargaining wheel-spinning. Arguing over rules and procedures will be replaced by endless negotiating.

In Kanter's view, the company is just another marketplace, not fundamentally different from the firm's product markets. Each employee is driven solely by an economic vision of work and seeks to maximize his or her utility through exchange relations with bosses, peers, and subordinates. The organizational climate becomes one of deal-making. In this environment the power of hierarchy fades, replaced by the power of rhetoric, but a very constrained rhetoric. The manager only prospers to the extent that she convinces other managers and subordinates that a deal will lead to benefits. Since the probability of rhetoric-driven success in deal-making is low, many deals must be negotiated. The venture capitalists' one-in-ten rule applies. Nine out of ten deals go sour, but the tenth deal should cover the losses or time wasted in the other nine. The new American manager thus is frantic in her search for opportunities, and the organization becomes abuzz with deal-making. Membership in multiple networks, formal and informal, is sought, since the more people you know, the more deal-making opportunities you have. Knowledge must be generalized to foster intelligent communication with other dealers. If the organization needs specialists, it can raise the status of blue collars, who will now become "knowledge workers" and consider themselves to have made a good deal. If the workers don't want to be knowledge workers, there is always artificial intelligence. The firm finds an expert, institutionalizes his or her expertise on a computer, and makes the software wisdom available to the deal-makers, who have no time to actually learn something on their own.

Although an aura of American nuttiness pervades this scenario, the general perspective is simply the market model applied to work. Work is an input to attain one's interests, and it results from exchange. It is allegedly a more efficient way to do things than work as a response to values, power, rules, calling, emotion, etc.

Supervising all of this—because they have been given huge monetary incentives to do so—are the senior executives, who examine deals to see if "added value" is being created for the owners. These people are the only watchdogs left in the firm. Less senior managers are integrators, facilitators, collaborators, and negotiators—hustlers in service to themselves, competing for scarce resources. They form strategic alliances with peers and workers, an activity which Kanter refers to as "trust-building". What she means by trust is the establishment of mutual recognition of the other party's interests in a deal so that good-faith bargaining can occur. It is not the trust of mutual obligations described above. But a marketplace atmosphere like this is not conducive to trust-building of any kind. Employees become "bolder about speaking up, challenging authority and charting their own course." They "complain loudly about corporate support departments and reject their use in favor of external service providers." They "shock corporate executives by criticizing upper management behavior."[26] One wonders how a worker forges good-faith bargaining links with other workers who are prone to lash out whenever they feel that their interests are thwarted.

We need to come back down to earth from Planet Kanter. The explosive dynamics of the new workplace described by her are just that—explosive—and doomed to fizzle out. Workers and managers driven solely by an exchange vision of work have no sense of equity (the concept of a "fair day's work" would be foreign to them), and their idea of trust is impoverished. Trust is not just good-faith bargaining but rather a sense of mutual obligation willingly entered into by each party. Trust of this kind is driven by character, not negotiation, and it is crucial to the maintenance of an organization. People must tend to be upright and honest—in other words, value-driven instead of interest-driven—if coordinated work is to occur. Without real trust, enormously costly monitoring of behavior is required. Beyond the cost of monitoring untrustworthy workers who will not deliver a fair day's pay without lengthy and also costly negotiating lies the problem of knowledge. There simply is not time for people who are constantly deal-making to master any set of skills or to build up a set of beliefs and facts which are the bases for decisions. It has been clear for several years now that expert systems on computers are not going to solve the knowledge problem, freeing managers to negotiate endlessly. Nor is the idea of creating clusters of highly paid knowledge workers of much value. Kanter, in calling for a new workplace, resurrects the old, in which accountants, lawyers, systems people, researchers, designers, engineers, and producers exist in isolated communities within the organization. The only difference is that in the old model these specialists often were content, influenced by their sense of work as a calling or a profession. This vision does not exist in Kanter's new workplace, and her knowledge workers will be prone to abandon their callings and start dealing like everyone else.

Rosabeth Moss Kanter began her career as a sociologist studying communes. Here is her take on work in 1972:

The fact is that people work for causes and challenges beyond making sure they will eat or be paid. In a commune they work because the effort may be intrinsically satisfying, may be chosen work; or they work because they are committed to the other people in the group and want, positively, to do their share to ensure the collective welfare and, negatively, to avoid the disapproval of people they love.[27]

In her early work, then, she makes it clear that, while communes are not always practical, they have much to tell us in a conversation about how labor markets might function. The approach of her communal workers to their toil is very much in the air today as a characteristic of the emerging organizational workplace, and Kanter's 1989 thinking in terms solely of an economic model suggests a narrowing and even an impoverishing in her thought. Both her contribution to the conversation about work and the implied conversations her managers will have during work seem constrained, artificial, and uncompelling.

HOMO ECONOMICUS IS IN TROUBLE

In the 21st century, markets will continue to function, and individuals will truck and barter just as they always have done. But attempts will increase to remove or curtail exchange relations in many areas where they now exist, and the force of these attempts will be augmented by the weak defense of markets mounted by their defenders, burdened as they are by a rational-man model that seems more of a caricature than a useful guide. Models can be of three kinds. An isomorphic model maps onto reality, so that x in relation to y in the model describes reality. A subway map is isomorphic. An idealized model describes a created reality. *Looking Backward*, the novel discussed in the last chapter, presents such a model of U.S. society. A simplified model takes complexity out so that clear thinking and useful explanations can be developed. Economists claim that the rational-man model is simplified while doing research, but then they often present it as isomorphic when discussing public policy or societal behavior. However, consider the bomb-in-the-brain problem. A technique has been developed to implant a small computer attached to an expensive grenade in your brain. The computer monitors your body and can tell, with complete certainty, if and when you are about to contract a disease which will produce a slow, excruciatingly painful death. As soon as it makes such a judgment, if it ever does, a signal is sent to the grenade, which explodes and kills you without pain. Would you purchase such a machine and have it implanted? The rational-man model says yes, you would, because the benefits of a quick death outweigh the costs of a slow, painful one. Yet we all know that no one would do such a thing. Something is wrong with the model.

Take another example. Economist Steven E. Landsburg in *The Armchair Economist* (1993) argues that seatbelts in cars actually foster accidents because increased safety removes the incentive to drive carefully.[28] He advocates mounting a spear on the dashboard pointing at the driver's heart as a way of creating a rational expectation that careless driving may be quite dangerous to one's vital organs and that the cost of recklessness outweighs the benefit of getting there faster. Here the rational-man model turns from a simplification to an isomorphic representation yielding behavioral guidelines. It isn't that his proposal is wrong or silly; in fact, it probably would work to reduce reckless driving without our having to remove seat belts from cars. What's wrong with this way of thinking and advising is that Landsburg uses a stylized model supposedly designed to foster theorizing as a source of normative recommendations. I happen to agree with everything he says. I am not troubled by his shifting from "I believe x is causally related to y" to "You should do y because x exists." Other people get infuriated, however, at the presumptuousness, posturing, and grandstanding Landsburg and similar imperial economists exhibit. The bomb-in-the-brain thought experiment and a hundred like it tell us how limited the homo economicus model is and how modest its adherents ought to be. Yet they allegedly insist on forcing their model on all human endeavor in a thoroughly unwarranted manner. A backlash is inevitable, particularly if the trends identified in Chapter 2 towards a more spiritual and autonomy-seeking existence continue in this country. People do not wish to be told that they are driven mechanically by an internal cost-benefit calculating machine and little else.

The microeconomic, rational-man theory of human choice behavior does not account for habitual, emotional, value-driven behavior. It does not have anything to say about exploratory choices—testing the waters—or choices made for the sheer joy of choosing. The latter is referred to as the "utility of the moment." The theory is quite useful in the investigation of economic behavior, but as a normative model legitimizing exchange relations, cost-benefit analyses, and "everything-is-or-ought-to-be-a-market" approaches for all human endeavors, it invites scorn. As one wag put it, economists and market defenders have an "irrational passion for rational calculations."[29] Keynes once noted, "If economists could manage to get themselves thought of as humble, competent people, on a level with dentists, that would be splendid."[30] Economists ought to be humble, because the model has a difficult time explaining the fundamental roots of economic growth. Is it fostered by:

- Freeing up animal spirits—perhaps by government and educational institutions trumpeting the importance of the entrepreneur and encouraging young people to take a chance and follow the dream? To some extent, this is already happening.

- Increasing rhetoric in support of the market model so that every schoolchild learns to downplay his or her natural inclination towards community and affiliation and to value self-interest and rational behavior?

- Reducing government's propensity to regulate, religion's propensity to require ritual behavior, and other institutions' constraints on exchange so that trucking and bartering will be liberated?

- Persuading individuals to find callings for themselves that value work, reduced consumption, and accumulating savings to fund investment? In the Elizabethan era, those in a calling by law were required to wear a certain kind of clothing to signal their status to others and to constantly remind the wearers of their position. In some U.S. school districts, schoolchildren early on are compelled to adopt garb of this kind. Are they being prepared for callings? Does that foster economic growth?

We are not only unsure of the fundamental roots of economic growth, but we also know little about the day-to-day processes through which growth occurs. The classical economic model says that when rational man, markets, property rights, information, and so forth all are functioning as they ought, an optimal equilibrium occurs. As long as nothing changes, the equilibrium condition continues. Thus even if societal conditions are unsatisfactory and even outrageous, they must be considered optimal. This was what Hayek argued early in his career, and it infuriated Keynes. Current conservative economic thinking is much less rigid than it was in Hayek's day, but still it is burdened by the static nature of the model. Further, in the hands of management gurus like Rosabeth Moss Kanter, prescriptions for behavior within the confines of the model become downright weird, with everyone urged to truck and barter endlessly and to do little else. Kanter has shown in her career that she knows better, and her organization as marketplace thinking probably has changed by now, but lots of gurus-in-waiting and some economists are ready to take her place. Other economists try to make the model more sensible by adding on theories about signals and implicit contracts which reduce market time so that production can occur. This is all to the good and undoubtedly will continue. But what is needed is a movement towards the market as conversation model and away from the narrower market as exchange paradigm. In this perspective, which really is that of political and institutional economics, markets foster well-being in society because behind them is (1) a functioning democracy that tolerates and encourages discourse, and (2) sets of institutions which help the individual tell the society her needs and desires and society tell the individual its requirements. All of these communications will be laden with norms, values, commands, requests, informing, convincing, and interests. Economic explanations within this expanded-process paradigm do not lend themselves to mathematical modeling, so rigor has to be given up. But so what, if a more realistic economics deflects the coming surge of attacks on the market model. The cost of the loss of mathematics will be outweighed by the gain of a stronger defense of the economic model. Here is a sign pinned to a downtown beggar:

Wars	2
Legs	1
Wives	2
Children	4
Wounds	2
Total	11

Just like the beggar, economists use mathematics to make their points, but like the beggar they have and should use other point-making rhetorical tools. Their opponents certainly do, as we will see in the following chapters.

NOTES

1. Keynes made this statement in a lecture on April 17, 1933. Quoted by Robert Skidelsky, *John Maynard Keynes, The Economist as Savior, 1920–1937*. (New York: Penguin Books, 1995), 477–478. At different times Keynes also occasionally attacked free trade in certain goods and commodities because imports hindered a move towards national self-sufficiency.

2. Quoted by Michael Ignatieff, *Isaiah Berlin, A Life* (New York: Henry Holt, 1998), 36.

3. Lawrence B. Lindsey, "The 17–Year Boom," *Wall Street Journal*, 27 January 2000, 16.

4. Robert B. Wilson, "Exchange." In John Eatwell, Murray Milgate, and Peter Newman eds. *The New Palgrave, The World of Economics* (New York: W.W. Norton, 1991), 237. Reading the prose that economists generally use to discuss important human issues is like wading through wet sand, and *The New Palgrave*, while a valuable resource, is no exception.

5. F.A. Hayek, *The Fatal Conceit, The Errors of Socialism* (Chicago: University of Chicago Press, 1988).

6. Hayek, op.cit., 31.

7. Hayek, op.cit., 64.

8. Hayek, op.cit., 76.

9. Hayek, op.cit., 82.

10. John Maynard Keynes, *The General Theory of Employment, Interest, and Money* (San Diego: Harcourt Brace, 1964), 33.

11. Keynes, op. cit., 150. The following quotes are from 152–164.

12. "Negro Slavery and the South," *De Bow's Review*, 1849, 7, September, 220. Quoted in John W. Blassingame, *The Slave Community* (New York: Oxford University Press, 1979), 227, 280.

13. See Blassingame, 280 ff.

14. Another important discussion of the slave "calling" is contained in the diary of Thomas B. Chaplin, a South Carolina cotton planter. See Theodore Rosengarten, *Tombee, Portrait of a Cotton Planter* (New York: William Morrow, 1986).

15. Adrian Furnham, *The Protestant Work Ethic* (London: Routledge, 1990), 276.

16. Max Weber, *The Protestant Ethic and the Spirit of Capitalism* (New York: Scribner's, 1958), 56–57.

17. Estimates are from Juliet B. Schor, *The Overworked American* (New York: Basic Books, 1991), 45.

18. Jon Elster, *Alchemies of the Mind, Rationality and the Emotions* (Cambridge: Cambridge University Press, 1999), 102. See also Colin F. Camerer, *Behavioral Economics* (Princeton: Princeton University Press, 2001).

19. Daniel M. Hausman and Michael S. McPherson, "Economics, rationality, and ethics." In Daniel M. Hausman, ed., *The Philosophy of Economics* (Cambridge: Cambridge University Press, 1994), 252–277.

20. For a sampling, see Daniel J. Kahneman, J. Knetsch, and R. Thaler, "Fairness as a Constraint on Profit Seeking," *American Economic Review*, 1986, 76, 728–741, and Amos Tversky, P. Slovic, and D. Kahneman, "The Causes of Preference Reversal," *American Economic Review*, 1990, 80, 204–217.

21. The bible for imperial economics is Gary Becker, *The Economic Approach to Human Behavior* (Chicago: University of Chicago Press, 1976). Becker's melding of behaviorist psychology and economics tends to create a stylized individual who might be called a purposeful pigeon.

22. Elster, op. cit., 285.

23. A noted Japanese scholar, Chalmers Johnson, has been quite active in this discussion. See Chalmers Johnson, et al., *The Industrial Policy Debate* (Cambridge: Harvard University Press, 1992) and *MITI and the Japanese Miracle* (Palo Alto: Stanford University Press, 1990). Johnson has at times advocated a U.S. government department of industrial policy to coordinate all the networks.

24. Donald N. McCloskey, *Knowledge and Persuasion in Economics* (Cambridge: Cambridge University Press, 1994), 367 ff.. See also his masterpiece, *The Rhetoric of Economics* (Madison: University of Wisconsin Press, 1985).

25. Rosabeth Moss Kanter, "The New Managerial Work," *Harvard Business Review*, 1989, 67(6), November-December, 85–92.

26. Kanter, op.cit., 90.

27. Originally from *Commitment and Community: Communes and Utopias in Sociological Perspective*. Excerpts reprinted in Yorick Blumenfeld, ed., *Scanning the Future, 20 Eminent Thinkers on the World of Tomorrow* (London: Thames & Hudson, 1999), 265.

28. Steven E. Landsburg, *The Armchair Economist, Economics and Everyday Life* (New York: Free Press, 1993).

29. See Mark Blaug, *The Methodology of Economics* (Cambridge: Cambridge University Press, 1994), 230 ff.

30. In "Economic Possibilities for Our Grandchildren." Quoted by Deborah A. Redman, *Economics and the Philosophy of Science* (New York: Oxford University Press, 1993), 155.

BIBLIOGRAPHY

Becker, Gary. *The Economic Approach to Human Behavior*. Chicago: University of Chicago Press, 1976.

Blassingame, John W. *The Slave Community*. New York: Oxford University Press, 1979.

Blaug, Mark. *The Methodology of Economics*. Cambridge: Cambridge University Press, 1994.

Blumenfeld, Yorick, ed. *Scanning the Future, 20 Eminent Thinkers on the World of Tomorrow*. London: Thames & Hudson, 1999.

Camerer, Colin F. *Behavioral Economics*. Princeton: Princeton University Press, 2001.

Elster, Jon. *Alchemies of the Mind, Rationality and the Emotions*. Cambridge: Cambridge University Press, 1999.

Furnham, Adrian. *The Protestant Work Ethic*. London: Routledge, 1990.

Hausman, Daniel M., ed. *The Philosophy of Economics*. Cambridge: Cambridge University Press, 1994.

Hayek, F.A. *The Fatal Conceit, The Errors of Socialism*. Chicago: University of Chicago Press, 1988.

Ignatieff, Michael. *Isaiah Berlin, A Life*. New York: Henry Holt, 1998.

Johnson, Chalmers. *The Industrial Policy Debate*. Cambridge: Harvard University Press, 1992.

———. *MITI and the Japanese Miracle*. Palo Alto: Stanford University Press, 1990.

Kahneman, Daniel J., J. Knetsch, and R. Thaler, "Fairness as a Constraint on Profit Seeking." *American Economic Review*, 1986, 76, 728–741.

Kanter, Rosabeth Moss. "The New Managerial Work." *Harvard Business Review*, 1989, 67(6), November-December, 85–92.

Keynes, John Maynard. *The General Theory of Employment, Interest, and Money*. San Diego: Harcourt Brace, 1964.

Landsburg, Steven E. *The Armchair Economist, Economics and Everyday Life*. New York: Free Press, 1993.

Lindsey, Lawrence B. "The 17–Year Boom." *Wall Street Journal*, 27 January 2000, 16.

McCloskey, Donald N. *Knowledge and Persuasion in Economics*. Cambridge: Cambridge University Press, 1994.

———. *The Rhetoric of Economics*. Madison: University of Wisconsin Press, 1985.

Redman, Deborah A. *Economics and the Philosophy of Science*. New York: Oxford University Press, 1993.

Rosengarten, Theodore. *Tombee, Portrait of a Cotton Planter*. New York: William Morrow, 1988.

Schor, Juliet B. *The Overworked American*. New York: Basic Books, 1991.

Skidelsky, Robert. *John Maynard Keynes, The Economist as Savior, 1920–1937*. New York: Penguin Books, 1995.

Tversky, Amos, P. Slovic, and D. Kahneman, "The Causes of Preference Reversal." *American Economic Review*, 1990, 80, 204–217.

Weber, Max. *The Protestant Ethic and the Spirit of Capitalism*. New York: Scribner's, 1958.

Wilson, Robert B. "Exchange." In John Eatwell, Murray Milgate, and Peter Newman, eds., *The New Palgrave, The World of Economics*. New York: W.W. Norton, 1991.

CHAPTER **4**

THE CHALLENGE OF JUSTICE: "WE WANT WHAT'S FAIR"

Capitalism and the extended order market model, regardless of their manifest success, are under attack. The American trends towards greater individualism and spirituality noted in Chapter 2 are to some extent in conflict with an economic system characterized by some as antisocial, vulgar, divisive, and philistine. Moreover, as described in Chapter 3, the defense of the system by some of the 20th century's most prominent economists was half-hearted at best and at worst downright bizarre. The stage is set for new models to guide investment, production, distribution, consumption, and attitudes to all these. The individual, the "I," is the primary social unit under the market system, who proclaims to the world, "What do I want? I want more, and I'm eager to trade for it." In four new models, "we," representing groups, a polity, or globalized humankind, emerges:

- *The Justice Model*: "We want what is fair."
- *The Order Model*: "We want stability, both in social life and the environment."
- *The Virtue Model*: "We want behavior that is right and good."
- *The Sovereignty Model:* "We want what's ours."

I will discuss justice and the challenges it creates in this chapter, with each of the following three chapters devoted to one of the other models.

CRITICS, CHRISTIANS, AND PROGRESS

Consider the deluge of criticisms of the market model and capitalism that comes from left-wing, right-wing, and no-wing sources. Capitalism is said to foster lifestyles based on the Puritan work ethic, which removes joy and spontaneity from life. Few remember that it was the implied promise of the business system in 1900 to continue the ethic that fostered a century of legitimacy for the corporations. Accusations also are often made that capitalism evokes a consumerist mentality which crowds out values in the single-minded pursuit of material possessions. When one points out that it appears to be a contradiction to attack a joyless work ethic and a joyful materialism at the same time, critics respond by shifting the argument to the unlivable dualities of existence forced on individuals under capitalism. When market defenders claim that markets allocate resources efficiently, critics note that ideas of fairness and justice should guide allocation, especially since market allocation seems to be flawed—why are some exceptionally rich and some outrageously poor? Defenders then argue that markets are discovery procedures and that information cannot be shared in society in any better way. Critics point to the Internet, where all the information in the world is given away free, seemingly for the sheer exhilaration of sharing. In discussions of labor markets, critics say that pay should reflect merit, with merit to be based on any number of criteria: victimhood rooted in gender, ethnicity, or sexual orientation; equity in income distribution; moral stature, as measured by church membership or recorded good works; job characteristics, with those doing dirty work paid more; skills, as measured by years of school or credentials earned; a need, with desires somehow split off. The list goes on, and none of the critics is in the least bit bothered by the inevitable conflicts that arise. They prefer endless negotiation over criteria to the endless exchanges of the markets.

Even worse, Christian tradition rarely has offered anything more than grudging support for market economics. As Sir Samuel Brittan notes, the Church "has sometimes been on the side of feudal reaction, sometimes of a vague, egalitarian socialism, occasionally on the side of the corporation, but only rarely . . . has it had much good to say for competitive capitalism."[1] A Christian supposedly would feel guilt if she let her self-interest be her prime guide to preferences. Although self-interest is clearly the strongest of motives, it is the "higher" motives which ought to drive genuine Christians. With sufficient good will, a benevolent outlook, and a concern for others, Christians ought to be able to coordinate producing and consuming activities, share information needed for these activities, and motivate each other to be efficient and effective—in other words, to do what markets do, only better. One who responded that Christians have not been very good at these things in the 1,500 years or so they have had to develop their skills would be told, quite gently, that a new Christianity is emerging. As I noted in Chapter 2, they might very well be right, but would it be able to take on market functions?

Critics and Christians did not get much attention in the United States during most of the 20th century because the public firmly believed in the

inevitability of progress. Somewhere along the way, however, progress began to fade. Who now believes "that mankind has advanced in the
past—from some aboriginal condition of primitiveness, barbarism, or even
nullity—is now advancing, and will continue to advance through the fore-
seeable future?"[2] Or, more appropriately, who now is willing to get up in
front of a group and say these things? Perhaps the rough edges of the cruder
capitalism cut progress into pieces. Perhaps capitalism's success gave us
the luxury to cast off ideas that we in fact need if we are to get any better off.
Perhaps all that talk of primitiveness is seen as a code for slurs on nonwhite
people. Ominously, perhaps Alexis de Tocqueville's early critique of capitalist democracy as being destructive of progress finally had its effect. In the
second volume of *Democracy in America*, Tocqueville claimed that democratic practices and institutions produced a society "at once agitated and
monotonous" and the relentless pursuit of money "soon makes [Ameri-
cans] wearisome to contemplate."[3] In this environment the arts and con-
templation would languish and alienation set in. Similarly, Henry Adams
worried that materialism and mechanization had eroded the worthy spirituality of an earlier age, a theme strongly invigorated in the 20th century
with the publication of Jacques Ellul's *The Technological Society* in the 1960s.
Ellul, a French thinker, saw technology as increasingly determining human
values and choices in ways that fostered meaningless consumerism, alienation, and authoritarianism.[4]

The idea of progress as advance gave way, at least in some circles, to mid
20th-century anguish over a perceived stagnation. Robert Nisbet quotes
part of the outline for Hoxie Neale Fairchild's *Religious Trends in English Poetry, 1920–1965* (1968):

Hollow men eating their Naked Lunches in the Wasteland while awaiting Godot.
Botched civilization. Sick world . . . No life beyond the grave. . . . No integrating
myths. No worship. No reality independent of the disinterested observer. No objective, sharable truth or truths. No scale of values. No norm of human nature . . . No
boundaries between the rational and irrational, normal and abnormal . . . Solipsism.
Nothing to discipline our emotions . . . Life patternless, purposeless, meaningless.[5]

In response, one is tempted to say, "Bummer" or "Have you thought about
moving to Cleveland?" However, this kind of extreme, sarcasm-inviting
despair generated serious pronouncements that not only was Western and
American collapse destroying civilization, it was being exported to con-
taminate, corrupt, and despoil other societies, and the people our madness
created would, like Frankenstein, come back to terrorize us.

If stagnation was bad, economic growth was presented as menacing the
very idea of human survival. One of the most influential thinkers along
these lines was Fred Hirsch, whose *Social Limits to Growth* set off debates in
graduate classes throughout the United States in the 1970s. Beginning with
the premise that "the analytical framework that the economist has come to

take for granted . . . has become a hindrance in understanding some key contemporary problems," Hirsch proceeded to argue against economic freedom and for "a structural need to pull back the bounds of economic self-advancement."[6] What he seemed to call for was a highly bureaucratized society with strict regulations to dampen consumption and the incomes that support consumption. His argument was based on the premise that "as demands for purely private goods are increasingly satisfied, demands for goods and facilities with a public (social) character become increasingly active."[7] Consumption of a private good like a candy bar benefits the individual with no effect on society. Social goods, such as cars, affect both individuals and society, and as more cars are bought, pollution and congestion create social costs so that the sum of individual benefits gradually is offset by aggregate social costs. Hirsch also discussed positional goods, such as education, whereby purchase tends to raise the status of the buyer. But if everyone obtains a college degree, one's status remains the same and educational expenses produce no gain. The increasing frustrations experienced by well-off consumers in the rich industrial world illustrate the "paradox of affluence" as the modern economy transforms itself from a self-interest-satisfying engine into a "frustration machine."

Hirsch was right in the sense that consumers do experience unanticipated frustrations when the joys of a new Mercedes or a degree from the state university are less than expected, but he failed to recognize that individuals have a habit of redefining utility. If a college degree no longer confers high status, consumers still are happy if the educational experience equips them with marketable skills. If driving a car produces long waits on congested highways, the product's perceived attributes shift from speed to comfortable isolation in comparison to public transport. Nevertheless, *Social Limits to Growth* was a powerful addition to a chorus of complaints that economic growth—progress—was fostering disaster. Environmentalists began to offer highly contrived models suggesting that many resources were scarce and nonrenewable and that we were using them up at a rate which soon would foster disaster. Talbot Page's *Conservation and Economic Efficiency* (1977), a publication of the influential Resources for the Future group, highlighted the prodigality of the United States and noted the difficulty of establishing criteria for deciding on optimal resource depletion rates. This and other works implicitly argued that if we do not know when economic growth dependent on resource depletion becomes dangerous to human survival, then perhaps a no-growth approach ought to be taken.

Progress, then, and the capitalist, market paradigm associated with it were under attack by the end of the 20th century. Allegedly, they evoked a joyless work ethic and consumption which was, depending on who was talking: the wrong kind of joy, concerned as it was with piling up trivial things; unfair, in that worthy folks often came up short; unchristian, since it put self-interest above charity, love, and brotherhood, fostering a sense of meaninglessness and stagnation; frustrating in that social costs detracted from personal utilities; and dangerous to human and animal survival. Most people kept right on getting and spending, as they always had done, but more and more they were being bombarded in magazines, movies, books, radio, and television with alternative models.

JUSTICE: "WE WANT WHAT'S FAIR"

Those who would replace market exchange as the process through which goods, wages, resources, and services are allocated in society often present justice as an alternative, with the impartial and consistent application of democratically determined principles of fairness ensuring that each of us gets what he or she is due. An early advocate of this idea was Pierre-Joseph Proudhon, who argued that human betterment and work should be somewhat separate issues.[8] True, work will always be a miserable activity, the response to mankind's lot, but it need not be quite as awful as it currently is. What is needed to alleviate the work burden is the abandonment of economic exchange. Instead of a wage being based on the level and extent of toil offered by the worker, it will be tied to the dictates of justice. An employee's remuneration will correspond to his needs and merits, not his output or work performance. Thus a good person in need will receive salary even though laid up for months with illness or accident. A laborer's wage will not fall below a certain proper amount, even though supply and demand considerations call for the price of labor to fall to subsistence levels. Justice requires this, as well as, of course, also requiring that the worker accept his lot and work responsibly if able.

It is justice which dictates that a certain level of happiness be maintained in workers by employers, and justice which demands that a worker respond to his human lot with toil. The economic link correlating toil with happiness through the medium of exchange is broken. This violation of economic "law" infuriated Karl Marx.[9] It intrigued John Stuart Mill:

What doctrines of justice are there, on which the human race would more instantaneously and with one accord put the stamp of its recognition, than these—that it is just that each should have what he deserves, and that, in the dispensation of good things, those whose wants are most urgent should have the preference?[10]

Mill at first argued that Proudhon's theory cannot be rejected on *a priori* principles. None exist. If justice does not prevail, it is because of the impractical nature of its dictates and hostile customs, not the inherent falseness of the idea. By 1879 he had changed his mind and returned to the economic model governing labor markets:

In the case of most men the only inducement which has been found sufficiently constant and unflagging to overcome the ever-present influence of indolence and love of ease, and induce men to apply themselves unrelaxingly to work for the most part in itself dull and unexciting, is the prospect of bettering their own economic condition. . . . To suppose the contrary would be to imply that with men as they now are, duty and honor are more powerful principles than personal interest.[11]

The separation of pay from work by making each respond to justice rather than to each other remains a powerful idea today. Not only is it attractive to union leaders, feminists, and socialists, but it pleases some Christian conservatives, who recall the "just price" debates of scholastics during the Middle Ages. A wage should be set by a fair-minded person representing prevailing insights into just compensation. Employees, also responding to justice, should work hard.[12] Modern arguments in favor of "comparable worth" are based on this model. Here, a woman's paycheck is not a matter of bargaining. Instead it should be assigned based on a fair value—what men get in roughly similar jobs. Left unstated, we should note, is the obligation of the woman to work hard because justice demands it, rather than because she has negotiated high pay for hard labor. The comparable-worth debate is simply Proudhon's theory carried forward 150 years and applied to a practical problem, the sorry state of women in the workforce.

We saw in Chapter 2 that Sinclair Lewis's *Babbitt* portrayed a world of 1920s American businessmen terrified by European socialism. What probably bothered them the most—if J.S. Mill had trouble with it, how could mere mortals cope?—was Proudhon's justice model as reflected in the pronouncements of guild socialists of the time. The key discussion was that of Walter Lippmann in his masterpiece, *Public Opinion* (1922).[13] Here he considered G.D.H. Cole's *Social Theory*, a tract emanating from the Fabian social movement in Great Britain.[14] Cole had argued that present governments were simply instruments of coercion that ought to be replaced by a guild socialism with no sovereign power in control. Instead, a "Commune" would act as a coordinating body responsive to local and state communes. Guild socialism would abolish property rights and see to the setting of prices and the allocation of labor and resources so that a just equality of incomes would result. Guiding the communes and the Commune would be democratically elected representatives from the factories and workplaces of society. The idea is that to carry out the functions of society, the functionaries (the workers) must be in control, either directly or through their trade unions, guilds, and communes. Aside from noting the obvious unworkability of the scheme, Walter Lippmann identified the fatal flaw. How can the aggregate self-interests of functionaries turn themselves into societal actions which answer to just principles of equality? How do democracy and justice coexist without some superordinate authority, such as a constitution, a coercive state, or enforced property rights, seeing to it that justice prevails and all are treated fairly?

Cole was one of the great socialists, and his ideas have been quite influential. Here is Professor Joyce O. Hertzler of the University of Nebraska in her 1928 college text, *Social Progress*:

The democratization of industrial enterprise is one of the most important single steps before us. The workers must have the inner satisfactions, the spiritual values, that come from the sense that they are free and masters of their own destinies.[15]

Hertzler does not call for total worker control of industry (one will not sell many college texts that contain such calls), but she does identify "the necessity of socializing business," with the first step in the process being the ending of "the sway of the laissez-faire philosophy." She specifically cites Cole's *Social Theory* in her bibliography and concludes that U.S. society is woefully deficient in the degree of justice demonstrated in the economic realm. A correct future will require that we observe "ethically recognized principles of justice in distributing the proceeds of our industry."[16] Similar thoughts on justice dominate other important works early in the 20th century, including Charlotte P. Gilman's *Human Work* (1904), W. Weyl's *The New Democracy* (1918), and R.H. Tawney's *The Acquisitive Society* (1920).

By the end of the century, Ralph Nader had become the most prominent advocate of justice as a substitute for market exchange. Although noted as a defender of consumers, Nader exhibited Proudhonist and guild socialist tendencies in his eagerness to abolish or alter the forces of capitalist coercion. The U.S. Congress is foremost among these, and Nader has targeted that body in several of his crusades. During the 1999 World Trade Organization protests, for example, the Web page of Public Citizen, Nader's organization, referred to Congress' approval of the WTO in 1995 as a "perversion of democracy" perpetrated by a "lameduck Congress, comprised of fired and retired Members of Congress—many eyeing their next private sector job opportunities."[17] For Nader, the pressures of globalization are causing "shock liberalization" that is unjust to small farmers, oppressed female workers, dislocated workers, and infant industries. A just Congress would foster democratic policymaking to enforce human rights, encourage nuclear nonproliferation agreements, and develop improved health, environmental, consumer protection, and food safety regulations. In reality, Nader sees the WTO and its base of congressional supporters as illegitimate, too powerful, beholden to corporate interests, overly legalistic, and lacking in social concern. He and his advocates want to emasculate institutions standing in the way of justice in favor of strengthening both popular sovereignty in the United States and "open and truly inclusive" nongovernmental organizations (NGOs). These would curtail the powers of multinationals and large government bureaucracies so that input from all "interests" would be heard and debated. All of this sounds very much like the guild socialist model, in which guilds and workers' groups feed popular discourse and vote results to the communes (small countries and NGOs in Nader's new order), who in turn advise some sort of Commune on how to order things fairly. Republican forms of government and representative democracy fade out of the picture, as do lobbyists, campaign contributors, spin doctors, and corrupt politicians.

Nader's was but one of many attacks, all advocating justice rather than market exchange, on the global trading system at the end of the 20th century. The system allegedly fosters militarism, fragmentation of indigenous cultures, environmental destruction, and demeaning and violent treatment of workers. It is said to support a capitalist world governing structure enforcing principles of profit, competition, and planned obsolescence rather than values of solidarity, mutual cooperation, and autonomy. It takes the place of colonial and church powers in earlier periods in fostering a homogenization of diverse cultures, a pervasive consumerism, and a growing dependence of individuals on corporations. Although spectacular gains in jobs and incomes have occurred, these benefits do not outweigh unjust and inhumane working conditions and the fragmentation of communities. This is the general message of Public Citizen, the International Confederation of Free Trade Unions, the Ruckus Society, the Third World Network, Peoples' Global Action, and hundreds of other groups to whom the Internet has given a voice. While they often disagree, they are united in service to the justice model.

What they want from governing bodies, however constituted on either national or international levels, is a system that is democratic, transparent, and broad in its concerns. It must adhere to core labor standards, environmental protection, and precautionary laws designed to stifle innovations whose risks are imperfectly understood. This kind of thinking would have kept penicillin off the market, but it also would have kept the *Titanic* from putting to sea without further study of the effect of ice on ships' hulls. The system also must encourage development of local industries and local agriculture. Down deep, the justice advocates believe that support for market mechanisms of exchange as the basis for the growing welfare of humankind is badly misguided and doomed to inevitable failure since markets are bound to be captured by forces of "patriarchy" (the term is used by many groups) and multinational corporations, neither of which is driven by considerations of justice. Globalization indeed has evoked efficiency, lower prices, high-quality goods and services, and greater choice for consumers, but because these benefits are not responsive to or derived from principles of justice, they cannot endure. Now, in the 21st century, the justice advocates say, we must confront the market system with, as People's Global Action (PGA) puts it, "rage and rejection."[18] PGA calls for nonviolent civil disobedience to foster dismemberment of the "illegitimate world governing system" but it reserves the right, ominously, to pursue "other forms of action."

What we will see in the 21st century is an attempt to move us away from the idea of justice as a set of practices ensuring the protection of individual freedom towards discussion of justice in terms of a theory of society. John Stuart Mill, in *Utilitarianism*, warned against this shift:

The moral rules which forbid mankind to hurt another (in which we must never forget to include wrongful interference with each other's freedom) are more vital to human well-being than any maxims, however important, which only point out the best mode of managing some department of human affairs.[19]

However, as we saw earlier, this is the same Mill who momentarily fell under Proudhon's influence and was willing to seriously consider his theory of a justly structured society as a replacement for the more liberal market-based society. As the paradigms of Proudhon, guild socialism, and modern justice come up against the reemergence of Walt Whitman's autonomous Americans (discussed in Chapter 2), sparks will fly, and multinational corporations will be caught in the middle. They are going to get burned.

JUSTICE AND PRIVATE PROPERTY

The first places they are going to get burned are in the legal and political arenas where discussions of property rights occur. Inspired by justice concerns, an expansion in the concept of private property is occurring which is going to give quite a bit of power to NGOs in their dealings with corporations.

Modern Western ideas in support of private property are not strongly rooted either in legal reasoning or in economic theory. They emerged out of efforts by the Catholic Church in the Middle Ages to weaken local rulers by making it difficult for families to secure heirs and by promoting the right of individuals to bequeath property as they wished. Through bequests, the Church ended up owning half of Western Europe, but an unintended consequence was the growing importance of the idea that individuals had the right to use, alter, lease, enjoy, and transfer property as they saw fit.[20] Today this right appears to be firmly entrenched in law, but in fact a good deal of controversy exists over several issues. The legitimate role government should have in regulating the exercise of property rights has been debated endlessly. Equally important have been discussions on the relationship between a person and a thing and the definition of a "person." If a person in the form of a corporation owns a forest, does it have an obligation attached to its right of possession to act as a steward on behalf of some other right possessed by society or nature? This kind of question introduces principles of justice into the debate.

Contemporary supporters of private property believe that economic relations in a market-driven society require a set of legal relations, including property rights. But beliefs of this kind, however commonsensical, historically are quite rare. Marx held that law and by implication property rights were mere superstructure erected on a base of naked power. Those with economic power get to make the laws, and their veneration of property is simply a manifestation of a will to solidify power.[21] While there is some truth in Marx's analysis, current anti-property thinkers take a different tack. They recognize the priority of law but seek to use it to diminish control and weaken exchange relationships if they hinder the pursuit of social goals such as equality, justice, and sustainable development. For example, Ralph Nader wants to check corporate power through passage of a "Corporate Democracy Act to give all stakeholders in corporate decision-making a real voice in corporate governance."[22] Employees in a labor market relationship with the corporation would shift to some extent, in their stakeholder role, towards an ownership role in that they would have a legal right to take part in decisions about how to use corporate property. Nader also wants laws promulgating Citizens' Utility Boards. A Board would have the right "to enclose notices inside certain company and state mailings to invite the public to become voluntary members of the C.U.B."[23] In effect, a corporation would be forced to yield some of its control over its assets to an organization bent on further eroding that control.

What Nader and his supporters are saying is that if property rights exist in law because they are useful in fostering market relations, they also can be useful in furthering just relations in society, even if market relations are occasionally hindered. One defense against this compelling argument is to restate an old explanation of property rights as partially rooted in human nature rather than in use value. This is the general point of John Locke's *Second Treatise of Government*, published in the late 17th century. To thwart a person's use and control of the fruits of his labor would be to thwart humanity itself, even on behalf of justice. "Upon the sacredness of property civilization itself depends—the right of the laborer to his hundred dollars in the savings bank, and equally the legal right of the millionaire to his millions," said Andrew Carnegie in *The Gospel of Wealth*.[24] In *Capitalism: The Unknown Ideal*, Ayn Rand declared, "It is only on the basis of property rights that the sphere and application of individual rights can be defined in any given social situation."[25] Rand's ideas on property rights as inherent in human nature were ably defended in this book by Alan Greenspan, who contributed an essay. The trouble with the human-nature defense, however, was that few bought into it. Proudhon had claimed that "property is theft" and thus not natural at all. More recently, as we saw in Chapter 3, Hayek noted that property relations are merely learned behaviors which in fact violate the human propensity towards collectivism and altruism. In his view, only use value legitimizes property rights.

Neither human nature nor utilitarian theories have been successful in nailing down the place of private property in the social structure. This failure makes it difficult to counter the claim that the task of society is to make humans virtuous in service to justice rather than interest-bound and property-focused in service to themselves. Such a claim is not being made by Ralph Nader, who simply wants to extend property rights to the service of justice, but he and his defenders run a small risk of playing into the hands of anarchists like Proudhon or communitarians like Marx who want to weaken and then kill off property rights and the market exchanges that depend on these rights. A much larger risk exists, however, in that the notion of a "person" who enjoys property rights can be extended in ways that allegedly serve the cause of justice. Naderites might come to argue that laws should recognize the existence of an abstraction like "the ecosystem" as a legal person enjoying property rights.

A NEW GLOBAL "PERSON"

Property has been described as a "bundle of rights" including the right to use, to exclude others from use, to alter, to enjoy the fruits of the property, and to transfer the ownership to another.[26] While individuals, groups, corporations, and the state mostly have possessed these bundles defined in terms of land, labor, capital, knowledge, processes, and things, a new paradigm has emerged in which abstractions like the "ecosystem" ("Mother Nature") are perceived by some as being able to enjoy property rights. Thus the ecosystem "owns" the environment, and an individual or business that hinders, alters, or destroys the environment or environmental processes is seen as violating property rights. In the 20th century the idea developed that the state should act as a property owner of, say, public lands in a steward role on behalf of the ecosystem. In this century it is likely that the ecosystem itself will emerge in the eyes of some as an owner of a bundle of rights known as the environment and that various NGOs will fight to have this vision enshrined in law. And if Mother Nature becomes real as a legal person, why not loose collections of people known as "victims," "indigenous peoples," and "people of color"? NGO advocates for justice might argue that these reifications ought to be considered legal persons entitled to property rights.

Early in the 20th century, economists argued that the state would have to regulate some exercises of property rights (e.g., emitting polluting smoke from a factory chimney) to promote the best overall use of resources. By century's end, unfettered property rights were back in fashion in the economics profession, thanks to the Coase Theorem. Ronald Coase had noted in 1960 that government interference is not needed, since conflicts over rights can be negotiated, with one party compensating the other for infringement without any change in society's economic output relative to what would occur under governmental regulation. At least in terms of economic well-being, Coase implied, collectivist and interventionist paradigms argued by justice advocates are unnecessary. Nice things would happen simply by allowing property owners to engage in exchange relations with each other.

This kind of thinking, that anything can be negotiated, plays right into the hands of those seeking justice for Mother Nature and other abstractions. While regulatory intrusions, thanks to Coase, may decrease in the coming decades, nothing will prohibit self-appointed representatives of the ecosystem, victims, the "gendered," and indigenous peoples from demanding compensation from corporations for alleged infringements of their "clients'" rights brought about in hiring practices, factory location, and manufacturing operations, and litigating if payment or redress is not forthcoming. If the costs of litigation become too onerous, then perhaps the Supreme Court will take on the task of defining a legal person more clearly than law and philosophy now do. For example, persons broadly are considered by some philosophers to be "those beings whose suffering (in the sense of being the objects of the actions of moral agents) permits or demands moral evaluation."[27] This concept is used to argue for the person-like rights of animals, and it could be argued on behalf of reifications before the Court. Even the threat of this kind of finding at some future point will be enough to persuade corporations to negotiate with NGOs. Perhaps a corporation that has not hired enough native peoples in a locale will be asked by an NGO to compensate the aggrieved "person," the indigenous people, by funding educational development in the community. Such things go on now, but they are done in the name of charity, public relations, noblesse oblige, and get-off-our-backs. They might be done in future in accord with the idea that property-rights holders in a conflict should and must negotiate if they want to avoid litigation or regulation. The Coase Theorem, plus the idea that the ecosystem can be a legal person, may set off serious attacks on business property rights by NGO advocates for justice in the coming decades. The fact that Mother Nature, the gendered, victims, and indigenous peoples are in every country makes the issue a global one. If Mother Nature is harmed by a U.S. multinational in Brazil, her U.S. defenders could threaten a suit in the United States if compensation was not made. After all, Mother Nature resides in America as well as in Brazil.

THE FAIR TRADERS

The oldest reified person of them all is the worker, and his labor union representatives and NGO advocates are using Proudhonist and new property-rights models in their battle to turn free trade into fair trade. From Proudhon and the guild socialists they have taken the idea that worker relations with owners in a just system should be based not on exchange but on fairness. Unlike the socialists, however, they are sticking with the idea of property rights, but property rights conceived of in the new way described above. In the trade-related formulation, the U.S. worker in the aggregate "owns" the set of jobs held by employees, and foreign workers cannot take those jobs away. To do so would be unfair and unjust. If foreign workers complain that their standard of living cannot rise unless they are free to work at jobs producing goods for the U.S. market, American labor leaders will tell them, with an argument based on the "lump-of-labor" fallacy described in basic economics textbooks, as well as on the property-rights claim, that it is unfair for workers of one society to appropriate jobs owned by workers in another society without permission. Far better for them to join with their U.S. brothers and sisters in demanding that developing-country capitalists raise wages and improve working conditions to just levels in the jobs the foreign workers "own."

Actually, the idea of owning a job may be novel in this country, but it is pervasive elsewhere. A Mexican classmate of mine in my MBA program during the 1970s was planning on returning and inheriting his father's civil service job, which had been in the family for several generations. In Japan's parliament, the Diet, perhaps 20 percent of members are children of former members. In an African country during the late 1980s, an American manufacturing manager of my acquaintance managed to double productivity in his small plant due to new machinery. He promptly doubled wages. Just as promptly, his workers started showing up for half the week, with their relatives taking their places the other half. All of these examples suggest that people are quite comfortable with the idea that a wage-based job or some organizational position can be owned, in the sense of having disposal rights attached to it.

U.S. labor leaders have been called hypocrites who simply want trade barriers to protect their members' jobs and are using trumped-up claims about justice to further their own selfish ends without concern for foreign workers. There is some legitimacy to this charge, but many labor activists seem genuinely committed to the rights model. As Teamster president James P. Hoffa put it,

We demand a set of core labor standards that guarantee workers the right to stand up, to organize and to work collectively to better their lives and the lives of their children. If a trade agreement can protect the rights of a corporation, then it surely can address the needs of ordinary workers.[28]

More pointedly, Jay Mazur of the Union of Needletrades, Industrial, and Textile Employees announced, "A first step toward that goal is building labor rights, environmental protection, and social standards into trade accords and the protocols of international financial institutions—and enforcing them with the same vigor now reserved for property rights."[29] According to Mazur, globalization based on the market model does not allow for accountability, follows undemocratic processes, and does not even result in balancing labor supply and demand. An approach in which workers obtained what was rightfully theirs in each society would be better, and he advocates a globalized union movement to "forge effective links with overseas partners, coordinate industrial actions, lobby governments, take legal action, and simultaneously publicize all this activity in more than one country."[30] This movement is one of many internationalizing efforts launched by unions over the last hundred years, but it is the first rooted in a theoretical model likely to generate unified support. The model's message is simple: You, the worker in each country, own your job. It cannot be taken from you by a worker in another country, and your ownership entitles you to a just, decent compensation.[31]

WILL THE UNITED STATES BECOME FRANCE?

Will the 21st century in the United States see a decline in the resonance of the idea of progress, a growing criticism of capitalism, and a rage for justice driving new ways of thinking about property, jobs, and trade? If so, the United States will have become France of the late 20th century. When Axa, the largest French insurance company, took over the state-run insurer in 1999, it discovered mounting losses from policies issued to protect families with mentally handicapped children. When it attempted to double the premiums, public outrage erupted. The social affairs minister noted that a corporation's social responsibility "conflicts with the logic of profit and providing maximum value for shareholders."[32] In other words, the cause of justice and that of capitalism are not complementary. Axa quickly withdrew the increase. In a second 1999 incident, a tanker carrying oil to be sold to Totalfina, a Franco-Belgian oil group, broke up and sank off the Brittany coast, causing extensive pollution. Although Totalfina had no legal responsibility, public outrage tended to blame the company, and environmentalists began a campaign to boycott the firm's products until it made reparations. The president of France criticized corporations like Totalfina for their "mad drive for profits," implying a connection between a capitalist, market model and unjust avoidance of moral responsibilities. Totalfina caved in, as did Michelin in a third incident during the year. The tire company made the mistake of announcing a 10 percent cut in its workforce simultaneously with a sharp increase in profits. Legislation soon was introduced in the French parliament to restrict a company's freedom to dismiss people when making profits. It soon was recast to give employees more control over company policy.

Just one year's worth of incidents in France illustrates the French public's toying with ideas that capitalism and justice are not compatible and that employees should have something akin to ownership rights in their companies. Could the United States eventually go down this road? It is easy to say no because France is built on a revolutionary idea of justice and the United States is not.

Out of this chaos of shadow, this tumultuous flight of clouds, spread immense rays of light parallel to the eternal laws—rays that have remained on the horizon, visible forever in the heaven of the peoples, and which are, first, Justice . . . [33]

One would scarcely expect to hear this kind of talk, Victor Hugo's, from Benjamin Franklin or Thomas Jefferson. Yet while Americans care more about freedom than justice, they can become mightily aroused by injustice. Here is a short American poem from around 1900:

> The golf links lie so near the mill
> That almost every day
> The laboring children can look out
> And see the men at play.

This anonymous effort suggests an American depth of feeling about per-ceived injustice and its connection to capitalist endeavor. It isn't all that dif-ferent from France.

WHAT DO THE JUST WANT?

Justice advocates attack capitalism as we know it because it allegedly fosters economic stagnation, which is bad. But when it evokes economic growth, they say that alienation, meaninglessness, and global attacks on the environment occur, which also are bad. Clearly capitalism cannot win, and its opponents have proposed a number of alternatives, depending on their ideology and theology:

- *Muscular Christianity:* In this model dedicated Christians become heavily in-volved in coordinating economic life in service to God's just cause. A naysayer who points out that Iranian religious authorities pursued this path for many years and failed in the 20th century will be dismissed. Iranians, he will be told, are not Americans and not Christian.

- *Naderite Proudhonism:* Proudhon was an anarchist whose anti-institutionalism in the name of justice is too extreme for Americans. In a nicely filtered version preached by reformers like Ralph Nader, justice replaces exchange in labor mar-kets and drives corporate governance. The old idea of a "just price" comes into its own again, as well as worker and consumer power in corporate deci-sion-making and a yielding of the power of elected bodies to NGOs who are ene-mies of corporate "patriarchy."

- *Your Landlord Is Mother Nature:* Instead of attacking property rights as Proudhon did, justice advocates want to use them to support the causes of equality and sus-tainable development, among others. One approach is to extend the definition of a legal "person," who can own property under the law, to reified concepts like the ecosystem, the gendered, victims, and indigenous people. NGOs acting on their behalf could argue their various justice concerns under the guise of defending ownership rights, either before courts or in negotiations with other property owners in the form of corporations.

• *Worker Ownership of a Nation's Jobs:* The justice model allows some union leaders in the United States to argue that it would be unfair for foreign workers producing goods for the American market to threaten jobs "owned" by U.S. workers. Instead, they should receive just wages and security for the jobs they own in their own societies. Rampant U.S. protectionism here is not selfishness and narrowness; rather it is supposedly a noble spur to leaders in other countries to turn to just relations with their workers.

NOTES

1. Samuel Brittan, *Capitalism with a Human Face* (Cambridge: Harvard University Press, 1995). A utilitarian with a meliorist tendency, Sir Samuel admits that even among sophisticated business journalists, "I find great resistance to the allocational and market-clearing functions of pay and prices" (49).

2. Robert Nisbet, *History of the Idea of Progress* (New York: Basic Books, 1980), 4. Nisbet was on scene in the 1960s and 1970s when intellectual fashions changed and progress discussions began to provoke throat-clearing and embarrassed or scornful side glances.

3. Alexis de Tocqueville, *Democracy in America*, J.P. Mayer, ed. (New York: HarperPerennial, 1969). The quotes are on 614–615.

4. Jacques Ellul, *The Technological Society*, trans. W. Lovitt (New York: Vintage, 1964). Henry Adams' attacks on modernism are in *Mont-Saint-Michel and Chartres* and *The Education of Henry Adams: A Study in Twentieth-Century Multiplicity*. In these works he argues (1) that a dualism between spirituality and a scientific perspective exists, (2) that the optimal balance occurred during the era of medieval Christianity, and (3) that things have been going downhill ever since.

5. Cited by Nisbet, 328–329. See Hoxie Neale Fairchild, *Religious Trends in English Poetry, vol. VI, 1920–1965, Valley of Dry Bones* (New York: Columbia University Press, 1968).

6. Fred Hirsch, *Social Limits to Growth* (Cambridge: Harvard University Press, 1976), 2, 190.

7. Hirsch, op. cit., 4.

8. Pierre-Joseph Proudhon, *Selected Writings*, Stewart Edwards, ed. (New York: Anchor Books, 1969).

9. See Karl Marx, *The Poverty of Philosophy (a reply to "La Philosophie de la Misère" of M. Proudhon)* (Chicago: C.H. Kerr & Co., 1910).

10. John Stuart Mill, "Thornton on Labour and Its Claims (1869)." In G.L. Williams, ed., *John Stuart Mill on Politics and Society* (New York: International Publications Service, 1976), 310–311.

11. J.S. Mill, "The Difficulties of Socialism (1879)," op. cit., 339.

12. See Henry W. Speigel, "Scholastic Economic Thought." In John Eatwell et al., eds., *The New Palgrave, The World of Economics* (New York: W.W. Norton, 1991), 627–633.

13. See Walter Lippmann, *Public Opinion* (New York: Free Press, 1949), Chapter 19.

14. G.D.H. Cole's ideas are still in print in *Guild Socialism Restated* (Piscataway, NJ: Transaction, 1980). Also see *Social Theory* (New York: Frederick A. Stokes Company, 1920).

15. Joyce O. Hertzler, *Social Progress* (New York: Century, 1928), 426.

16. Hertzler, op. cit., 430–431.

17. The quotes in this section come from Public Citizen's home pages at www.citizen.org during October–December, 1999.

18. The quotes here are from PGA's website, www.agp.org/agp/en/ PGAInfos/ during October–December, 1999.

19. Cited by John Gray, "The Light of Other Minds," *Times Literary Supplement*, February 11, 2000, 12.

20. See Nathan Rosenberg, *How the West Grew Rich: The Economic Transformation of the Industrial World* (New York: Basic Books, 1986) and Deepak Lal, *Unintended Consequences* (Cambridge: MIT Press, 1998).

21. I am drawing here on Tom Bethell, *The Noblest Triumph, Property and Prosperity Through the Ages* (New York: St. Martin's Press, 1998).

22. Ralph Nader, "Democratic Revolution in an Age of Autocracy," *Boston Review*, bostonreview.mit.edu/BR18.2/nader html, no date.

23. Ibid.

24. From *The Gospel of Wealth*. Quoted by Bethell, op. cit., 174.

25. Ayn Rand, *Capitalism: The Unknown Ideal* (New York: New American Library, 1967), 259.

26. Bethell, op.cit., 344.

27. Edward Johnson, "Moral Status." In Robert Audi, ed., *The Cambridge Dictionary of Philosophy* (Cambridge: Cambridge University Press, 1995), 513. Johnson refers to what are called "moral patients"—the objects of moral concern. Other philosophers occasionally include personhood in this concept and discuss the rights of animals, plants, etc., as perhaps having some characteristics of persons.

28. James P. Hoffa, "The 'Battle in Seattle' Puts Worker Rights Center Stage," *Teamster*, 2000, 97 January/February, 1.

29. Jay Mazur, "Labor's New Internationalism," *Foreign Affairs*, 2000, 79, January/February, 79.

30. Mazur, op.cit., 86.

31. For a similar model, see Margaret Jane Radin, "Property and Personhood," *Stanford Law Review*, 1982, 34, 991–996. She argues that tenants may be thought to have property rights evolving out of long tenancy. In effect, they would own their rentals.

32. See Robert Graham, "Capitalism fails to win French hearts," *Financial Times*, 6 March 2000, 4.

33. Victor Hugo, *Ninety-three* (New York: Carroll & Graf Publishers, 1998).

BIBLIOGRAPHY

Bethell, Tom. *The Noblest Triumph, Property and Prosperity Through the Ages*. New York: St. Martin's Press, 1998.

Brittan, Samuel. *Capitalism with a Human Face*. Cambridge: Harvard University Press, 1995.

Cole, G.D.H. *Guild Socialism Restated*. Piscataway, NJ: Transaction, 1980.

————. *Social Theory*. New York: Frederick A. Stokes Company, 1920.

Ellul, Jacques. *The Technological Society*, trans. W. Lovitt. New York: Vintage, 1964.

Fairchild, Hoxie Neale. *Religious Trends in English Poetry. Vol. VI, 1920–1965, Valley of Dry Bones*. New York: Columbia University Press, 1968.

Graham, Robert. "Capitalism Fails to Win French Hearts." *Financial Times*, 6 March 2000, 4.

Gray, John. "The Light of Other Minds." *Times Literary Supplement*, 11 February 2000, 12.

Hirsch, Fred. *Social Limits to Growth*. Cambridge: Harvard University Press, 1976.

Hoffa, James P. "The 'Battle in Seattle' Puts Worker Rights Center Stage." *Teamster* 2000, 97, January/February, 1.

Hugo, Victor. *Ninety-three*. New York: Carroll & Graf Publishers, 1998.

Johnson, Edward. "Moral Status." In Robert Audi, ed., *The Cambridge Dictionary of Philosophy*. Cambridge: Cambridge University Press, 1995, 513.

Lal, Deepak. *Unintended Consequences*. Cambridge: MIT Press, 1998.

Lippmann, Walter. *Public Opinion*. New York: Free Press, 1949.

Marx, Karl. *The Poverty of Philosophy* (A Reply to "La Philosophie de la Misère" of M. Proudhon). Chicago: C.H. Kerr & Co., 1910.

Mazur, Jay. "Labor's New Internationalism." *Foreign Affairs*, 2000, 79, January/February, 75–90.

Mill, John Stuart. *John Stuart Mill on Politics and Society*, ed. G. L. Williams. New York: International Publications Service, 1976.

Nader, Ralph. "Democratic Revolution in an Age of Autocracy." *Boston Review*, bostonreview.mit.edu/BR18.2/nader.html, no date.

Nisbet, Robert. *History of the Idea of Progress*. New York: Basic Books, 1980.

Proudhon, Pierre-Joseph. *Selected Writings*, ed. Stewart Edwards. New York: Anchor Books, 1969.

Radin, Margaret Jane. "Property and Personhood." *Stanford Law Review*, 1982, 34, 991–996.

Rand, Ayn. *Capitalism: The Unknown Ideal*. New York: New American Library, 1967.

Rosenberg, Nathan. *How the West Grew Rich: The Economic Transformation of the Industrial World*. New York: Basic Books, 1986.

Speigel, Henry W. "Scholastic Economic Thought." In John Eatwell, et al., eds., *The World of Economics*. New York: W.W. Norton, 1991, 627–633.

Tocqueville, Alexis de. *Democracy in America*, ed. J.P. Mayer. New York: Harper Perennial, 1969.

CHAPTER 5

THE WAY OF ORDER: "WE WANT STABILITY"

In 1999 Coca-Cola developed a vending machine programmed to raise prices during hot weather. Within a few months Coca-Cola's stock price had fallen 20 percent. Could it be that admitting that demand influenced prices turned away consumers, who did not want to hear the dirty little secret aired? Or was it the fact that EU regulators began investigating Coca-Cola's alleged anticompetitive practices in Europe? Probably both. Pursuing the economic model in a sense is required by U.S. law, but not talking about it is required by consumers, who like to think that the world is a stable, orderly place, with prices inherent in the makeup of a product—like color or taste—and thus unchanging. The rage for order in all of society, including economic life, was announced by a Chinese poet in 250 B.C.:

> Therefore, in the Government of the Sage:
> He empties their minds,
> And fills their bellies,
> Weakens their ambition,
> And strengthens their bones.
>
> He constantly causes the people to be
>   without knowledge and without desires.
> If he can bring it about that those
>   with knowledge simply do
>   not dare to act,
> Then there will be nothing that is not in order . . .
>
> Heaven and Earth are not humane;
> They regard the ten thousand things

as straw dogs.
The Sage is not humane;
He regards the common people as straw dogs.[1]

Plenty of Sages still remain in the 21st century, not just in China, and they will want very much to foster a more ordered existence for a variety of reasons ranging from the political to the environmental.

The kind of views expressed in an old American folk-religion tune are not congenial to the order-seekers:

1200 miles its length and breadth,
The Foursquare City stands.
Its gem-set walls of jasper shine,
Not made with human hands.
100 miles its gates are wide,
Abundant entrance there,
With fifty miles of elbow room
On either side to spare.

When the gates swing wide on the other side,
Just beyond the sunset sea,
There'll be room to spare as we enter there,
Room for you and room for me.
For the gates are wide on the other side,
Where the flowers ever bloom.
On the right hand, on the left hand,
Fifty miles of elbow room.

Sometimes I'm cramped and crowded here,
And long for elbow room.
I want to reach for altitude,
Where fire flowers bloom.
It won't be long till I shall pace
Into that city fair,
With 50 miles of elbow room
On either side to spare.

Americans want the freedom of elbow room in the Foursquare City. It is not the city of the Sage, where a kind of menacing equilibrium prevails and change is not much thought about as long as basic needs are met. The stage is set, then, for a 21st-century battle between American individualists and Sages over the nature of globalization.

The poem of the Sage is an early statement of a social paradigm much discussed in Asian circles from Singapore and Kuala Lumpur to Tokyo. In the 1970s it was called the "Pacific Way," but today it goes by the name "Asian Way." Although forced into hiding by the Asian Crisis of 1997–1999, Asian Way advocates will be back, arguing even more strongly in the coming decades that capitalist societies are disorderly and in need of modification. They will be supported by European supporters of the so-called Third Position and radical environmentalists who demand sustainable development focused more on moving to and maintaining stable optimal conditions rather than on economic development of the "extended order" kind advocated by Hayek.

CAPITALISM AS CHAOS

The theme of capitalism as chaotic is not new, having been introduced by Marx:

Constant revolutionizing of production, uninterrupted disturbance of all social conditions, everlasting uncertainty and agitation distinguish the bourgeois epoch from all earlier ones. All fixed, fast-frozen relations, with their train of ancient and venerable prejudices and opinions, are swept away, all new-formed ones become antiquated before they can ossify. All that is solid melts into air.[2]

Other critics noted that as the capitalist model evoked growing disorder, the power of government grew. For some this power was intolerable. According to Proudhon,

To be governed is to be watched over, inspected, spied on, directed, legislated, regulated, docketed, indoctrinated, preached at, controlled, assessed, weighed, censored, ordered about . . . noted, registered, taxed, stamped, measured, valued, patented, licensed, authorized, endorsed, admonished, hampered, reformed, rebuked, arrested.[3]

The twin horrors of out of control capitalism and overly controlling states led in the 20th century to what Arnold Toynbee called the "Third Position" (or the Third Way), a middle-ground, social democratic model which we will examine below in Europe and as it has worked itself out in the much-admired social structuring of Japan after World War II.[4] While currently in the throes of economic stagnation, Japan and its models are out of favor, but they are likely to return to fashion in the coming decades since they promise both economic progress and social order.

Mainstream defenders of capitalism argue that market mechanisms are better than any other method in providing a system of signaling through prices to alert suppliers of resources as to what is needed by consumers and what is not. As long as price information and other signals can and do flow freely, the well-being of a nation's citizens should be maximized.[5] Since well-off citizens are more orderly than the less well-off, social disorder will not be a problem and the state need not intrude. On paper in the form of highly mathematicized statements of general equilibrium theory, this model works quite well, but it requires a world in which markets are freely competitive, information is available to everyone, and everyone uses all the information in a sensible manner. In reality, as a growing body of critics argue, many markets are uncompetitive, information is often lacking, and individuals and firms have a disturbing habit of ignoring useful data in favor of, say, what is either vivid or representative of preconceived, ill-conceived notions. Throw in the tendency of humans towards herd behavior and the stage is set for booms and busts, widows and orphans betrayed and bewildered, multimillionaires whose wealth is based on sheer luck, and a troubling sense that we are endlessly on the verge of chaos.

Spurred on by these observations, some economists and social theorists are moving towards a theory of capitalism based on Darwinian natural selection theory, in which random variations evoke natural selection. In the 20th century this view first was popularized by Joseph Schumpeter, who noted, "The essential point to grasp is that in dealing with capitalism we are dealing with an evolutionary process." He had no illusions about the process being orderly: "Capitalism, then, is by nature a form or method of economic change and not only never is but never can be stationary."[6] As businesses are expanded or started by entrepreneurs, innovators, corporations, and even governments, a wealth of information about products and services floods society, where it washes up against the needs, desires, and expectations of individuals living within the constraints of cultural and institutional forces. In natural selection theory, a process not under the control of any individual, group, or state then ensues, in which the "fit" products and firms survive and the unfit perish. It is not quite the invisible hand, in which information politely travels back and forth in exchange relationships. Rather it is more like an invisible gardener, who ruthlessly culls the field of plants and weeds that are deemed neither useful nor pretty. The problem is that the gardener has no particular sense of what should or should not survive and is easily swayed by his own, the plants', the weeds', and bypassers' needs, desires, and expectations—which in any given bypasser often are in conflict with one another.[7] Economic life in this kind of environment is seen by some people as unpredictable and chaotic, and their distaste is not offset by the fact that the gardener's good selections mostly outweigh his bad.

The signaling model of capitalist economies, being unrealistic, is giving way to a natural selection model which presents the world as messy and unattractive. Third Position advocates accept the selection model but add government and NGOs to it to provide order and stability.[8] In this chapter I want to examine (1) European models, (2) Asian approaches that emphasize fitness based on government influence in the natural selection process, and (3) environmentalist thinking rooted in the defense of ecological equilibrium.

THE EUROPEAN THIRD WAY

Third Way social models are alternatives to the strongly individualistic and market-oriented societies of the United States and Great Britain and the command economies of totalitarian states. In continental Europe they are referred to as "social democratic" by some and in Germany as "corporatism" or the "social market economy." What they have in common are redistributionist welfare policies, restrictions on competition, controls on labor markets, and a pervasive rhetoric of self-approval, especially in comparison with the United States. The goals of Third Way nations involve the reduction of poverty, the promotion of equality and integration, stability, autonomy for individuals, and orderly community. Measures of success include a high percent of households above a poverty line, equal income distribution, low divorce rates, employment stability, access to education and jobs, low income variability for households, and other criteria.[9] In Germany, the corporatist model is associated with labor representation on large company boards, which also must consult workers' councils on such things as pay, benefits, and overtime. As one might imagine, German hourly wages are some of the highest in the world, but so is German productivity. Throughout Europe, unemployment rates are much higher than in the United States, probably in response to layoff-inhibiting regulations in most countries that influence firms to avoid hiring, substitute capital for labor instead, and require overtime from workers during high-demand periods. Order for the many, it appears, comes at a price of disorder for the few.

In Sweden, Third Position thinking has equated social order with the quality of life, defined as "the individual's command over resources in the form of money, possessions, knowledge, mental and physical energy, social relations, security, and so on, through which the individual can control and consciously direct his living conditions."[10] While this sounds like an innocuously praiseworthy tribute to autonomy, the statement contains an implied anti-institutionalism. For example, Swedish society in the forms of family, business, or church ought not to pressure individuals to work if they choose not to and are willing to accept a lower income. The state provides income to these people as a matter of course:

According to social democracy, state activities are not merely a supplementary mechanism, but one on a par with the market. . . . Various social provisions are seen as the rights of citizens in this perspective. The state should, therefore, provide . . . a good standard of living regardless of income and family size.[11]

If an individual does work, the model calls for the state to ensure that the workday is rich in "relationships with work-mates" and short enough to provide "opportunities for leisure-time activities."[12] In some cases, Swedish workers may leave a workplace to pursue personal goals during the workday without informing the employer.

Intellectually, the Third Position is rooted in the writings of Jean-Jacques Rousseau on the "natural man" who acts in accord with his own impulses and reason and ought not to be interfered with by society; the ideas of Voltaire and Montesquieu on the variability of laws and social structures in shifting environments; and the insight of Madame de Staël that government power could be used to manipulate institutions in service to individual liberty. Nevertheless, behind the social market economy is the profound fear in European elites of rioting in the streets. As late as the 1950s, French police in Paris carried machine guns and occasionally used them to kill demonstrators. The practice stopped when people viewed the practice on television, and police came to the realization that care, concern, and melioration worked better than bullets in keeping the masses off the avenues. Even with unemployment rates sometimes over 10 percent and an underclass that has never worked and will never work, France is virtually free of violent demonstrations.

German corporatism offers a model of economic coordination likely to expand throughout Europe in the coming decades and eventually to offer itself to Americans as an alternative to the uncoordinated messiness of the U.S. system. In contrast to American companies, the ideal, and sometimes even real, German firm sees its duty in contributing to a stable, prosperous social order rather than narrowly maximizing shareholder value. To keep shareholder pressure low, most capital is raised from banks, which are more interested in a client's earnings before interest and taxes than its net income and often urge clients to grow revenues rather than profits since growth evokes more lending. The growth focus is supported by large, well-funded trade associations that provide research and development funds for small companies so that high quality subcontractors and suppliers will be available to service large firm growth. Also supportive are the labor unions, which trade off no-strike promises for high wages and job security so that growth is not stalled. The government does its part by orchestrating a huge vocational training apparatus in which joint school-employer apprenticeships cover 60 percent of potential workers. And works councils foster stakeholder dialogue and consensus revolving around the formula that high wages, job security, and high skills equal high competitiveness.

The corporatist model sounds like economic paradise, but it is not, and a brief look at who senior corporate managers are and what they do tells us why. The typical German executive in a large corporation probably is an engineer or a technician with a strong focus on efficiency. This is because the social market model emphasizes the development of a skilled workforce to produce today's middle technology products rather than yesterday's low-tech or tomorrow's high-tech output. The disorder of entrepreneurship and innovation do not fit in well, so they are downplayed. What's left to manage, besides relations with bankers and unions, is costs, since only cost-cutting and productivity increases can provide adequate profits to keep the system going. Marketing becomes simple in planning, although terribly difficult in execution. Consider Mercedes-Benz. It is unable to produce a low-priced car, so it must persuade the public that its quality and reputation are great enough to justify its high prices. Even if it succeeds, it finds itself locked out of mid-range and low-end markets. The company is trying desperately to break out of this bind by investing heavily in developing-region locales like Alabama, where labor and other costs are low, and by repositioning its brand image. Its high-end image, however, could be hurt. Other German firms also are fleeing the country, suggesting that corporatism may be a recipe for stagnation rather than stability and job losses rather than job security. Nevertheless, it all looks good to observers in the United States who are eager for alternative social models to replace the U.S. version.

THE ASIAN WAY

Japan is the undisputed leader in Asian Way social ordering. Since World War II, a series of paternal, therapeutic governments led by the Liberal Democratic Party and supported by big business have gathered most power in the society to themselves in the name of assuring material well-being while downplaying raucous individual virtues of self-reliance and autonomy. In place of disorderly freedom and unrestrained capitalism, these regimes have offered equality, planning, and benevolent paternalism under a two-pronged agenda. First, a rigorous control of education inculcates values associating personal liberty with disorderly hedonism and selfish licentiousness. Second, economic growth is fostered as a means to obtaining security and an orderly existence rather than the "happiness" of the American consumer. Immerse yourselves in corporate life, Japanese workers are told, and you will have jobs for life. This program is a variant of Third Position thinking. Retained is the rejection of both unrestrained markets and overly restraining Marxism and an emphasis on well-being, but the ideas of personal autonomy and self-fulfillment energizing European thought are very much in the background. As in Europe, however, the fear of social unrest is very much present.

The Asian Way model in Japan developed after the Pacific War in response to a desire prevalent among the people to mobilize themselves in service to achievable, peaceful, and progressive goals. Japanese leaders, mindful of the chaos of recent Japanese history, instead offered an exchange in which their clever management would provide economic growth and security in return for the downplaying of personal autonomy in favor of corporate groupism and a vague commitment to what used to be called the "national essence"—a kind of racial and cultural force allegedly propelling the society towards greatness.[13] However, this is a bargain that cannot be kept for long. As Francis Fukuyama noted in *The End of History and the Last Man* (1992), individuals cannot forgo their need to experience self-esteem for long without feelings of shame. Moreover, "When other people treat them as though they are worth less than [their own sense of self-worth], they experience the emotion of anger."[14] Shame and anger can foster dramatic changes in a society, and some kind of movement is occurring in Japan as the people reassert themselves. Women especially are voting with their purses, and Japanese consumption has been stagnant for a decade.

Fukuyama's point was that historical inevitability posited the merging of science, technology, economic development, and individualist democratic freedom. All societies, Japan not excepted, eventually must move toward this "end-of-history" convergence.[15] Be that as it may, the economic coordination practiced by government and big business elites for fifty years attracted much admiring comment and a stream of "why-can't-we-be-like-them" books beginning with Ezra Vogel's *Japan as Number One* (1979). The specifics of Japan's Asian Way are well known:

- Strong networking among firms was encouraged in the form of *keiretsu* and the practice of cross-shareholding. The result was a reduction of risks for managers, who always could count on help from allied firms in times of trouble. Low domestic risk enabled global expansion risks to be assumed.

- Government tolerance for price-fixing and other anticompetitive practices also reduced business risks.

- Company unions whose sole goal was job security for their members and who were individually too small to fund any strike efforts ensured a steady supply of quiescent workers. For many years in Japan wage increases were substantially less than productivity increases, and high cash flows were available to fund investment and international expansion. The downside was that labor became a fixed cost as job security promises were kept.

- In addition to some financing from cheap labor, big companies could count on easy access to loans from large banks that were little more than government servants tasked with carrying out policies.

These, and other elements of the system, evolved as mechanisms to drain risk out of the market model so that corporations could accept lower returns on investment and thus do more of it. Over and over again in Japan, one heard the term "orderly competition" as the solution to the allegedly wasteful and chaotic capitalism of the United States. Economic life was structured to benefit the people in their roles as managers and employees rather than as stockholders and consumers. Dividends were miniscule, no real mergers and acquisition markets were allowed to develop, various practices put constraints on venture capital and entrepreneurialism so that established firms had little to fear from new entrants in an industry, government regulations kept costs high so poorly funded upstarts were bound to fail, and consumers were encouraged to see exceptionally high prices as a small burden to bear in return for stable employment, orderly and sustained economic growth, and high-quality goods.

By the 1990s the system had gone into decline, to some extent for the very reasons that had explained its earlier success. When ill-conceived monetary contraction engineered by the ministry of finance in 1989–1990 evoked recessionary conditions, Japanese consumers did what people lacking autonomy and confidence in themselves would be expected to do—they stopped buying and increased savings. Although various government stimulus programs persuaded them to spend on occasion, the trend was clear. A "liquidity trap" began to develop in which, as consumers reduced spending, companies could not find opportunities and reduced investment. As people feared for their jobs, they began to save even more. Prices soon fell, encouraging consumers to hold off on purchases until prices came down even further. A terrifying downward spiral began to develop in which consumer retrenchment fostered company retrenchment, which in turn brought out more consumer retrenching, and so forth. As these processes played themselves out in Japan, security promises that no longer could be kept broke the "fate-sharing" bonds of trust between companies and employees. Collective bargaining at arm's length by no-longer-passive unions began to emerge, as did a breakup of *keiretsu* relations among firms tired of holding equity that was constantly falling in value and paying high prices to network suppliers when global markets offered better deals. Saddled with about a trillion dollars of bad loans, banks began to cast off the shackles binding them to the government and to assess loan applications in terms of supply and demand. The government, stung by corruption charges and harassed by reformers among the elites, pulled back. All of these events ensured that Japan eventually would resume growing again as companies became more efficient, more flexible, more responsive to consumers, and less burdened by government-induced regulatory costs.

However, if Japan ever does once more become an economic star in the 21st century, we can count on seeing a resurgence of arguments that the Asian Way model offers a better, more ordered way for Americans. We know what the arguers will propose, since their ancestors proposed these things in the 1980s. A U.S. Department of Industrial Policy will be called for to plan for responsible growth and to carry it off with control over credit allocation by banks and the ability to subsidize high-technology innovation by favored companies, which will then expand internationally to dominate world markets, thus ensuring high-wage jobs for lots of American workers.[16] Strategic and often anticompetitive alliances of the *keiretsu* kind will be taught in business schools and tolerated by government as the be-all and end-all of clever managing, with little discussion of the rigidity and high costs often associated with them. The role of consumer will be criticized as the selfish exercise of untoward desire, while the worker role will be offered as the prime activity in society. Trade barriers will be seen as the way to eliminate unemployment and to punish other nations for daring to thwart U.S. companies in their foreign activities. All of this will be clothed in a rhetoric of the need to create a decent, orderly community in which individuals will no longer need to worry about income dips and bouts of unemployment.

THE STEADY-STATE WAY OF THE ENVIRONMENTALISTS

A growing number of environmentalists have joined forces with the Asian Way variety of industrial policy advocates, especially in their admiration for trade barriers:

Protectionism—shielding an inefficient industry against more efficient foreign competition—is a dirty word among economists. That is very different, however, from protecting an efficient national policy of full cost pricing from standards-lowering international competition.[17]

Free trade in this view causes immense environmental harm. As developing-country firms ignore costly pollution-control standards, they produce goods at lower unit costs than those of firms in the United States. As these goods flood into the United States, American firms find that they cannot compete on price without lowering their own costs. These firms lobby Congress for relief from environmental protection regulations, with the result that the ecosystems in developed countries are soon as damaged as they are in developing countries with no standards or standards that are not enforced. Only trade barriers can save the environment, by relieving pressure on U.S. firms and Congress to lower standards and by pressuring developing nations to raise theirs. This model sounds good, but it suffers from a lack of empirical support. Moreover, as trade barriers come down, developing countries become richer, and richer citizens typically demand cleaner air and purer water.[18]

Regardless of data calling it into question, the anti-trade model presents a compelling argument, especially when it is associated with what is called "the steady-state economic paradigm," which requires "a sustainable scale of total resource use" involving constraints on consumption so as not to threaten the "regenerative and assimilative capacities of the biosphere."[19] Free trade harms ecological sustainability in two ways, by allegedly pushing standards down and by fostering economic growth. Growth is the real villain in the steady-state world, and anything that hinders growth in support of the existing ecological order—or some pristine preexisting ecological order—is all to the good. Increases in gross national product (GNP) are said to foster decreases in "natural capital," defined as nonhuman species and their habitats. Fringe environmentalists, called "deep ecologists," want to reduce humanity's threat to the ecosystem. They push for ruthless population control or even forced enclave living, the movement of humans onto reservations, but the moderates, if that is the right term, seek a halt in GNP growth or even a mandated decline. Since citizens in a democracy are currently unlikely to vote themselves into genteel poverty, they must be educated to see the true path, the way, and part of that education will focus on singling out the multinational corporation as the dangerous mechanism of accelerating growth, increasing incomes, and expanding consumption in the world.[20]

The bible of the way is Paul Hawken's *The Ecology of Commerce* (1993). Although he wants to motivate rather than regulate corporations into changing their wayward practices, Mr. Hawken is quite clear in his beliefs:

The promise of business is to increase the general well-being of humankind through service, a creative invention and ethical philosophy. Making money is, on its own terms, totally meaningless, an insufficient pursuit for the complex and decaying world we live in.[21]

"Business is destroying the world," he claims, because the existing market model of economic growth "lacks any guiding principles to relate it to such fundamental and critical concepts as evolution, biological diversity, carrying capacity, and the health of the commons."[22] Maladaptive and predatory economic practices accelerate species' extinction, damage human health, create stress and anguish for workers, and harm air quality, water, and forests. What is needed is a new "ecological commerce" focused on steady-state sustainability, mostly through conservation of resources. Businesses must be persuaded to change their goal from competing in order to earn profits to competing in order to conserve and increase resources.

We face "an ecological and social crisis whose origins lie deep within the assumptions of our commercial and economic systems."[23] The crisis calls for a change in the way the public looks at economic activities so that a biological rather than a monetary point of view comes to dominate. Such a development, for Mr. Hawken, requires a major redesign of the institution of business. The key elements are systemic change to reward long-term restoration activities of corporations while penalizing short-term exploitation. Change mechanisms will involve subsidies and regulatory processes that encourage innovation, especially from small companies, large corporations being too unwieldy. Trade barriers will play their part, putting a halt to "resource-consumptive luxuries such as Chilean strawberries and nectarines flown in daily during New York winters." As New Yorkers face the unendurable, presumably they will begin to establish hothouse production of organic fruits, perhaps in the wastes of Hoboken and the surrounding areas, although since these are wetlands designated for protected species, Central Park may have to be developed for agriculture.

As Dr. Herman Daly, at one time an environmental economist with the World Bank, puts it,

The term *sustainable development* therefore makes sense for the economy but only if understood as *development without growth*. . . . Currently the term *sustainable develop-*

ment is used as a synonym for the oxymoronic *sustainable growth*. It must be saved from this perdition.[24]

It would be nice if everyone in the world could enjoy American-style living standards, but Dr. Daly claims that, given the already outrageous human exploitation of the ecosystem, increased purchasing power for the world's poor is impossible. It is far better to reduce U.S. living standards so that the developing peoples can claim a bit more through wealth distribution, augmented by rigorous population control. The first step to take is to institute severe taxes on resource extraction to foster conservation of energy. Other environmentalists in the no-growth, steady-state path advocate: efforts to increase use of solar power, human-powered machines for transportation (formerly known as bicycles and tricycles), enforced settlement patterns that encourage walking, a movement away from factory production and back towards local crafters and artisans, and food production focused on perennial polyculture, aquaculture, and permaculture.[25]

ENVIRONMENTALIST IDEOLOGY

Environmentalists come in different packages, from the catch-and-release whaling advocates of Greenpeace, through the scare-mongering lawyers of the Natural Resources Defense Council (who damaged the apple industry with the claim that alar sprayed on apples could cause cancer), to the Nature Conservancy, which purchases land from private owners to keep it from being overexploited. These people are not all party to the deep ecologists' faith in disruptive and even violent actions to save the earth, but all of them share some common beliefs to a greater or lesser degree:

- *Humans are not part of nature.* This assertion comes in two forms. First, the world ecosystem exists for species and habitat; humans have a separate existence that can threaten the ecosystem. Second, modern humans in industrial societies have drifted away from the communitarianism of indigenous peoples, who live in harmony with nature through submission to the ecosystem. As Al Gore put it, we in America inhabit a "dysfunctional civilization" that intrudes on the rights of nature (recall the last chapter's discussion of the reification of nature as a legal person entitled to the right to own property).[26]

- *Government has a communitarian role.* American political theory mostly is based on various forms of liberalism, in which governments' roles are to maintain public order so that individuals can pursue their needs and desires and, in more recent formulations, to ensure equal opportunity for all. In contrast, communitarian theory maintains that the most basic rights and needs are not those of individuals but rather of the collective. Environmentalists interpret this to mean the ecosystem, while Marxists see the collective in terms of class, and fascists of race. In a democratic society, the government cannot simply order people about in service to the needs of the ecosystem. But it can and must mobilize values in society so that protection of the collective's rights becomes the willing responsibility of individuals. For Al Gore this is the "central organizing principle for civilization" and requires an "all-out effort to use every policy and program, every law and institution, every treaty and alliance, every tactic and strategy, every plan and course of action . . . to halt the destruction of the environment and to preserve and nurture our ecological system."[27]

- *A global citizen must emerge.* Governments must do their part, but since the ecosystem is worldwide, individuals must redirect their allegiance from national to global institutions. Here is where NGOs come into their own, since no constituted world government exists or is likely to exist. However, in the "think global, act local" model of environmentalists, NGO-led world citizens must work diligently to protect the ecosystem within their domain. In agriculture, for example, the citizen tries to push multinational corporations out of local farming because they allegedly ruin land through overfertilizing and drive away small farmers producing needed local staples. Former Sierra Club president Adam Werbach, in *Act Now, Apologize Later* (1997), for example, urged environmentalists to work against both international and intra-national food trade, claiming that Safeway stores in Idaho should carry only Idaho-grown potatoes.[28]

- *Precaution is more important than progress.* Risk is the probability of a known loss occurring, and in standard formulations the greater the risk, the greater the required net benefit an undertaking should provide. However, under conditions of great uncertainty the model breaks down.[29] If a long time lag occurs between an action and its effects on the environment, one never can be sure when a risk assessment is correct. In addition to the temporality problem, a spatial one exists; actions taken in the United States, for example, may impact the Canadian environment. One cannot be sure about this, and neither can one be sure about the possibility of cumulative effects, in which seemingly minor environmental degradations build up to the point where some major damage occurs. When these uncertainties are added to the certainty that most bad degradation effects will go unreported, risk assessment becomes nearly worthless.

Two responses are available to this failure, *tax and shame* and *command and control*. Under tax and shame, a mix of policies sidesteps the risk-assessment problem. Instead, economic growth is advocated in conjunction with increased public awareness. As households become richer, they demand a cleaner, safer, sustainable environment. Governments respond with increased taxes on such things as carbon emissions as an incentive to get corporations to reduce them. Ecolabeling requirements keep public awareness levels high, as do periodic shaming revelations on big offenders by local, national, and international NGOs. However, no-growth, steady-state advocates argue that increased GNPs will make things worse and that risk/benefit trade-offs are not acceptable under conditions of great uncertainty, especially when the survival of the world's ecosystem is at stake. They call for increased government control guided by the precautionary principle, and their views gradually are becoming embedded in international agreements.

According to the Sanitary and Phytosanitary Agreement (SPS) which forms part of the World Trade Organization's rules, "In cases where relevant scientific evidence is insufficient, a Member may provisionally adopt sanitary or phytosanitary measures on the basis of available pertinent information. . . ." And the Cartagena Protocol on Biosafety, agreed to in 2000 in Montreal, states, "Lack of scientific certainty . . . shall not prevent that Party from taking a decision . . . in order to avoid or minimize such potential adverse effects."[30] Both versions of the precautionary principle allow import bans as long as risk assessment is subsequently undertaken. However, since assessments often cannot be authoritative, bans on trade in many agricultural and chemical products may become permanent. European outrage over imports of products known as genetically modified organisms (GMOs), for example, has led to precautionary principle bans based on the assertion that biological diversity in the ecosystem is threatened. Presumably similar bans on within-country production and trade also will become more common.

- *Science is dangerous.* Ever since science fiction movies of the 1950s first resurrected Mary Shelley's idea that scientists' desire for knowledge is dangerous, some environmentalists have attacked science as pumped up with vanity and inadequate to deal with serious ecosystem concerns. In criticizing the WTO's reliance on risk assessments, Ralph Nader's Public Citizen complains that the SPS Agreement "exalts the role of science far beyond the point it is appropriate, attempting to eliminate all 'non-science' factors from standard setting."[31] Moreover, waiting for science to come up with answers on risks is foolish; far better to follow the path of proactive prudence. Public Citizen calls for highly politicized discussions of potential ecosystem threats based on the idea that power must reside in the realm of the polis, not the academy. NGO-influenced societal values should outweigh scientific assessment in determining legal and regulatory protections, and the chief value is and will be precaution. The highest possible standards covering both products, inputs, and processes should be set as the global floor, not the ceiling, by international agreements augmented by congressional and state legislation. This kind of precaution reflects not just a fear of unknown terrors but a profound distrust of industries and the scientists industry leaders are alleged to control. Supposedly these people are capable of almost unimaginable foolhardiness in pursuit of their own narrow and short-term goals of profits for business captains and distinctions for scientists. An early Greek scientist, Democritus, once said, "I would rather discover a causal relation than be king of Persia." Today, an environmentalist might say, "What does it profit a scientist to know the secrets of nature if in knowing it she helps destroy it?" The real Frankenstein was not the creature, after all, but its creator.

THE WAYS OF ORDER

In the 21st century, the Third Way of Europe, the Asian Way of Asia and Japan, and the Steady-State Way of environmentalists will combine to mount a prolonged attack on ideas of growth, change, innovation, mobility, consumption, leisure, and science. The way of order will be preached by self-appointed sages offering individuals a life well lived in terms of stability rather than progress. Capitalism will be described as a system bordering on chaos in which ruthless processes of natural selection foster ever-recurring bouts of unemployment and social unrest. The three ways alternatively will advocate stability, predictability, and an orderly existence either with or without economic growth. Sadly, they will provoke unrest instead. Here are three possible scenarios:

- *The European Third Way will trade off high unemployment for high stability with growth.* Controls on the functioning of labor markets such as no-layoff regulations, the encouragement of low labor mobility, and workers on boards of directors will evoke high wages, job security, and high unemployment. Cadres of the unemployed will turn into the unemployable and, as in Paris now, will be shunted off into public housing reservations ringing each of the great cities in Europe. The specter of rioting will haunt leaders and their well-off, middle-class supporters.

- *The Asian Way will trade off individual autonomy for high stability and economic growth.* The prime unit of society will be the employee rather than the consumer or the citizen. He and she will yield allegiance to collectives in the form of corporations, which will treat labor costs as fixed, and to the government, which will allocate credit and subsidies in accord with industrial policy. Trade barriers will protect firms from foreign competition and allow them to build up cash flow to finance economic dominance in global markets, with global profits used to keep the domestic system running smoothly at full employment. But hostility from abroad will evoke anxiety, as will domestic social unrest driven by individuals' shame and guilt over the autonomy they have surrendered.

- *Steady-state environmentalists will trade off high unemployment, autonomy, and economic growth for ecosystem stability and sustainability.* Under the guidance of the belief that human capital must defer to natural capital, severe constraints on consumption will be implemented. Driven by distrust of the actions of multinational corporations, leaders will break them up and institute trade barriers. Because of the precautionary principle, the highest possible environmental and conservation standards will be promulgated. As individuals secretly seek to consume, to trade, and perhaps to cut down a tree here and there on the ecosystem's land, they will be punished severely. Rebellion will be ever in the air, and massive reeducation campaigns will be needed to control unrest.

NOTES

1. Robert G. Henricks, *Lao-Tzu Te-tao Ching: A New Translation Based on the Recently Discovered Ma-wang-tui Texts* (New York: Ballantine, 1989), 192, 196. This is the kind of order Hayek argued against in his "extended" order model.

2. The quote is cited in *The Economist*, 31 December 1999, 38.

3. The quote is cited by Eugen Weber, "Killing Gestures," *New Republic*, 13 March 2000, 46.

4. Toynbee's ideas are analyzed by William H. McNeill, *Arnold Toynbee: A Life* (New York: Oxford University Press, 1989).

5. See John Kay, "Invisible Hand or Chaos," *Financial Times*, 8 December 1999, 14.

6. Joseph Schumpeter, *Capitalism, Socialism and Democracy* (New York: Harper, 1950), 82.

7. The evolutionary perspective is the theme of R. Nelson and S. Winter, *An Evolutionary Theory of Economic Change* (Cambridge: Harvard University Press, 1982). Also see Sidney G. Winter, "Natural Selection and Evolution." In John Eatwell et al., eds., *The New Palgrave, The World of Economics* (New York: W.W. Norton, 1991), 493–501.

8. See Joseph E. Stiglitz, *Whither Socialism?* (Cambridge: MIT Press, 1996) for a good Third Position discussion.

9. A key discussion of these models is in Robert E. Goodin, Bruce Headley, Ruud Muffels, and Henk-Jan Dirven, *The Real Worlds of Welfare Capitalism* (Cambridge: Cambridge University Press), 1999.

10. Robert Erikson, "Descriptions of Inequality: The Swedish Approach to Welfare Research." In Martha Nussbaum and Amartya Sen, eds., *The Quality of Life* (Oxford: Clarendon Press, 1995), 72. See also Assar Lindbeck, *The Swedish Experiment* (Stockholm: SNS Forlag, 1997).

11. Erikson, ibid., 80.

12. Erik Allardt, "Having, Loving, Being: An Alternative to the Swedish Model of Welfare Research." In Nussbaum and Sen, op. cit., 91.

13. For a summary of this kind of talk, see Peter Dale, *The Myth of Japanese Uniqueness* (New York: St. Martin's Press, 1986) and my own interpretation in Jeremiah J. Sullivan, *Invasion of the Salarymen* (Westport, CT: Praeger, 1992).

14. Francis Fukuyama, *The End of History and the Last Man* (New York: Free Press, 1992), xvii.

15. I am drawing here on the fine work of David Gress, *From Plato to NATO* (New York: Free Press, 1998).

16. See the strategic trade policies, involving heavy subsidies, proposed by Laura Tyson, *Who's Bashing Whom? Trade Conflict in High Technology Industries* (Washington, D.C.: Institute for International Economics, 1993). Also see a discussion of the benefits (and costs) of a "capitalist development state" in Chalmers Johnson, *Japan: Who Governs?: The Rise of the Development State* (New York: Norton, 1995). An admirer of an Asian Way system is James Fallows, *Looking at the Sun: The Rise of the New East Asian Economic and Political System* (New York: Random House, 1995).

17. Herman E. Daly, "Free Trade, The Perils of Deregulation." In Jerry Mander and Edward Goldsmith, eds., *The Case Against the Global Economy* (San Francisco: Sierra Club Books, 1996), 233.

18. See World Bank, *World Development Report 1992: Development and the Environment* (New York: Oxford University Press, 1992). See also Bjorn Lomborg, *The Skeptical Environmentalist* (Cambridge: Cambridge University Press, 2001).

19. Daly, op. cit., 235.

20. The filtering down of steady-state stasis ideas into elementary schools is described in Steven E. Landsburg, "Why I Am Not an Environmentalist: The Science of Economics Versus the Religion of Ecology," *The Armchair Economist* (New York: Free Press, 1993), 223–232.

21. Paul Hawken, *The Ecology of Commerce, A Declaration of Sustainability* (New York: Harper Business, 1994), 1.

22. Hawken, ibid., 3, 5.

23. Ibid., 201. The second quote in this paragraph is on p. 211.

24. Herman E. Daly, "Sustainable Growth? No Thank You." In Mander and Goldsmith, eds., op. cit., 193.

25. One well-known steady-state tract is Kirkpatrick Sale, *Dwellers in the Land: The Bioregional Vision* (San Francisco: Sierra Club Books, 1985).

26. See Chapter 12 of Albert Gore, Jr., *Earth in the Balance: Ecology and the Human Spirit* (Boston: Houghton Mifflin, 1992).

27. Gore, ibid., 273.

28. See Adam Werbach, *Act Now, Apologize Later* (New York: HarperCollins, 1997).

29. See U. Beck, *Risk Society: Towards a New Modernity* (London: Sage, 1992) and *Ecological Politics in an Age of Risk* (Cambridge: Polity Press, 1995).

30. Quoted from *World Trade Agenda*, 14 February 2000, 9.

31. See Public Citizen's site at www.citizen.org/pctrade/gattwto/1999.htm, 7 *ff.* as of 13 October 1999.

BIBLIOGRAPHY

Beck, U. *Ecological Politics in an Age of Risk.* Cambridge: Polity Press, 1995.

———. *Risk Society: Towards a New Modernity.* London: Sage, 1992.

Dale, Peter. *The Myth of Japanese Uniqueness.* New York: St. Martin's Press, 1986.

Fallows, James. *Looking at the Sun: The Rise of the New East Asian Economic and Political System.* New York: Random House, 1995.

Fukuyama, Francis. *The End of History and the Last Man.* New York: The Free Press, 1992.

Goodin, Robert E., Bruce Headley, Ruud Muffels, and Henk-Jan Dirven, *The Real Worlds of Welfare Capitalism.* Cambridge: Cambridge University Press, 1999.

Gore, Jr., Albert. *Earth in the Balance: Ecology and the Human Spirit.* Boston: Houghton Mifflin, 1992.

Hawken, Paul. *The Ecology of Commerce, A Declaration of Sustainability.* New York: Harper Business, 1994.

Henricks, Robert G. *Lao-Tzu Te-tao Ching: A New Translation Based on the Recently Discovered Ma-wang-tui Texts.* New York: Ballantine, 1989.

Johnson, Chalmers. *Japan: Who Governs? The Rise of the Development State.* New York: Norton, 1995.

Kay, John. "Invisible Hand or Chaos." *Financial Times*, 8 December 1999, 14.

Landsburg, Steven E. *The Armchair Economist.* New York: The Free Press, 1993.

Lindbeck, Assar. *The Swedish Experiment.* Stockholm: SNS Forlag, 1997.

Lomborg, Bjorn. *The Skeptical Environmentalist.* Cambridge: Cambridge University Press, 2001.

Mander, Jerry, and Edward Goldsmith, eds. *The Case Against the Global Economy.* San Francisco: Sierra Club Books, 1996.

McNeill, William H. *Arnold Toynbee: A Life.* New York: Oxford University Press, 1989.

Nelson, R. and S. Winter, *An Evolutionary Theory of Economic Change.* Cambridge: Harvard University Press, 1982.

Nussbaum, Martha, and Amartya Sen, eds. *The Quality of Life.* Oxford: Clarendon Press, 1995.

Sale, Kirkpatrick. *Dwellers in the Land: The Bioregional Vision.* San Francisco: Sierra Club Books, 1985.

Schumpeter, Joseph. *Capitalism, Socialism and Democracy.* New York: Harper, 1950.

Stiglitz, Joseph E. *Whither Socialism?* Cambridge: MIT Press, 1996.

Sullivan, Jeremiah J. *Invasion of the Salarymen.* Westport, CT: Praeger, 1992.

Tyson, Laura. *Who's Bashing Whom? Trade Conflict in High Technology Industries.* Washington, D.C.: Institute for International Economics, 1993.

Weber, Eugen. "Killing Gestures." *New Republic,* 13 March 2000, 46–49.

Werbach, Adam. *Act Now, Apologize Later.* New York: HarperCollins, 1997.

Winter, Sidney G. "Natural Selection and Evolution." In John Eatwell et al., eds., *The World of Economics.* New York: W.W. Norton, 1991, 493–501.

World Bank. *World Development Report 1992: Development and the Environment.* New York: Oxford University Press, 1992.

Chapter 6

THE RETURN TO VIRTUE: "WE WANT WHAT'S RIGHT AND GOOD"

Assume that you are the American head of Podiatronics' Asia Regional Headquarters, located in Tokyo. Your company sells shoes worldwide, and your job is to manage relations with Korean contractors who produce the shoes in Vietnamese factories staffed mostly by young women. You are visiting one of the factories, just outside of Hanoi, on an especially hot day, and you take off your jacket and put it on a chair next to the supervisor's desk on the factory floor. When you return to pick it up after a tour around the facility, you find that your wallet is missing. Annoyed, you tell the Korean factory manager, who is deeply offended by this affront to his honor. He immediately halts work and has his Korean assistants line up the 200 Vietnamese women in the factory's courtyard. There they are ordered to strip off all their clothes so that a search for the wallet can be made. Those showing reluctance are threatened with dismissal, so no one refuses and the women begin to strip.

What do you do as you watch this scene begin to unfold in front of you?

You might say, "Stop this at once. I am not the kind of person who tolerates such things, and neither is my company." Your statement suggests that you value tolerant, decent behavior as an end in itself. This is one variant of what is called virtuous behavior.

More likely, you will make a quick calculation involving the benefits of getting your money back and supporting an important subcontractor and the costs of damaging the employees' morale and perhaps evoking government wrath. These are major negatives, so you say, quietly, to the factory manager, "Please find an excuse to stop this. Nothing good will come of it, and the loss is minor. I will compensate you for any embarrassment with increased orders." This is called utilitarian behavior, and it is the most common way of ethical reasoning among American managers.[1] The problem is that it is uncommon elsewhere in the world. If you had pursued the virtuous path, the Korean would have been outraged, since his concept of virtue involves loyalty to one's family or family-like relationships, but he would have understood instantly that you were following the path of virtue. What people can understand they can live with, and he might even admire you for exhibiting a noble character.[2] In the new village-like global business era, Americans are going to have to return to earlier ideas of ethics associated with virtuous behavior or they are not going to be able to cope.

WHAT HAPPENED TO THE PURITAN COMPROMISE?

As I noted in Chapter 2, by 1900 big business in the United States often was associated with predatory, disruptive, and destructive behavior. What persuaded middle-class Americans to support corporations was not only the jobs and economic growth they provided but their requirement that employees and managers exhibit behavior characterized by prudence, diligence, thrift, loyalty, temperance, fair dealing, and truthfulness. This was the Puritan Compromise in which corporate activities of an occasionally unsavory nature were tolerated as long as ethical behavior rooted in ancient virtues was venerated. These virtues were associated not just with Puritan thought, but also with republican ideology of the kind preached by Benjamin Franklin and, much further back, with the cardinal virtues of medieval philosophy (prudence, courage, temperance, and justice) and the stoic philosophy of the noble Romans. This "virtue ethics," as philosophers call it, thus is deeply tied to the historical, cultural, religious, and political thought and institutions that make up the social fabric of American society and to the importance we attach to the individual's freedom to choose to be virtuous.

Virtuous behavior may be guided by learned social rules regulating behavior or by self-generated ideals, self-image, or goals. These last may be subsumed under the concept of character. The man or woman of character in business exhibits a disposition, signaled by virtuous practice, towards a praiseworthy life associated with human "flourishing."[3] Critics of a virtue-based ethics say the virtues often are in conflict and it's never clear what the virtue pecking order is. Should we be primarily loyal and lie at times for our employer? Or should we be truthful, even if our organization is harmed? Nevertheless, a business life based on virtue has a good many things going for it. Markets work better when individuals are virtuous, and virtuous behavior is often said to be in harmony with nature, including human nature—at least that is what the Roman stoics and modern environmentalists believe.[4] Add to this broad support the reality that every culture has a sense of a set of right and good behaviors that are virtually identical to the American and European list. The upshot is that an ethical system based on virtue was ideal for the continent-wide expansion of U.S. business in the 20th century and is ideal for its globalization in the 21st.

If all this is arguably so, what killed off virtue ethics in U.S. business life and replaced it with various forms of utilitarianism? By the 1920s writers like Sinclair Lewis in *Babbitt* began to portray the Puritan Compromise as a failure. Businessmen in this view had become facile apologists for money-grubbing and depended on a crude instrumentalism to legitimize their dealings. This theme of virtue's failure reappeared in the 1950s with the publication of David Riesman's *The Lonely Crowd* (1950) and William H. Whyte's *The Organization Man* (1956). Both authors described a highly bureaucratized society that pressured individuals into a social ethic characterized by loyal conformity, a faith in collectives rather than in individuals, and a passion for technological rather than ethical solutions to every problem. Indeed, technology had replaced virtue as the business system's engine in the ideology of the social engineering movement which had had great influence up to World War II.[5] It petered out when European fascists fixed on the movement's idea that individuals were malleable and could be manipulated in service to the state's goals, but the faith in technology remained. As Alasdair MacIntyre argued in *After Virtue* (1981), a managerial focus on technology requires a commitment to the natural pursuit of utility—that's what machines are for—that pushes off to one side the practices of virtue. What do prudence, courage, and temperance have to do with getting a fifty-ton sheet metal pressing machine to work more efficiently so that unit costs can be driven down and prices lowered to capture market share? Diligent and conformist loyalties to a complex system are important, but not as virtues contributing to a sense that an individual, free and autonomous, is part of a praiseworthy human flourishing. They are merely learned habits with corporate-use value.

The virtues also started to be associated with conservative Protestant fundamentalism and with European totalitarianism. After all, it was Robespierre who said, "Terror without virtue is bloody; virtue without terror is powerless." Chilling remarks like this convinced many people that the man or woman of character easily could be associated with extreme religious views at best or at worst with downright ideological barbarism. The best course of action for the American middle class seemed to be a bland hunkering down based on the precept "Do no harm" rather than "Do good and be moral." This was a particularly appropriate ethics for business, since as the century wore on corporations increasingly became targets for criticism rooted in accusations of harm to the environment, the cause of justice, democratic processes, indigenous peoples, peoples of color, and so forth. Corporate responses involved toting up all the good things done to offset the bad, and a harm-avoiding utilitarian ethics replacing virtue ethics was the inevitable result.

UTILITARIAN ETHICS

Utilitarian ethics is based on the net-benefits, greatest-happiness principle formulated by John Stuart Mill and, earlier, by Jeremy Bentham: Act always to evoke the greatest happiness, not so much in oneself but in the set of people affected by any actions. Contrast this approach with virtue ethics, in which the consequences of an act are ignored in favor of the praiseworthy nature of the actor's actions. As I noted earlier, virtue ethics are more common throughout the world than utilitarianism, and an example from Singapore drives home the point. Assume that you are an American manager in your U.S. company's Singapore office. One day you look out the window and happen to notice one of your employees carrying a large can of garbage out the door, heading for the dumpsters across the parking lot. A full gale is blowing, and you say to yourself, "Boy, is he going to get soaked." But instead of trudging across the lot, the employee dumps the garbage right outside the door. Just as he does it, a policeman comes around the corner. The employee rushes into the building, and the officer soon follows. A few minutes later he enters your office.

"Did you see the man who dumped the garbage?" he asks.

You hesitate to answer, weighing the utility of possible responses. If you tell the truth and say yes, the policeman will insist that you point the employee out. The employee will be carted off to jail and punished with a severe whipping. Afterwards, he will hate you, as will his friends in the office. However, if you lie and say no, the policeman will arrest you for lying to the police, since he saw you watching from the window. You will get whipped, but morale in the office will soar and you will be the hero of the moment. You conclude that the greatest happiness (or the smallest unhappiness) will result from lying; at the expense of a sore bottom, much can be gained. This is utilitarianism.

A virtuous American would not hesitate.

"Yes," you say, "I saw the man," thus exhibiting admirable truthfulness.

"He has broken the law," the policeman says. "Please point him out to me."

"I refuse," you respond, thus exhibiting loyalty to your employees.

The policeman says, "If you do not tell me, I will arrest you. You will be whipped in his place." You shake your head, exhibiting courage, and are led away.

In both cases you are going to have trouble sitting on a barstool for the next few weeks, yet the exhibition of virtue clearly is the better choice, even on utilitarian terms, than the calculation of benefits and costs. All parties will admire you, even the authorities, and you will admire yourself. Something fine and ennobling of humanity will have occurred. Why then, in the hundreds of times I have posed this kind of case to American students and managers, do they invariably choose utilitarianism?

WHY DO AMERICANS CHOOSE UTILITARIANISM?

American managers have something few employees possess in other countries. It is training, in collegiate schools of business, engineering schools, professional seminars, and on the job. And what they are trained to be is rational, with rational defined as being calculating in service to goals. As I have noted in earlier chapters, to be rational in most societies is to be coherent—to fit into the scheme of things and to act in accord with the order of the universe. This kind of rationality is not encouraging of net benefit calculations focused on the outcomes of possible choices. But Americans are trained in such a way that a utilitarian ethic seems natural and even commonsensical, especially when other ethics models appear deeply flawed. Exhibition of the virtues is seen at times as disruptive, too judgmental, and associated with extremism, and alternative ethics do not stand up very well either. One of the most common is *intuitionism*, the doctrine that "goodness" is not just the result of a feeling or a cultural value. Rather it exists as a reality which is the same everywhere and requires us to behave in accord with its rules. Intuitively, each of us is supposed to know what good conduct is, although we sometimes ignore the inner whisperings of our consciences and need to be reminded. Conscience in this paradigm does not tell us to act nobly and to be of good character. It simply says, "This is right and good. This is not." This approach is less demanding than a virtue ethics, yet it too has fallen into disfavor.

Intuitionism declined as an ethics model as multiculturalism gained influence in American schools and workplaces. Everyone is a member of a culture, cultures differ, and no culture is better than another, Americans were told. Your conscience is not a good guide, since it merely reflects your cultural values, which may be inappropriate in other societies. Here is a case to consider. You are a British manager in India in the days of the Raj. One day you notice that the workers in your factory are leaving and joining a group gathering in a public square. There you notice that a large coffin is sitting atop a funeral pyre, as is a very young woman who seems quite at peace with the world. In accord with the ancient custom of *suttee*, illegal but practiced here and there in India, the young woman, as the wife of the deceased man, will be burned along with his remains. What are you going to do? Here are some answers from MBA candidates at New York University's Stern School of Business:

"It's their culture, and we shouldn't interfere with their practices. As long as the girl is going along with it, I wouldn't do anything." This was the most common response.

"I would dock their pay for leaving the workplace without authorization." New Yorkers can be a tough bunch sometimes.

"I would immediately decide to take my vacation." This was my favorite response.

"It's murder, and I would do everything I could to stop it." Religious students—and these are few and far between—tended toward this answer.

Neither conscience nor virtue played much of a part in most responses. The majority of students simply accepted any behavior practiced frequently anywhere as legitimate for that culture and weighed the costs and benefits of either interfering or doing nothing. However, here is where students and American managers in foreign posts run into trouble. They want to tote up net benefits of their possible actions, but they often have no idea how prevalent local practices are or how dominant a value is. Since their calculations and actions often depend on reacting to these, they don't know what to do. Being of good character, virtuous, and conscience-driven are considered inappropriate, so they look for laws, rules, and codes of conduct. The more structured an environment, the easier it is to assess the utility of adhering to or violating its norms.

CODES OF CONDUCT

Neither the internal conscience nor the external virtues is the dominant guide for American managerial behavior in global business environments. Instead, right and good actions are those which, given the local culture's norms and constraints, maximize net benefits. But intimate knowledge of the local culture often is lacking. In the *suttee* example, how many people in the town actually approve of the practice? How many hate it and would like to see the elite take positions against it? In the absence of hard facts to input to the utility calculator, Americans abroad have turned to codes of conduct.

We can rank codes from high to low in terms of their focus on promulgating the good. At the highest level are sets of rules genuinely driven by a desire to be and do good or to avoid harm. Levi Strauss & Co. developed its "Global Sourcing Guidelines" in the early 1990s when company officials discovered that over 100 of their subcontractors in Bangladesh, Pakistan, and elsewhere were using child labor in an unacceptable manner. The guidelines state that the company will not subcontract in countries that tolerate unreasonable health and safety risks for workers and human rights violations.[6] In addition, it will subcontract only with firms exhibiting a commitment to environmental protection, safe and healthy workplaces, and employment practices associated with fair compensation and free association. Specific guidelines call for:

- A maximum sixty-hour work week with at least one day off per week.
- A minimum worker age of fourteen, with a recommendation for apprenticeship programs.
- No use of prison or forced labor.

- No hiring discrimination based on personal characteristics or beliefs.
- No use of corporal punishment or other forms of mental or physical coercion.
- A commitment to the betterment of community conditions.

Buried in these rules is a faith in behaving justly, but virtue is not the main driver of the Guidelines. Rather they help a manager to calculate benefits and costs of contemplated decisions. While the benefits of using prison labor supplied at low fees by the local police chief may be great, the cost of violating corporate rules is even greater, so a Levi Strauss country manager would have no trouble making a decision, regardless of what the local culture will tolerate, conscience dictate, or virtue demand.

At a level of their highest and best use, then, codes of conduct help a utilitarian ethic work reasonably well. The problem, however, is that they often are not used in the way Levi Strauss uses them. Codes of conduct may be used by professional bodies, industries, and corporations to foster some kind of professional image or public identity. Thus codes for engineers belonging to professional societies or engineering unions may require behavior which enhances the image of "engineer" and differentiates engineers from non-engineers. The fostering of ethical decisions is not absent from this model, but its real function is to raise the status and perhaps the incomes of its adherents. Consider the problem faced by a code-bound company like The Body Shop, which seems genuinely committed to a sustainable environment, animal protection, and the needs of workers, minorities, and women, yet nevertheless is constantly under attack for hypocrisy and failing to live up to its code.[7] Finally, at the lowest level of functioning, some companies publish codes simply as cover stories to deflect public criticism. Several big consulting firms have developed lucrative "ethics" practices helping companies with well-earned bad reputations. Elaborate investigations are conducted, codes are written, ethics training is required, whistle-blower hot lines are established, and "ethic officers" are appointed. The goal here is not good behavior or even defense of a good name; rather it often is the attempt to drown a bad name in a flood of stated good intentions.

No thoughtful person will take codes of this kind seriously, and neither will front-line managers. It is all perceived to be so much bafflegab coming from "the big glass house" of corporate headquarters. However, this hypocrisy taints well-meaning corporations like The Body Shop and Levi Strauss so that employees and the public never can be quite sure how committed the firm is to its code. This kind of uncertainty, always present, renders codes only of modest value as inputs to utilitarian calculations. Even worse, codes often are internally inconsistent, do not make clear which rules are weighted more heavily than others, are often changed, and frequently are quite different from the focus of other relevant codes. For example, the Caux Principles is an ethics code developed in the 1990s for international companies.[8] One of its rules requires that the work of the World Trade Organization in fostering free trade should be supported. Environmentalist-focused codes like that of The Body Shop might disagree strongly with that rule.[9] The biggest problem with codes is that they are inflexible. Once in print, a company is locked in. In 1996, Levi Strauss began curtailing its operations in China because of widespread human rights and other abuses. But by 2001 the company had fallen on hard times and was moving some production back to China. In the face of financial difficulties, the firm's "Guidelines" had become something of a burden. A similar fate befell The Body Shop. It was becoming clear that the costs and benefits of codes of conduct were turning negative as inputs to cost-benefit calculations in business decisions.

GLOBAL HARMONIZATION OF STANDARDS

If American managers persist in applying utilitarian ethics in their international activities yet do not know local norms or have much confidence in corporate conduct codes, they may at some point begin to move towards the justice and order-seeking positions of labor and environmental activists in advocating globally harmonized standards. Ethical decision-making in a utilitarian calculus would be relatively simple when the rules are the same everywhere and the costs of violations are known. Even better, a move of this kind would get Ralph Nader and the ecosystem defenders off managers' backs.

In many countries labor and environmental standards are quite low. Children are exploited, forced labor occurs, collective bargaining efforts are crushed, water sources are poisoned, and forests burned down. These practices enable a few manufacturers to keep costs down so that they can export price-competitive goods. Some economists, good utilitarians, see long-term benefits in this behavior, since the society's focus on pursuing a comparative advantage based on low labor and environmental costs ought to lead eventually to gains from trade, increases in well-being as incomes rise, and improved labor and ecosystem management. As I noted in Chapter 5, the worries of activists over this kind of behavior probably are exaggerated. Nevertheless, no one disputes that these practices go on, and few want to adopt the long-term, light-at-the-end-of-the-tunnel theories of extended order utilitarian economists. Although corporate managers also are utilitarians, they are compelled to right and good actions yielding right and good *now*, not in the long run. Their focus, moreover, is on the input to utilitarian calculations rather than the outcomes. If input information is sound, decisions can be defended as ethical, and that is what counts in a world where critics accusing them of being unethical are everywhere. A set of universal rules, therefore, is quite attractive.

Implied global rules concerning behavior towards children, minorities, women, and unions are contained in the United Nations' Universal Declaration of Human Rights and the U.S.'s Model Business Principles. The Convention on the Rights of the Child calls for work environments that do not hamper a child laborer's physical, social, cognitive, emotional, or moral development. Companies are urged to follow these practices and to avoid business with firms that do not. For the environment, the Basel Convention on Transboundary Movements of Hazardous Wastes and Their Disposal promulgates practices regarding wastes that have hazardous characteristics. Trade in endangered species is prohibited by the Convention on International Trade in Endangered Species. The Montreal Protocol on Substances That Deplete the Ozone Layer focuses on reducing production levels of chlorofluorcarbons, and the Climate Change Convention suggests restrictions on the use of fossil fuels that emit carbon dioxide.[10]

Other conventions, treaties, protocols, and principles exist, and an expansion of global standards probably would be well received by corporate executives, justice crusaders, ecosystem defenders, and Global Villagers. But movement along these lines is highly problematic. Developing countries are against standards set so high as to retard economic development, while the rich nations fear lowest-common-denominator approaches. Thus global agreement is unlikely on the level of standards required in the rules for labor and environmental management. Moreover, influential economists and policy analysts argue that countries differ in the regulatory regime optimal for achieving high economic growth and net benefits to workers and the environment. Global standards might be unethical practices in some nations, since net costs rather than net benefits would result. Even worse, universal standards, no matter how noble, could be seen as intrusions on national cultural practices and sovereignty. Finally, enforcement mechanisms are weak and likely to remain so. Clearly global standards are not going to be the salvation for American utilitarian ethics calculations in transnational business.

U.S. UTILITARIANISM IN CRISIS

When I was a boy, my friends and I enjoyed comic books full of grisly violence and not-nice aliens from decidedly non-suburban planets. The U.S. Congress investigated comic books' influence on the minds of children—one voracious young consumer interviewed was reported to have said, "When I grow up, I want to be an axe murderer"—and calls multiplied for regulations. The industry responded with its own ethics code, which in part required publishers to place a notice on each comic book that announced in block letters, "CRIME DOESN'T PAY!" This was utilitarian ethics at its finest, given the implicit argument that children should be made aware that a life as an axe murderer in the aggregate evokes net costs rather than net benefits and therefore should be avoided. Similar arguments have been made from time to time concerning film and television productions, and similar industry codes have been developed. But what if crime did pay? What if teenage sex and drug-taking was on balance more fun than harmful? What if child pornography had no negative effect on the performers or the viewers? This last argument is close to the position of the Society for Man-Boy Love, which, according to newspaper reports, has a newsletter and a publicist. Presumably the support for such amorous practices in parts of Plato's writings is quoted in the newsletter.

Americans in fact are a moral people and are more likely to behave virtuously than in response to a deeply flawed utilitarian calculus. They have created a mostly orderly society for themselves—crime rates in some European cities are higher than in most U.S. cities, they don't cheat much on taxes, they behave decently to each other, they are charitable, and they want their children to behave themselves because it's the right thing to do. Yet in their existence as economic creatures they invariably resort to utilitarian paradigms to justify their pronouncements on what is and is not ethical. Why didn't the comic book industry say, "Crime is bad" on its publications, since most Americans have strong and enduring beliefs about good and bad, right and wrong? Indeed, these beliefs are quite similar to those held by other peoples in the world, and, as with other peoples, the beliefs guide behavior. As I noted earlier, the answer is that an extended order society structured along bureaucratic and technological lines tends to justify decisions in terms of benefits and costs, especially when it fears excesses based on self-appointed defenders of virtue and abolishers of evil. But individuals in the United States, like their brothers and sisters elsewhere, generally try to be virtuous, even as they justify their actions with the utilitarian cover story. This kind of justifying is not common elsewhere and invites criticism.

Americans have no deep commitment to utilitarian ethics, since the model simply evolved alongside the rush in the 20th century to choose reason and technology as the tools to build a highly prosperous market society. We cannot give these up, nor should we. But we can push utilitarianism into the background where it belongs and let virtue and the dictates of conscience reemerge.

GLOBALIZATION, VIRTUE, AND CONSCIENCE

As U.S. trade and investment across borders grow in the 21st century, American managers will find that the utilitarian ethics that fits in so well with a market-based economy rooted in reason, calculation, technology, and bureaucracy does not fit in well where quasi-market conditions prevail in the midst of affiliation networks based on relations among people deemed to be of good character and thus trustworthy. Consider an American manager in Indonesia. She is likely to rely on an economic model in which all business relationships are exchange-oriented and emphasize constant bargaining and negotiation with customers, subordinates, superiors, suppliers, and channel members. She will deal fairly with them and expect the same because the benefits of right actions outweigh the costs—or so she will say to anyone who asks. Down deep she probably feels that her conscience requires fair dealing because it's the right thing to do, but announcing that to the world, except in the mouths of pious Chief Executive Officers (CEOs) or public relations flacks, is not cool. In any case, she will find that Indonesian managers live in a world where vertical relations are based on norms of reciprocity and allegiance in which those above (e.g., bosses and customers) provide benevolent patronage to those below, who in turn respond with obedience to the demands of those above. In their view, this is what virtuous behavior by people of good character demands. Horizontal relations are made up of trust networks in which business people share information and rely on each other for help. Even competitors can expect this behavior from each other because good character is expected to prevail.[11] Not all societies are like Indonesia, but more are like it than are like American business society.

To function as an ethical person in both a Global Village and an extended order economy, the American managers need not give up exchange-based relations. In fact, the Indonesians are going to have to give up their model and move more towards the market model, perhaps as modified by the justice-based or order-producing paradigms that may emerge. But most of the world's peoples rely on virtue ethics and character as guides to behavior and that is unlikely to change. Americans will feel pressure to stop legitimizing their dealings in terms of net benefits and to return to the older American ways, which are also the world's way. Unlike the challenges from justice and order advocates, the challenge from the world to return to virtue is not particularly destabilizing, since the whispers of conscience in American hearts point in that direction anyway. Moreover, even when Americans find that some virtues get emphasized a lot more in America, and vice versa in other settings, conflict can be muted by a mutual recognition of a common humanity rooted in a common morality. No such recognition occurs when conflicts arise because utilitarian calculations among parties differ, as they inevitably do.

THE CHALLENGE TO RETURN TO VIRTUE

Currently right and good behavior for American managers in global business is that which, given local cultures and various codes of conduct, maximizes net benefits for stockholders or perhaps stakeholders. However, what with the agonizing Americans have been exhibiting over ethics in business for decades, a utilitarian approach is not working very well. It is time to return to virtue ethics.

A model of ethical behavior guided by a respect for a set of virtues is deeply rooted in Western traditions and American republicanism, which calls for only minimal government regulation of social order in a society graced by people of character. American business once supported this model, and good companies required virtue and character in employees. This requirement helped legitimize business when it needed legitimizing a hundred years ago, and the model fostered efficient market functioning. But over the course of the 20th century we drifted away from a virtue ethics as a technological and bureaucratic focus on rational calculation evoked a calculation-based utilitarianism. Moreover, utilitarian ethics filled a void created as middle-class Americans grew reluctant to give allegiance to a model seemingly associated more and more with extreme religious and political behavior. In a rapidly globalizing world, virtuous behavior came to seem disruptive, and to be guided by one's conscience showed insensitivity to local cultures and practices. Utilitarianism, which posited right and good action as the result of an exquisitely sensitive toting up of benefits and costs, seemed more appropriate.

But calculating right and good in all the countries where Americans do business requires intimate knowledge of mysterious values, rituals, and practices. It is a very hard thing to do, so during the 1990s a movement developed in corporate circles and business schools to establish codes of conduct to drain off some of the uncertainty from ethics calculations. Nevertheless, some codes are mere exercises in hypocrisy and lack credibility, and good codes often are internally inconsistent and in conflict with other good codes. A universal code for everyone would be nice, but it isn't going to happen. Thus U.S. practitioners of utilitarian ethics in foreign settings face a dilemma. In many decisions whereby they try to calculate the action that yields net benefits to all concerned, they lack information and don't know how to weigh the information they have, given a somewhat mysterious local context. They are going to make many ethics decisions deemed unethical by interested observers.

A different ethics is needed, and a return to virtue is in order. It's true that adherence to a set of virtues creates problems as virtues conflict with each other, just as elements of conduct codes do. And like codes, virtues can evoke inflexibility. But unlike codes, virtues are not mere inputs to a decision. They are the noble goal of human behavior. What's more, all humans recognize the basic virtues (truthfulness, courage, etc.) and try, however imperfectly, to follow them. A virtue ethics thus has a gravitas lacking in codes of conduct, so its failings are more likely to be excused or tolerated in non-U.S. locales. The utilitarian approach may work well in the United States, where we have information on values and know what's what, but it does not function adequately abroad, and Americans in other societies who justify their actions with elaborate cost-benefit PowerPoint tables will be criticized for getting things all wrong at times and, every time, for not following the panhuman requirement to have and to exhibit good character. We must return to our roots, both in the United States and in international settings, and begin again to stress virtue, character, and conscience as the guides to business behavior. Since I basically am arguing here for the net benefits of a virtue ethics, I cannot reject utilitarianism as an ethics model. That is not the point. Rather, virtue again must become our dominant mode of ethical behavior, with consequentialist, utilitarian justifications for behavior playing a secondary role. Twenty-first century globalization challenges us here to go backward if we want to go forward, so backward we must go.

NOTES

1. See S.R. Premeux and R.W. Mondy, "Linking Management Behavior to Ethical Philosophy," *Journal of Business Ethics*, 1993, 12, 349–357. The roots of business utilitarianism are illustrated in Bouck White, *The Book of Daniel Drew* (New York: Doubleday, 1910). A modern defense of utilitarianism is in Leland B. Yeager, *Ethics as Social Science: The Moral Philosophy of Social Cooperation* (Northampton, MA: Edward Elgar, 2001).

2. Korean and Taiwanese subcontractors of Nike have been known to force workers to jog around the factory in stifling heat and lick the floor and to hit them with shoe parts. See Samantha Marshall, "On Today's Shop Floor, It Pays to Be Culturally Sensitive," *Asian Wall Street Journal*, 28 February–5 March 2000, 7.

3. I am drawing here from Jorge L.A. Garcia, "Virtue Ethics." In Robert Audi, ed., *The Cambridge Dictionary of Philosophy* (Cambridge: Cambridge University Press, 1995), 840; A.J. Ayer, *Philosophy in the Twentieth Century* (New York: Random House, 1989); and C.I. Lewis, *An Analysis of Knowledge and Valuation* (LaSalle, IL: Open Court Publishing, 1949).

4. See Bertrand Russell's discussion of stoicism in *A History of Western Philosophy* (New York: Simon & Schuster, 1972), 254–256.

5. See John M. Jordan, *Machine-Age Ideology: Social Engineering and American Liberalism, 1911–1939*. (Chapel Hill: University of North Carolina Press, 1994).

6. Levi Strauss & Co., "Global Sourcing Guidelines," no date.

7. See The Body Shop, "The Body Shop Approach to Integrated Ethical Auditing," The Body Shop International, 1995. Attacks on the company are discussed in Joan Bavaria, Eric Becker, and Simon Billeness, "Body Shop Scrutinized," *Insight*, 15 September 1994, and John Entine, "Green Wishing: Exploiting Idealism," *Utne Reader*, 1995, January. The Body Shop has been criticized for not doing enough for indigenous peoples, having poor relations with some franchisees, and for using non-natural ingredients. It has defended itself from some charges and announced changes in response to others.

8. The Principles are associated with *Business Ethics* magazine and the Caux Round Table.

9. Another such code is that of the Coalition for Environmentally Responsible Economies (CERES), established by over fifty companies in 1992.

10. Richard Schaffer, Beverly Earle, and Filiberto Agusti, *International Business Law and Its Environment* (Minneapolis: West Publishing, 1996), 690 ff.

11. The differences between quasi-market and market societies are explored in Karl Polanyi's *The Great Transformation: The Political and Economic Origins of Our Time* (Boston: Beacon Press, 1989).

BIBLIOGRAPHY

Ayer, A.J. *Philosophy in the Twentieth Century*. New York: Random House, 1989.

Bavaria, Joan, Eric Becker, and Simon Billeness. "Body Shop Scrutinized." *Insight*, 15 September 1994.

The Body Shop. "The Body Shop Approach to Integrated Ethical Auditing." The Body Shop International, 1995.

Entine, John. "Green Wishing: Exploiting Idealism." *Utne Reader*, 1995, January.

Garcia, Jorge L.A. "Virtue Ethics." In Robert Audi, ed., *The Cambridge Dictionary of Philosophy*. Cambridge: Cambridge University Press, 1994, p. 840.

Jordan, John M. *Machine-Age Ideology: Social Engineering and American Liberalism, 1911–1939*. Chapel Hill: University of North Carolina Press, 1994.

Levi Strauss & Co. "Global Sourcing Guidelines." No date.

Lewis, C.I. *An Analysis of Knowledge and Valuation*. La Salle, IL: Open Court Publishing, 1949.

Marshall, Samantha. "On Today's Shop Floor, It Pays to Be Culturally Sensitive." *Asian Wall Street Journal*, 28 February–5 March 2000, 7.

Polanyi, Karl. *The Great Transformation: The Political and Economic Origins of Our Time*. Boston: Beacon Press, 1989.

Premeux, S. R. and R.W. Mondy. "Linking Management Behavior to Ethical Philosophy." *Journal of Business Ethics*, 1993, 12, 349–357.

Russell, Bertrand. *A History of Western Philosophy*. New York: Simon & Schuster, 1972.

Schaeffer, Richard, Beverly Earle, and Filiberto Augusti. *International Business Law and Its Environment*. Minneapolis: West Publishing, 1996.

White, Bouck. *The Book of Daniel Drew*. New York: Doubleday, 1910.

Yeager, Leland B. *Ethics as Social Science: The Moral Philosophy of Social Cooperation*. Northampton, MA: Edward Elgar, 2001.

CHAPTER 7

THE CHALLENGE OF SOVEREIGNTY AND IDENTITY: "WE WANT WHAT'S OURS"

In late February 1997, over 300 delegates to People's Global Action (PGA) met in Geneva to discuss joint actions against the WTO, the IMF, the World Bank, the North American Free Trade Agreement (NAFTA), and the Maastricht Treaty, which established the European Union. Their goal was to develop a manifesto bearing witness to "the devastating social and environmental effects of globalization" brought about by "corporate control" of transnational corporations supported by the named international bodies.[1] What they yearned for was "solidarity" among "men and women of grassroots movements," including foes of privatization, women, small farmers, indigenous peoples "fighting for their cultural rights," students, anti-trade militants, environmentalists, fisher folk, animal rights activists, and "peace mobilizers." What these disparate groups had in common was a hatred of the "corporate empire" and admiration for those who had "destroyed the seat of Cargill in India or Novartis's transgenic maize in France."

In the midst of PGA's overblown rhetoric, all-encompassing zealotry, and a faith in the unifying force of shared sentiments, a "Peoples' Global Action Manifesto" did emerge, and one of the themes running through it is a faith in national sovereignty as an antidote to the WTO's and the multinationals' efforts "to strengthen their global control over political, economic, and cultural life."[2] Allegedly, "capitalist accumulation has always fed on the blood and tears of the peoples of the world," and a stop to this can be brought about by returning autonomy to these peoples, which to some extent refers to nation-states. This rage for national sovereignty, as we will see, generates passion not only among indigenous folk in developing countries and their well-fed supporters in suburban American colleges, but also among new Hegelians such as Patrick Buchanan, who see the pristine "spirit" of a nation as somehow tainted by expanding markets and border-crossing flows of goods, services, capital, and people. They fear the spread of technology, the mysterious workings of a global financial system that can strike with currency terror seemingly overnight, international bodies such as the WTO, and multinational corporations. But they also fear each other. The developing countries fear U.S. intrusions on their autonomy, and some Americans see danger across the Pacific as well as the Rio Grande. A developed country like Canada fears the cultural hegemony of its giant neighbor, while French groups fret over the loss of *gloire* in a mongrelized European Union. In the coming decades the sovereignty movements will call for trade and investment barriers, not to protect jobs so much but to defend a way of life, a culture, a tribe, or a religion. Also demanded will be abrogation of treaties, conventions, and agreements, as well as recognition of sovereignty-like status for groups modeling themselves on the Palestine Liberation Organization (PLO). As such groups multiply, so will their attempts to regulate business. The world appears to be on the verge of a strengthening of the national sovereignty paradigm, its broadening to include non-state bodies, and the reemergence of powerful ideologies revolving around the idea of the state as a spirit or a pure essence which must be protected from globalization's pollution.

SOVEREIGNTY: A VAPOROUS CONCEPT

It is easy to define sovereignty as "a state's externally recognized right to exercise final authority over its own affairs," but then the hard part comes.[3] What is a state? What does external mean, and who is doing the recognizing? What affairs are covered? And most important of all, who is "it"? Is "it" a corrupt governmental elite or is it all of the much put-upon inhabitants of the country? Is "it" the dominant tribal or religious group, or is it the noble defenders of the nation's spiritual essence, traditional culture, and ancient way of life? No one really knows the answers to these questions, and a "your-guess-is-as-good-as-mine" environment legitimizes just about any concept of national sovereignty. Indeed, a sense of internal and external must be established before an "it" can have any firm meaning. In quiet, nonturbulent times, one can define a Frenchman as one who says he is French and not be accused of uttering a tautology.[4] But more defensible definitions are in order in periods of flux. Our globalization era is one of those. The more the French are identified as European citizens, the more some of them will want to set up rules for who's in and who's out as "the French." Some of these rules will end up as trade and investment barriers designed not so much to hinder foreigners' economic activity but rather to affirm "Frenchness." Moreover, as globalization pressures the French to define themselves, various ethnic, gendered, tribal, religious, and economic bodies will come forward to claim priority as truly the "people" of France. To some extent this is what was going on at the 1997 People's Global Action meeting in Geneva, where, according to PGA press releases, special interest groups seemed at pains to proclaim themselves as the representatives of the people of Argentina, Chile, Indonesia, et al.

Globalization weakens the ability of groups to define and proclaim national identity and membership in the "people" of the nation, so they respond by louder and longer proclamations. The goal is to move the idea of the people inexorably towards the idea of the nation so that the sovereign status of the state becomes that of the nation's people, however defined. If small farmers in Indonesia can get the world to see them as the people of the Indonesian nation, benefits can flow from that recognition in the form of nation-building aid from the rich countries, charitable donations, loans from international organizations, and pleasurable status at international conferences for the people's leaders. One even can talk about the "peoples" joining together in a Global Village. Consider this statement from an official of Friends of the Earth, a people's advocacy group for farmers and others:

I think one of the common complaints is that many of these organizations don't listen as well as they say they'll do. *The Indonesians* [my italics] have a new saying for dealing with the World Bank: they invite us, they inform us, and then they ignore what we have to say.[5]

The implied message here is that "the Indonesians" are the people of Indonesia, who are the small farmers. They are the nation and should be trusted accordingly, perhaps with IMF membership, a place at the table of WTO deliberations, and recognition of their constraints on foreign corporations' activities in Indonesia.

The model for all of this is the Palestine Liberation Organization, which had neither territory nor recognition by nations, yet was granted observer status in the United Nations in 1974. In 1988, the group called for Palestinian independence and achieved mission status in the United Nations (UN). This sovereignty-like identity helped the PLO to obtain aid and, later on, some control over territory. The message is clear: Get the world to think of you as a sovereign people, then a nation, and then a recognized state, and good things will happen.[6] Similarly, the Chinese elites of Hong Kong always were subservient to British rule until the Peoples Republic of China (PRC) took over in 1997, yet so powerful was the group's rhetoric that the PRC awarded Hong Kong a good deal more autonomy than it probably would have had in the absence of years of talk about the "people" of Hong Kong and their sovereign rights.

Clearly being a sovereign people pays off, but it's a hard act to develop and hard to keep going. Other groups in the society also seek the "people" label and often are unwilling to accept the fact that one group has captured the flag. This has been the experience of the PLO, which is in constant battle with other people's groups in its territory. In the arena of global business, groups compete for sovereign-like recognition, which may lead to corporate largess, through the use of Web sites, public relations campaigns, and a vocal presence at demonstrations in Geneva, London, Washington, DC, and Seattle. Well-meaning advocacy organizations help this process along. The People's Global Action claims that globalization destroys "rural societies, dignity in labor, the environment, cultural diversity, and self-determination." Transnationals seek "control over political, economic and cultural life" of various peoples. Ralph Nader's Public Citizen (PC) wants an end to multinationals' "rent-a-nation" practices and power for "pro-democratic activists" among the people.[7] Indeed, PGA, PC, and like-minded groups often seem on the point of being overwhelmed by various peoples seeking to take the first steps along the road to a golden sovereignty.

We are in a world in which national sovereignty is seen by many in both developing and developed countries as an antidote to the poisonous activities of global forces, extended order capitalism, and abstractions associated with the market model (such as the global financial system). But the concept is tenuous enough to include many disparate groups seeking the benefits of sovereign-like identity as "the people," and lots of NGOs are now available to help them plead their case. There is nothing deeply wrong in all of this if genuine improvements in the lives of humankind result. History tells us that sometimes good things happen from upswings in sovereignty claims and sometimes bad things, but one thing is certain: The greater the battles over sovereignty or similar kinds of recognition or autonomy, the more groups will try to assert their identity—after all, one cannot be recognized without having a prominent identity—by defining inner and outer, internal and external, included and excluded. They will do this through rhetorics of exclusion (e.g., "They don't belong here"), inclusion ("We are special, unique, chosen, favored, worthy, etc."), and control ("Outsiders must do this; insiders must do that"). As globalization evokes more and more sovereignty worries and claims in the coming century, corporate traders and investors will have to endure much and exercise great care in their behavior.

The threats businesses will face as they penetrate various foreign markets will revolve around five claims made by sovereignty defenders, and I will discuss each in this chapter:

- *"No one is in charge."* Here the worry is that abstractions like "the global market," "the global financial system," or "the West" are sucking autonomy out of a poor nation.

- *"The multinationals are taking charge."* Sovereignty defenders or seekers claim that stateless, rootless corporations are inexorably gaining control of economic and political life in nations.

- *"The supranationals want to rule us."* Anxieties abound over the UN, WTO, IMF, NAFTA, the World Bank, and in Europe, the European Union.

- *"Our cultures are under attack."* Forces of globalization are seen as destroying ancient ways and values.

- *"We are losing our national spirit."* The Hegelian concept of nationhood is alive and well in the person of Patrick Buchanan and economic nationalists in the United States. For them foreigners pollute the societal essence.

"NO ONE IS IN CHARGE"

One of the advocates of small-country sovereignty is Mahathir Bin Mohamad, prime minister of Malaysia. "There must be an identity for that country which related to the indigenous people," he proclaimed in 1989. "We who are inside feel that we have a right to rule our own people."[8] True to the principles of inclusion and exclusion as defenses of sovereignty in a turbulent time, Mr. Mahathir makes it clear that long-term Chinese residents of Malaysia cannot be considered Malaysians with a claim to the autonomy of "the people." Only Malays have that right. But Chinese are only a tangible threat to identity and its benefits. A greater force, the West, is crashing about through Asia, and its policies, blunderings, and carelessness may threaten the order and prosperity of the people. In the wake of the Western dreadnought, identity and sovereignty might sink forever.

The threat to sovereignty comes from the West in the form of:

aid, loans, GSPs [Generalized System of Preference reductions of U.S. trade barriers for poor countries], currencies, labor unions, media, transnational pressure groups, non-tariff barriers, tariffs, technology, investment funds and know-how, global corporations, and a host of other institutions that can be manipulated to ensure that the development [of the rich nations] . . . is achieved, if need be, at the expense of the poor.[9]

The idea behind this tirade is called *dependencia*, and it originated among Latin American Marxists in the 1950s. In theory, the developed nations are running out of economic growth opportunities, and they inevitably will turn to the developing nations as markets for the products of their corporations. The first step in the process is the subversion of sovereignty in those nations so that no one is left in charge. Into this political and cultural vacuum will come the multinationals, representing rich-country interests.

Mahathir is not a Marxist, and he does not believe any conscious, coordinated policy is guiding the Western nations (Japan, probably because of extensive Japanese investment in Malaysia, is not seen as part of the problem). It is all just happening, with a million pinpricks here and there adding up to a terrible stab in the back. The providers of aid and loans, especially the International Monetary Fund, gradually will suck power away from the people's leaders. The developed nations will allow their currency values to fall so that the poor nations' currencies are overvalued, thus ruining their exporters'—and the nation's—chances for economic growth. If currencies fall dramatically, the West's corporations will try to buy up and control an economy's assets. When the Asian Crisis came along in 1997–1999 and all of these things happened in East and Southeast Asia, Mahathir and his supporters felt vindicated. The threat was real, and it had become manifest.

The way to counter the next and the next after that Asian Crisis' attack on sovereignty is regionalism among Southeast Asian nations in which "manufacturing can be planned for complementation and yet remain mutually profitable."[10] Without giving up national identity, the region's nations somehow will form a broader identity, evidenced in a mutual commitment to buy from each other rather than from the West. This effort will force multinationals to sell their goods and services at more reasonable prices, thus helping Asia to grow without losing control. This mushy idea, which by 2002 had gone nowhere, nevertheless found powerful support in Japan's ministry of finance. Even after sixty years of failure, some Japanese elites still yearned for a Greater East Asian Co-Prosperity Sphere with Japan calling the shots, and Mahathir's musings fitted in nicely with their plans.

Eisuke Sakakibara, a former vice minister in Japan, devoted his retirement to furthering the cause. His most detailed proposals called for the development of a liquid and efficient pan-Asian bond market, a regional currency, and an Asian Monetary Fund, empowered to serve as a lender of last resort in times of crisis.[11] This form of regionalism would push Western banks and Western-controlled NGOs right out of Asia, allegedly leaving Asian sovereignty intact.[12] The obvious desire of Japanese to expand their power into Asia fooled no one, but that was not really the issue. Asians like Mahathir simply wanted Western meddling and bumbling to stop threatening national identities. Perhaps the Japanese, who had shown themselves exquisitely sensitive to Asian needs, could be relied on to coordinate the salvation of local cultures from the Western consumerist onslaught (in the form of Western goods and Western "media," as Mahathir liked to put it). Perhaps not. The fear of no one being in charge could result in someone else taking control.[13]

"THE MULTINATIONALS ARE TAKING CHARGE"

In 1997 Peter Drucker argued that the sovereignty of developing nations had indeed become endangered, but not because of vast abstractions like the global financial systems. He noted that the emergence of floating currencies in most countries after the collapse of the Bretton-Woods system in the early 1970s had returned monetary control to country elites, and they then had proceeded to ruin their economies with untoward inflationary policies. This was the real threat to sovereignty, national identity, and the people.[14] But the problem easily was being resolved. As countries competed with each other to attract foreign direct investment, they would institute policies to reduce inflation, defend property rights and contracts, provide incentives for the development of business, and foster improved worker skills. If a nation did not do these things, it would not benefit from multinational capital's global movement and would decline. Drucker, as in so many of his pronouncements, is right in general. But as nations have disciplined themselves, some of their elites naturally have developed strong resentments and fears of multinational corporations taking control of their societies.

Multinational corporations are an easier target for sovereignty defenders than "the rich" or "the system." They are concrete, in the form of people and physical structures, and they are organized in such a way as to render them suspicious to governments. The difficulty, according to Raymond Vernon, lies in "the right of a parent corporation created by the act of one sovereign state to own and manage a subsidiary created by the act of another sovereign state."[15] Will AT&T's Brazilian subsidiary be run to benefit Brazil, or will it be compelled to serve AT&T's global interests, perhaps to Brazil's detriment? Or will it simply carry out a government's policies? An example of this latter issue occurred in 1995 with Japan and the United States when Daiwa Bank's New York subsidiary uncovered evidence of massive fraud. It immediately notified corporate headquarters in Tokyo, which informed the ministry of finance (the alleged friend of regionalism). Bank executives were told to keep a lid on the scandal for a few weeks for policy reasons, and so, in conflict with U.S. law, U.S. Federal Reserve officials were kept ignorant of what had happened. When they eventually learned of the fraud, their outrage led to a forced shutdown of most of Daiwa's U.S. banking operations.

If the powerful United States can become so worked up over foreign multinational activities, imagine the anxieties of developing-country governments. Some of them may come to see their nations as moving towards themselves becoming "wholly-owned subsidiaries" of large corporations with a corresponding loss of autonomy and identity. A walker through any large city in the developing world will encounter endless signs proclaiming the presence of Coca-Cola, KFC, Mobil, Xerox, Microsoft, and other corporate giants, and some of them will mistake advertising strength for political and cultural power and will want to fight back. In 1999 militant French farmers destroyed a McDonald's restaurant in Millau and a McDonald's in Brittany was fired on. In 2000 this restaurant was bombed, resulting in the death of a twenty-seven-year-old female employee. In fact, between 1995 and 2000, McDonald's stores were the target of violent protests in over fifty countries.[16] The company is a convenient symbol of corporations' supposed attack on national sovereignty, culture, identity, and even health.

Although McDonald's certainly is blameless, developing-country citizens are not irrational in having concerns about multinationals. At their worst they can inspire Bhopal-type horrors, but even ordinary business practices may cause harm. When multinationals arrive, they compete for skilled workers, driving up wages to the detriment of local firms. Or interest rates may be driven up as multinationals bid for local bank loans. In fact, however, multinationals generally seem to do more good than harm. They create jobs, bring in new technology, and contribute dollars to nations often short of them. But any problems they cause, no matter what the net benefits, may evoke charges that they are destroying, corrupting, or seeking to dominate a society. In Nigeria, Royal Dutch/Shell, worried about local unrest near its oil fields, appealed to officials for protection during the mid-1990s. The results were disastrous, as police and military units used the request as an excuse to mount a campaign of repression against political dissidents. Whole villages were laid waste and prominent leaders executed. Shell, accused of complicity with corruption and denial of the people's rights, was severely criticized. Even a simple and legitimate request for property-rights protection, then, may be seen as an attack on a society.

"THE SUPRANATIONALS WANT TO RULE US"

During his presidency, George Bush proclaimed a new world order in which supranational institutions such as the United Nations, the World Bank, and the International Monetary Fund would work together with the support of the major nations to bring peace and economic growth to the world. This harmless rhetoric should have joined the "great society" and the "new frontier" in the dustbin of history's slogans, but it seemed to be taken seriously by the leadership of the IMF, which had been floundering about for years in search of a mission. Originally established to make short-term hard currency loans to help countries get over balance-of-payments rough spots threatening the fixed currency system created at Bretton Woods, the IMF found itself with little to do when the system collapsed, floating rates emerged, and balance of payments became self-adjusting in most cases. It first shifted towards making longer-term loans to solve macroeconomic problems and then, in the 1990s, began making demands for social change as a condition for a loan.

Alarm bells went off all over the developing world, and a new term, *transgovernmentalism*, began to be heard.[17] Although intended to refer to the development of a more networked, coordinated world in which national sovereignty would be fostered by helping it to become more effective, developing-country leaders and elites began to worry that a positive spin was being put on what in fact was a menacing development. This was especially so since one of the U.S. elites, Professor Samuel Huntington of Harvard, had proclaimed a coming battle among civilizations in *The Clash of Civilizations and the Remaking of World Order* (1997). Were the IMF's actions the first step, covered in the happy talk of Hollywood Martians ("We come in peace. We are your friends...."), in infiltrating enemy lines? Attacks on the IMF began to mount from both developing-country and American critics. One of these latter actually got into a fistfight with an IMF executive during a seminar at the Chicago Federal Reserve ("You can't fight in here. This is the Federal Reserve."), and demonstrations against the organization mounted. Finally, U.S. officials decided that something had to be done and began calling for the IMF to stop making what were in effect sovereignty-threatening loans and to return to the short-term variety.

While all of this was going on, the World Trade Organization had the bad sense to be born. Although mostly a club of nations agreeing to be bound by a set of trading rules with so many exceptions that it takes about 20,000 pages to state them, the WTO was perceived immediately by some as a threat to national sovereignty because it seemed to have something other supranationals lacked, power to require changes in a country's practices, laws, and habits if they interfered with the WTO's principles of nondiscriminatory, fair treatment of foreign goods and to some extent companies. The reality that the WTO is one of those transgovernmentals that defend sovereign rights by treating them with exquisite sensitivity in its rulebook did not halt massive demonstrations against the organization in London, Geneva, and Seattle. As a mingler in the crowd at the 1999 Battle of Seattle, I saw a city come to the point of complete anarchy for a few hours and then, thanks to the refusal of the great mass of demonstrators to ransack a town that had become defenseless, pull back. It was a close-run thing, and it suggests just how explosive the clash over transgovernmentals and national sovereignty could become.

"OUR CULTURES ARE UNDER ATTACK"

During the 20th century, German leaders in the 1930s proclaimed the defense of race and culture, and Serbian leaders in the 1990s sought to defend ethnicity and religion. The century was alive with various elites using cultural and related arguments to try to hold on to authority or to gain authority.[18] By century's end these groups often had joined together to attack globalization, and supporters in the United States were arguing that transnational corporations were the vanguard of a new imperialism. Under a deluge of consumer goods and advertising, a nation's people would be fragmented. Out of the group would emerge individuals, and not just individuals but consumers. As fishermen hurl their nets to gather in their prey, so expanding markets would spread over a society, with giant corporations then pulling the people one by one away from their webs of affiliation, values, and allegiance towards an atomized existence as self-interested utility seekers. Where once a person was embedded in a network of national identity, he now would be in thrall to personal salvation through gratification of desire. The worst part of the unfolding globalization process, according to its critics, is that most people do not even know what is happening to them. Most Japanese think of IBM Japan as one of the great Japanese companies, and young people in the world's great cities often are not aware that Mc-Donald's is an American corporation. Thus it is up to the critics, in their view, to shout loud and long if they are to save culture and identity from being homogenized and eliminated. The battle over cultural imperialism has been and will continue to be especially bitter, and the fact that both sides usually talk past each other only will make it more so. IBM Japan will note that it has created thousands of jobs and fostered a technological revolution in the country, while McDonald's will announce with pride that it provides a safe, clean, reliable food service, often where none existed before. Culture defenders will say that IBM, McDonald's, and other giants slowly are gaining control of information channels. The next step will be to control values so that, say, the people are taught to view existing food rituals and symbols as old-fashioned and quaint. The gaps in meaningfulness that develop quickly will be filled in with McDonald's consumerist ideology.

A Nazi leader once said, "When I hear the word culture, I reach for my revolver." For "Nazi leader" substitute "U.S. economist" and you get some idea of the dislike and downright contempt some economists have for cultural studies and culture-bound ideology. For them the world is made up of individuals purposefully seeking to attain their selfish interests. Moderates among economists will say that, while cultural values do not mediate the process, they can establish preexisting "exogenous" tastes. True believers, the "imperial economists," come very close to arguing that individuals mostly are undifferentiated across time and space and that they possess mostly identical sets of needs and desires.[19] Business is the satisfaction of those, and it thus ought to be the same everywhere. This is a recipe for standardized products produced under scale economy conditions by multinational corporations in a globalized extended order. While economists, like all of us, are prone to exaggerate the explanatory power of their models, there is a good deal of reality in what they say, and what they say terrifies and enrages those who defend sovereignty in terms of inclusion and exclusion associated with culture-bound identity.

As an example of the conflict, consider the case of the people of Ladakh, a harsh and barren land on the Tibetan Plateau in northern India.[20] The inhabitants grew barley, wheat, apples, apricots, and vegetables using stone-age technology within the context of "a remarkably rich culture, one that met not only their material wants but their psychological and spiritual needs as well."[21] This all began to change in 1975 when the Indian government opened up the region to foreign tourists. Then Western films and television appeared. Soon what anthropologist Helena Norberg-Hodge calls a "cultural inferiority complex" began to develop. The media presented an implicit ideology in which humans dominate nature rather than nature them. Progress was emphasized (ironically, the very thing politically correct Americans no longer discuss in polite company) and supported with attractive images of powerful youth, beauty, and high fashion. Village life began to look primitive, and toil in the fields for Ladakh youth somehow shameful.

Thus primed, the Ladakhis were ready for the fruits of comparative advantage, the economic theory which relates maximum well-being to a nation's emphasis on producing that which it is comparatively best at and trading for the rest. Ladakhis were best at tourism rather than agriculture, so the people began to replace local food production with imports from elsewhere. A community-based economy rooted in subsistence farming began to change into a consumer society dominated by cross-border trade. An economist would say all of this is good and even inevitable. Short of walling off Ladakh and prohibiting radio, film, and television usage, what else was there to do? Moreover, most Ladakhis voted with their pocketbooks and accepted the transition. They recognized that benefits of increased material well-being come with culture-altering costs, but like individuals everywhere, they chose higher purchasing power over culture.

Critics like Norberg-Hodge argue that globalization of this sort is corrupt, since many imports are the result of producer subsidies that Ladakhis don't receive. It is not progressive, since displaced agricultural workers cannot be absorbed by tourism and end up unemployed and poor. It robs people of their self-esteem, since their cultural identity is made to look inferior. It fosters conflict, as local leaders lose influence and a scramble for power breaks out. And it encourages dehumanizing passivity where once autonomy flourished.

Traditionally, village life included lots of dancing, singing, and theater. People of all ages joined in . . . now that the radio has come to Ladakh, people do not need to sing their own songs or tell their own stories . . . [22]

A cynical defender of globalization might say that Norberg-Hodge is the kind of person who would advocate retention of slavery so that the "happy darkies" culture of plantation life could be preserved. Norberg-Hodge, the displaced village elders, and various developing-country thinkers would angrily reply that the fragmenting of culture destroys autonomy and sovereignty. With sovereignty's decline is a loss of recognition and a fading into anonymity, and there is a word for powerless and anonymous people: *prey*. What good is increased purchasing power when your existence has been extinguished? Clearly no meeting of the minds is going to take place here, no reasoning together, and no consensus formation. Over the rest of this century the battle will be fought out as it was fought out in the preceding two centuries, with charges, countercharges, violence, and the inevitable victory of globalization. But multinationals are going to get caught in the middle of the struggle, and their managers will have to endure one crisis after another. No escape is possible.

"WE ARE LOSING OUR NATIONAL SPIRIT"

While defenders of developing-country sovereignty are busy attacking the rich, the system, the supranationals, the multinationals, and the destroyers of religion, ethnicity, and culture, economic nationalists in the United States are worried sick that the spirit and essence of the nation-state is at risk from globalization and foreign influences. Led by Patrick Buchanan, they call for trade barriers and restrictions on foreign investment as necessary for salvation of the American "soul."

All this talk of spirit, essence, and soul is ultimately rooted in the pronouncements of Georg W.F. Hegel, one of the most influential philosophers of the last two centuries. He argued that the individual is not as important as the collective spirit, the *Geist*, as embodied in the nation-state. The truly rational person finds a meaningful existence, according to Hegel, only in giving allegiance to the nation, which exists on a higher level than the merely political, economic, tribal, or cultural. As Karl Popper notes, this way of thinking requires that "the various nations must be conceived as personalities."[23] The people, their values, and institutions are merely the reflection of the state's personality, or, as it often is called, the national character. No sovereignty defender we have thus seen goes this far in separating the nation from its parts, and in discussing new Hegelians like Pat Buchanan, we leave the realm of practical politics, interests, and ethnicity and enter the hothouse world of passionate ideology. It is a world where international corporations and businesspeople might be at great risk in the coming decades.

The Hegelian state is the incarnation of the spirit, and this vague concept has been made manifest in a number of ways. Sometimes reference is made to the race or the people, sometimes to the land (or, today, the ecosystem), and occasionally to the leader, the Great Man who stands above the petty bourgeois with their trivial economic pursuits. Crucial to the ideology, however, is the belief that the state by its very essence can exist only through its contrast to other individual states. This is more than just a definitional issue in which what is excluded is not what is included. Rather the nation's existence and essence requires it to be in a perpetual state of war with other states. If a state is not moving forward to be omnipotent, it soon will be moving backward into nonexistence.

We now come to Pat Buchanan, consumed with fears that America is moving backward.

As we noisily boast of America's "leadership," tough-minded rivals laugh behind our backs and loot us blind. . . . [24]

. . . nations are rivals, antagonists and often mortal enemies. . . . No superpower can rely on foreign trade for the necessities of national survival—and remain a superpower.[25]

Globalization here is not increasing incomes, amelioration, or even a happy interdependence in the Global Village. It is a threat to the national spirit born of increasing trade and investment, which add up to robbery and soul-destroying dependence. The chief purveyors of decay are the transnational corporations. "A transnational has no heart or soul. It is an amoral institution that exists to maximize profits, executive compensation, and stock dividends."[26]

In Buchanan's ideology, a U.S.-headquartered transnational like General Motors is dangerous because it refuses to serve U.S. state interests. A foreign transnational not only does not serve U.S. interests but often is compelled to serve its own nation, which usually is well aware that the *Geist* requires conquest. This nation (Buchanan means Japan) can "laugh behind our backs" because it sees how hilariously naïve we are and how ripe for the plucking. America has made the war all so wonderfully, pleasantly easy to win.

In the midst of the war of nations, increases in the flow of goods, services, and capital are sapping America's ability to campaign successfully.

A nation sells its soul for a cornucopia of foreign goods. First the nation gives up its independence: then its sovereignty, and finally its birthright—nationhood itself.[27]

For Buchanan, one need look no further than Canada for proof of the ongoing descent into national nonidentity under a deluge of U.S.-made magazines, movies, television shows, and products. To those who call for trade and investment liberalization with the slogan, "There shall be open borders," he responds,

Tear down the border posts! Throw open America's doors to all who wish to shop here, sell here, move here, live here. Nationality means nothing. . . . For the United States that is the end of History.[28]

The American version of Hegelianism in the writings of Patrick Buchanan goes something like this. History is identity, and identity is the root of sovereignty. In turn, sovereignty is required for security, and security requires dominance. If America runs a huge trade deficit and endures enormous inflows of foreign capital, its economic dominance in the world will be lost. National security will decline, and sovereignty will be threatened. The U.S. national identity will begin to fragment, and with its collapse, American history will be rendered meaningless. At this point the *Geist* will evaporate, as will the people's reason for being. We must resist this horrific progression with all our might.

"One nation's rise entails another's decline," Buchanan notes, and glob-alization, which negatively affects America more than others, is hastening the decline.[29] The solution is *economic nationalism*, a set of policies whose goal is the maintenance of U.S. sovereignty. Sovereignty requires activities to foster economic security, which is achieved when the nation has no need to rely on foreign goods or foreign investment. Import barriers should be raised, and the nation should run a trade surplus—if it even trades at all—to create jobs and higher wages. The country should give up member-ship in those supranational organizations which foster free flow of goods, services, and capital. The United States should institute "consumption taxes" on the products of countries that have "run up . . . trade surpluses at our expense."[30] In addition, these tariffs will produce revenue for the gov-ernment, thus reducing its reliance on the income tax. As foreigners rather than citizens pay for government services, Americans' "economic free-dom" will increase. After all, "in the nineteenth century, when tariffs ran as high as 50 percent, there was far greater economic freedom than today, when tariff rates approach zero."[31] An especially high import tax at the bor-der, the "equalization tariff," would halt the exodus of transnational pro-duction from American to Third World locales to reduce unit costs through the use of cheap, "conscript" labor.

All of this, and a lot more not discussed here, is allegedly required to save the American soul. Globalization is seen as undermining the United States' ability to defend itself in the nations' struggle for dominance and strengthening that of its competitors. One wonders why Pat Buchanan, like Hegel before him and his fascist admirers afterwards, does not advocate real war, with tanks and guns and other tools of that sort, to accomplish the same ends. It would all be over a lot faster than in the slow, agonizing strug-gle described in the economic nationalists' model.

ANTIDOTES TO GLOBALIZATION'S ALLEGED POISON

A state asserts its nationhood and national identity by controlling entry into its territory and regulating those allowed to enter. What Jeremy Rifkin calls the "forces of global commerce" and the "new global network econ-omy" are allegedly threatening these sovereignty-marking practices by pushing to dismantle barriers and, once inside, to take control of societies.[32] The elements of the network are faceless entities like the market model, in-ternational finance, and "the rich" and supposedly barefaced liars and de-ceivers known as multinational or transnational corporations. Both the faceless and the barefaced are said to be aided and abetted by the supranationals in the form of the UN, the WTO, the IMF, and the World Bank. All of these inside and outside powers are accused of threatening the political, economic, cultural, and spiritual unity of both developing and de-veloped nations. And the discourse which makes up the conflict between the global and the national is rendered increasingly more complex by the growing number of sovereignty-like claims from various classes, tribes, religious groups, and culturalists within states and their NGO representatives without.

The march of globalization will continue over the coming decades, sovereign states probably will adjust, and the claims of sovereignty seekers will come and go. Yet all of this turmoil will evoke uncertainty, risk, and harm to internationally-minded companies.

- *NGOs will make increasingly outrageous demands on corporations.* Right now the various autonomy and recognition seekers of the world outnumber NGOs likely to be of help, and compete for their attention. All of this demand should bring out more supply, and the number of NGOs with a global advocacy focus will soar. Public Citizen and the People's Global Action already have been joined by the Ruckus Society, the Direct Action Network, and the Revolutionary Anti-Capitalist Bloc. At some point the NGOs will begin to compete for the attention of various "peoples," and they will do it by showing themselves to be tough, relentless opponents of the easiest target available, the corporations.

- *As the rationale for trade and investment barriers grows, so will barriers.* Freer flows of goods, services, and capital began to occur in the latter half of the twentieth century, first, because U.S. post-1945 companies faced no foreign competition and wanted liberalization. Then, second, when the U.S. economy boomed in the 1990s, other countries supported trade to gain access to American markets. Barrier defenders mostly focused on job protection in their arguments, with limited success. But the 21st century will see more powerful claims made for constraints. Liberalization opponents will say that porous borders call into question the very idea of sovereignty which, if damaged, can threaten a way of life, a culture, and identity itself. Moreover, autonomy or rights-seeking groups will demand targeted barriers to help them affirm their sovereignty-like claims. French farmers, for example, will demand limits on food imports based on the assertion that their very existence is threatened without them. As they achieve their goals, their stature and power in France will grow far beyond what their small numbers alone would have produced.

- *Anti-Americanism is likely to grow.* In France it is fashionable to see the United States as both a cultural pariah and a geopolitical bully. Some Americans resent this and respond in kind—Mark Twain once said that the motto of France is "Liberté, Egalité, and Adulteré." The U.S. is accused of manipulating globalization through its control of the IMF; through flooding the world with its movies, fast food, and novels; through its direction of NATO; and through the foreign investments of its corporations. Similar anxieties are heard in Japan, Mexico, Canada, China, Russia, and various developing countries. As America's economic, military, and political power grows in the coming decades—a virtually inevitable process—harassment of Americans abroad will increase. At some point, U.S. multinationals may find it in their interests to locate their headquarters outside of the United States or to restructure themselves into networks of affiliates with no national identity.

- *Regionalism will increase.* Incessant attacks on the WTO and other supranationals will drain them of power, fostering a turn more towards trade and investment rule-making in regional agreements. This movement will be supported strongly by developing-country leaders like Mahathir Bin Mohamad of Malaysia, who envision increased power in regional rather than global alliances, and by the United States, with its interest in NAFTA and new, NAFTA-like clones.[33]

- *Efforts to control capital flows will increase.* A nation often sees its autonomy as involving control of its monetary policy and avoiding instabilities caused by variability in the value of its currency. As globalization pressures grow and sovereignty worries multiply, an increasing number of nations will try to control capital flows across their borders in support of their monetary and exchange-rate policies. At worst, blocked currency policies might emerge, in which currency could not be removed from the issuing country, or controls on profit repatriation might increase. More limited controls on capital might be more frequently used, such as those instituted by Malaysia in the 1990s and the United States in the 1960s.

- *Culturalist pressures will push multinationals towards more localized products.* John Mueller describes the anxieties of national culture defenders who worry that "the distasteful will drive out the refined, the machine-made the handcrafted, the schlock the subtle, the gross the quaint, the factory-made the artisan-fashioned, the bland the distinguished, the fast the laid-back, the mediocre the splendid, the K-Mart the corner emporium, the engineered McDonald's the homey greasy spoon."[34] People who hold this view are not going to change their minds, no matter what kind of argument is presented to them, so multinationals will have to adapt if they want to avoid trouble. Terms like "localization" and "mass customization" will become more common as manufacturing is pressured to become more responsive to country-by-country demand and cultural factors within a country.

NOTES

1. *PGA Bulletin*, www.agp.org/agp/PGAInfos/bulletin1.html, March 1997.

2. "People's Global Action Manifesto," ibid.

3. Roxanne Lynn Doty, "Sovereignty and the Nation: Constructing the Boundaries of National Identity." In Thomas J. Biersteker and Cynthia Weber, eds., *State Sovereignty as Social Construct* (Cambridge: Cambridge University Press, 1996) 142.

4. See Eric J. Hobsbawn, *Nations and Nationalism Since 1780* (Cambridge: Cambridge University Press, 1992).

5. Statement of Andrea Durbin, Director in International Programs, Friends of the Earth, 16 April 2000, in the *New York Times*, 6.

6. The benefits of international legal recognition of state sovereignty are illustrated in Stephen D. Krasner, *Sovereignty, Organized Hypocrisy* (Princeton: Princeton University Press, 1999). Krasner shows how muddled the concept is, with no clarification in sight.

7. See Public Citizen's Web site at www.citizen.org/pctrade/gattwto/1999.htm for comments along these lines.

8. Mahathir Bin Mohamad, *Regionalism, Globalism and Spheres of Influence* (Singapore: Institute of Southeast Asian Studies, 1989), 34, 35.

9. Ibid., 14.

10. Ibid., 16.

11. Eisuke Sakakibara, speech at World Bank Headquarters, Washington, DC, 19 April 2000.

12. For another Japanese view on regionalism as a solution to the sovereignty problem, see Kenichi Ohmae, *The End of the Nation State: The Rise of Regionalism* (New York: Free Press, 1996). Ohmae claims that the nation-state and the global economy cannot coexist. He calls for the enhanced autonomy of natural economic zones of 5 to 20 million people. Clearly this is not the regionalism envisioned by Mahathir or Japan's ministry of finance.

13. For a view that growing regionalism is due to a decline in U.S. influence and guidance rather than rich country blundering, see Robert Gilpin, *The Challenge of Global Capitalism* (Princeton: Princeton University Press, 2000).

14. Peter Drucker, "The Global Economy and the Nation-State," *Foreign Affairs*, 1997, 76, No. 5, 159–171.

15. Raymond Vernon, "Seeds of Conflict, The Global Spread of Corporate Enterprise," *Harvard International Review*, 1995, Summer, 26.

16. James L. Watson, "China's Big Mac Attack," *Foreign Affairs*, 2000, 79, No. 3, 127.

17. See Anne-Marie Slaughter, "The Real New World Order," *Foreign Affairs*, 1997, 76, No. 5, 183–197.

18. See Jack Snyder, *Democratization and Nationalist Conflict* (New York: W.W. Norton & Company, 2000).

19. See Gary Becker, *The Economic Approach to Human Behavior* (Chicago: University of Chicago Press, 1971).

20. The story of Ladakh is told with all the passion of the cultural true believer by Helena Norberg-Hodge in "The Pressure to Modernize and Globalize." In Jerry Mander and Edward Goldsmith, eds., *The Case Against the Global Economy* (San Francisco: Sierra Club Books, 1996), 33–46.

21. Ibid., 34.

22. Ibid., 40.

23. Karl R. Popper, *The Open Society and Its Enemies*, Vol. 2 (Princeton: Princeton University Press, 1996), 52. Popper's great discussion of Hegel is the source of my comments on Hegel's works. Note that Sir Karl refers to Hegel several times as a "clown" and holds his ideas partially responsible for the European mayhem caused by Hegel-influenced Nazis in 1939–1945.

24. Patrick J. Buchanan, *The Great Betrayal* (Boston: Little, Brown and Company, 1998), 8.

25. Ibid., 45.

26. Ibid., 55.

27. Ibid., 72.

28. Ibid., 74.

29. Ibid., 65.

30. A demand of Mr. Buchanan's reported by the Japanese government-financed *JEI Report*, 21 February 1996, 2.

31. Buchanan, op. cit., 295.

32. Jeremy Rifkin, *The Age of Access* (New York: Tursher/Putnam, 2000). Rifkin sees local cultures as national assets that must be protected from globalization's destructive tendency.

33. Some observers see a future in which governments, realizing that development is impossible without multinational investment, form regional blocs to develop attractive, multi-country incentive packages. See H. Peter Gray, *Global Economic Involvement: A Synthesis of Modern International Economics* (Copenhagen: Copenhagen Business School Press, 1999).

34. John Mueller, *Capitalism, Democracy, and Ralph's Pretty Good Grocery* (Princeton: Princeton University Press, 1999), 47. Professor Mueller, defending the market model, notes that it provides global goods and services which are "cheaper, better, more abundant, and more widely dispersed." Support for this claim is contained in Richard A. Easterlin, *Growth Triumphant: The Twenty-first Century in Historical Perspective* (Ann Arbor: University of Michigan Press, 1996) and W. Michael Cox and Richard Alm, *Myths of Rich and Poor, Why We're Better Off Than We Think* (New York: Basic Books, 1999).

BIBLIOGRAPHY

Becker, Gary. *The Economic Approach to Human Behavior*. Chicago: University of Chicago Press, 1971.

Buchanan, Patrick J. *The Great Betrayal*. Boston: Little, Brown, 1998.

Cox, W. Michael, and Richard Alm. *Myths of Rich and Poor, Why We're Better Off Than We Think*. New York: Basic Books, 1999.

Doty, Roxanne Lynn. "Sovereignty and the Nation: Constructing the Boundaries of National Identity." In Thomas J. Biersteker and Cynthia Weber, eds., *State Sovereignty as Social Construct*. Cambridge: Cambridge University Press, 1996.

Drucker, Peter. "The Global Economy and the Nation-State." *Foreign Affairs*, 1997, 76, No. 5, 159–171.

Easterlin, Richard A. *Growth Triumphant: The Twenty-first Century in Historical Perspective*. Ann Arbor: University of Michigan Press, 1996.

Gilpin, Robert. *The Challenge of Global Capitalism*. Princeton: Princeton University Press, 2000.

Gray, H. Peter. *Global Economic Involvement: A Synthesis of Modern International Economics*. Copenhagen: Copenhagen Business School Press, 1999.

Hobsbawn, Eric J. *Nations and Nationalism Since 1780*. Cambridge: Cambridge University Press, 1992.

Krasner, Stephen D. *Sovereignty, Organized Hypocrisy*. Princeton: Princeton University Press, 1999.

Mahathir Bin Mohamad. *Regionalism, Globalism and Spheres of Influence*. Singapore: Institute of Southeast Asian Studies, 1989.

Mueller, John. *Capitalism, Democracy, and Ralph's Pretty Good Grocery*. Princeton: Princeton University Press, 1999.

Norberg-Hodge, Helena. "The Pressure to Modernize and Globalize." In Jerry Mander and Edward Goldsmith, eds., *The Case Against the Global Economy*. San Francisco: Sierra Club Books, 1996, 33–46.

Ohmae, Kenichi. *The End of the Nation State: The Rise of Regionalism*. New York: Free Press, 1996.

Popper, Karl R. *The Open Society and Its Enemies*. Vol. 2. Princeton: Princeton University Press, 1996.

Rifkin, Jeremy. *The Age of Access*. New York: Tursher/Putnam, 2000.

Slaughter, Anne-Marie. "The Real New World Order." *Foreign Affairs*, 1997, 76, No. 5, 183–197.

Snyder, Jack. *Democratization and Nationalist Conflict*. New York: W.W. Norton & Company, 2000.

Vernon, Raymond. "Seeds of Conflict: The Global Spread of Corporate Enterprise." *Harvard International Review*, 1995, Summer, 25–30.

Watson, James L. "China's Big Mac Attack." *Foreign Affairs*, 2000, 79, No. 3, 125–135.

CHAPTER 8

WORK AND WORKERS IN THE 20TH CENTURY

Who said that work is an ongoing social process in which a manager should demonstrate "that personal consideration for, and friendly contact with, his workmen which comes only from a genuine and kindly interest in the welfare of those under him"? And, echoing this view of toil as involving elements of human community and fellow feeling, who said that work is "an end in itself, the meaningful expression of human energy"? The first quote is from Frederick W. Taylor, the second from Karl Marx.[1] The idea of labor as a necessary part of the process of living was congenial to both right-wing (Taylor) and left-wing (Marx) thinkers in the 19th century and also fit in well with the basic American belief in the autonomous individual acting reasonably to choose a meaningful existence within a democratically governed community. Yet, as I noted in Chapter 2, this idea faded into the background in the 20th century. It is making a big return in the 21st century, and, because it accords with human nature, the move to seeing work as part of living in a sensible, meaningful way will be both an American and a global phenomenon challenging corporations to adapt. In this chapter, I will discuss confused and infeasible 20th-century approaches to managing work and workers and focus on the 21st-century move back to the human norm in the next chapter.

WHAT DOES IT MEAN TO WORK?

In a Huntsville, Texas, factory, 120 workers sit at their sewing machines, producing top-of-the-line work pants. Malingering is rare, and relaxed chats at the coffee urn do not interfere with the high productivity of the plant. Nevertheless, the work is hard, and as one of the workers noted, "When you hit Friday's shift, and arrive at the end of the week, why, everybody's looking forward to the weekend." The only problem that interferes with the smooth flow of toil by the laborers is that every so often one of them is taken out, strapped down on a table, and killed by lethal injection.[2]

The factory is a unit of Texas Correctional Industries at the Huntsville State Prison, and the workers all are death-row inmates. Why are they working? Some do it for economic reasons. Their work earns them privileges such as larger cells. Others were brought up to value productive toil and are responding to that value with work. And some simply immerse themselves in the timeless flow of the assembly line. A few probably do it for all three reasons: as an input to an economic exchange, as an output which is a response to some value or cue, and as a process of human experiencing which is an end in itself. I will be arguing that the input and output models of work that prevailed in the 20th century are going to be downplayed in the 21st as the process view becomes dominant.

We can see just how complex working is if we look at the plight of the nonworking. According to one of the leading researchers in the field, "The psychological health of unemployed people is significantly below that of people in jobs."[3] Why is this so?

- Is the gain in leisure from unemployment more than offset by the loss of income to enjoy leisure? An economist would define the low "health" of the unemployed as simply unhappiness at thwarted desires. Work here is input to an economic exchange.

- Is working a response to some cultural, family, or personal value, with non-working a betrayal of the obligation implicit in the value? An anthropologist or social psychologist would associate the unemployed's poor state with a sense of shame. Work here is an output, an effect of some cause.

- Is working a meaningful end in itself, with unemployment related to a sense of meaninglessness—the existential dread so feared by some philosophers? This is the process view.

We really do not know the answers to these questions, although I am claiming that all of the answers presented have merit, with the first two views overly emphasized in the 20th century and the third downplayed.

The extended order idea that work is solely an economic exchange relationship within the context of a market model, in which an individual willingly puts himself under the direction of another in return for some reward, is a thoroughly modern one. It certainly is not something ancient people believed. In *The Ancient Economy* M.I. Finley notes that both Greek and Roman writers, following their own ideology, generally treated wage labor as an unseemly form of dependence. "The condition of the free man, " wrote Aristotle, "is that he not live under the constraint of another."[4] Cicero had a similar but more sophisticated view:

Now in regard to trades and employments, which ones are to be considered liberal and which ones mean, here is the more or less accepted view. First, those employments are condemned which incur ill-will, such as those of collectors of harbor taxes and money-lenders. Illiberal, too, and mean are the employments of all who work for wages, whom we pay for their labor and not for their art; for in their case their very wages are the warrant of their slavery.

He goes on to list the kinds of workers he is referring to: wholesalers, craftsmen, fishmongers, butchers, cooks, poulterers, fishermen, and performers. Anyone engaging in physical labor or sharp-dealing trade is considered base because work is base. Acceptable, even noble, work is associated with those whose toil brings benefit to society, such as farmers and importers who bring food to Rome, and doctors, architects, and teachers who enrich human happiness in one way or another.

Ancient working, of whatever kind, was not quite an economic activity, at least in the modern sense. As Finley puts it, "Technical progress, economic growth, productivity, even efficiency have not been significant goals since the beginning of time. So long as an acceptable life-style could be maintained, however that was defined, other values held the stage." Working to the ancients was mostly a ritual which was an end in itself associated with one's status and identity. Low-status people were wage slaves and high-status people did it freely, but both groups were more focused on processes of being than economic becoming. Working here is simply what one does.

These noneconomic, noninstrumental views of work are still quite prevalent, only now the focus is often on work as an output—a response to something—rather than a process. One of the major problems of the modern industrial era has been the development of an ideology "which could provide a satisfactory reason for work, which could motivate the employee to carry out his master's instructions with zeal and serve his interests with enthusiasm."[5] Here are some of the elements of the ensuing 19th- and 20th-century rhetoric:

- People of good "character" work hard. A sign of good character thus is hard work.

- In society it is the duty of employers to exercise paternal regard for their employees, whose duty in turn is to work hard.

- In organizations managers know best how to create efficient operations, which benefit all parties. This expertise legitimizes managerial authority and requires employees to respond with hard work.

- Hard work, more than ability or luck, is the instrument of success. Thus workers who want to improve their lots must work hard. This idea of work is not really instrumental. Instead of offering hard work in return for some benefit, the worker simply expends great effort in response to the rule that hard work equals success.

All of these ideas have several things in common. They envision work as an output, a response to something, either to character, duty, legitimate authority, or a rule for success. They also have in common a rejection of an economic theory of labor. It became clear in the 19th century—and is equally clear today—that the idea of work as solely part of an economic exchange could not be defended, since no one could come up with empirical evidence to support a theoretical exposition of just what work as solely exchange would look like. The claim of some economists (such as Nassau Senior, the first holder of Oxford's chair in political economy, and the editors of *The Economist* at different times) that work was nothing more than exchange flew in the face of reality and set off a reaction in the form of claims such as those listed above that work was never an exchange but was rather a response to something. Since this bifurcation in the theory of work occurred, neither side has spoken to the other. One has only to go to the cafeteria in a modern business school to see evidence of this. The economists eat together at their table and the organizational behaviorists (the contemporary advocates for work as response) dine at theirs. Crossover is unheard of, as is any attempt at integrating theories, and hapless students are subjected to completely contradictory theories of work and motivation in their classes. The same problem has beset workers in organizations during the last century.

The work behavior of modern managers is among the most difficult one could imagine, for they must mobilize labor in terms of work theories which are inadequate and incompatible. As P.D. Anthony notes, "Capitalist theory will explain why men work, but the explanation will not encourage work, at the lower levels, of sufficient energy and intensity to meet the capitalists' own interests. It provides a motive which is insufficient to overcome bounds set by reality (insatiable economic needs [as economic theory would have it] in a dustman can only lead to lunacy or despair), by fatigue, or by boredom."[6] Managers cannot succeed through allegiance to an explanation of work as solely an economic, instrumental act. To do their jobs they have had to get workers to engage in work for both instrumental and noninstrumental reasons. In the 20th century they could have offered work as part of a process of living to augment its existence as an economic exchange. Instead, heavily influenced by academic theorists, they tended to see work as a response to a managed stimulus in addition to work as a purposeful act to attain an income goal.

In sum, American corporations and the academics in business schools who study them have tended to ignore the process idea of working. Basically, they early on adopted views of work as either an economic exchange input and then later as an output response to some stimuli.

This idea that working is that which occurs after manipulation is as powerful today as it was forty years ago. For example, the fad of the moment is team-building in which the fundamental work unit becomes the group.

The group then creates pressure on the individual to perform. The whole approach is simply the Alcoholics-Anonymous technique writ large, in which the AA group shames the member into avoiding backsliding. The AA and the work group are not social ends in themselves, meaningful as human experiencing in their own right. They are simply controls designed to bring out desired behavior. While there is nothing inherently wrong in all of this—human nature after all in part involves responding to stimuli—one senses that something is missing. Alcoholics know this and see AA as but a way station. Managers often do not exhibit this sophistication. To them, a fair day's work is one in which laborers respond willingly and happily to manipulation. It is an impoverished notion.

THE SEARCH FOR BEHAVIORAL CONTROL

The modern version of the idea that work is solely a response for most people most of the time emerged from the efforts of Elton Mayo, Chester Barnard, and a group at the Harvard Business School known as the Harvard Circle.[7] Chester Barnard wrote, "Organization results from the modification of actions of the individual through control . . . or influence. Deliberate conscious and specialized control is the essence of executive function." On the receiving end of control are "persons as objects to be manipulated by changing the factors affecting them. . . ."[8]

These "factors" are always shifting across individuals, tasks, and time. Managing, then, becomes the search for successful control. It is even more complicated because control is not always deterministic. Workers have free will and occasionally use it, although mostly their work is a response to rules, habits, scripts and various cues and triggers. For the Harvard Circle, the keys were (1) to identify and create those environments in which the work-as-output vision dominated, and then (2) to find out what to manipulate within that environment to bring out the desired level of work. The laborer's work response is not automatic, but rather is a chosen act of tension reduction. Because of feelings and desires evoked by the manipulation of stimuli, workers generally can be counted on to undertake work to relieve pressure to make their desires come true. This paradigm has become the mainstay of managerial training in how to motivate employees as it is taught in departments of management in business schools by organizational behavior experimentalists. Since employees do make choices within the models, it is often characterized as a humanistic, liberal approach to managing. However, it is by no means the genuinely humanistic model of economists, which does not rely so much on control as it does on information collection to learn workers' purposes and on information dissemination to alert them to offered rewards in exchange for work. Humanism, basically, focuses on autonomous individuals freely seeking to achieve their purposes.

Theorists such as Mayo called for the emergence of a highly trained (at Harvard) managerial elite who would be effective at crafting suitable environments and manipulating stimuli.[9] The so-called human relations movement, using such terms as "industrial harmony," "higher productivity," and "benefit of all mankind," soon developed as a cadre of researchers acting on behalf of the "elite."[10] These consultants and professors have examined group dynamics, attitude formation, corporate culture, rhetoric, and many other issues in their search for control knowledge. Regardless of the path, however, their basic unstated premise is that workers naturally work as a response to something.

INTERNAL CONTROLS AND SELF-DEVELOPMENT

The Harvard Circle sought to develop models in which manipulation of external environments and stimuli evoked desired work efforts. An equally powerful set of theories focused on individuals developing internal stimuli, triggers, and cues. In the United States, for example, sustained, motivated work was seen for a long time to be a response to "character" (this is not the idea of character as associated with virtue that I discussed in Chapter 6), a vague term encompassing enthusiasm, self-confidence, simplicity, frankness, energy (often called "pep"), courage, foresight, judgement, determination, and self-control.[11] After World War II such books as *How to Win Friends and Influence People* added new attributes to the man of character. He (not she) now also was accommodating, interactive, and communicative. These qualities were under the control of the employee and directed his work. Today's popular psychology, now including women as well as men among those who are capable of having character, offers a steady stream of advice on "self-development" which is in direct conflict with models of work as an externally manipulated response or as a purposeful, instrumental act in service to interests. In the new ideology the "developed" worker—the man or woman of character with a new label—constructs an internal control room and then happily lets it dictate work effort and direction. The "underdeveloped" employee is supposedly not capable of happiness and success, since his selfish, grasping purposefulness is destabilizing in the coherent world of modern industry. Moreover, if he has not developed, he will fall prey to the controllers, an un-American lot eager to enslave him in one way or another.

These ideas of character and self-development are more a reaction to the undemocratic theories of Chester Barnard and Elton Mayo and to economic exchange models of work rather than thoughtful descriptions of work visions that people really have. Nevertheless, they imply a theory which seems to say (1) that humans are born with an instrumental vision of work which is wrong, a kind of original sin, and (2) that they also are born with the ability voluntarily to install a new work vision in place of the old one if they try hard to do so. This new vision will be associated with work as a response to a development-focused character, which in turn will lead to happiness, motivated work, and success.

What happens when managers, who both in U.S. and non-U.S. settings tend to like the ideas of internal and external controls, follow these theories? The usual scenario has been played out a thousand times, and most employees are familiar with it. First, some kind of external behavioral or culture control is attempted, usually through a rhetoric intended to develop team values that foster hard or creative work. This happened in Bank of America in the late 1980s. Then, when some necessary layoffs call the rhetoric and the corporate "culture" values into question, a new control model is tried. Often the self-development paradigm then is installed, and huge training costs are incurred to help employees develop self-esteem, character, or some other internal generator of the desired work effort. When people do not change much, the management turns to careful selection of workers with a suitable character or work ethic. Since these are hard to find in a big city full of rootless people, the work-as-response model is abandoned and the work-as-economic-input model is adapted. The wages offered are increased. This is even more costly than training, so it is dropped. Everything then begins all over again, usually with a new management proclaiming a "new" rhetoric of team values. The fact that American society is prosperous probably has very little to do with the muddled ideas about work, workers, and motivation that come and go in corporations and business schools, but one wonders how much longer such confusion will stay in the realm of the merely harmless.

WORK CONFUSES ECONOMISTS

The idea of work as a response to an external or internal stimulus acting in a cause-like manner leaves little room for homo economicus, who lives in a world where the conscious purposes of workers in exchange relations generate work. To some extent economists have brought this problem on themselves, since their extended order theories of labor have been inadequate to fully describe what really goes on in a workplace.

The first problem for economists is that they have little interest in work. Their focus from the beginning has been on nonwork, which is often defined as utility, happiness, or the satisfaction of desire; on how to attain nonwork; and on who gains the most or least from nonwork. Activities during nonwork hours are referred to as consumption. To attain nonwork—which I will now call leisure—people enter into exchange relations in which they offer production activities called work in return for compensation, which allows them to enjoy leisure and consumption. It was Max Weber who provided a sense of scientific worthiness to the unformulated beliefs about work of 19th-century economists.[12] He characterized work—in contrast to the early Protestants about whom he wrote—as a rational-instrumental act available to almost any person, since most people are rational-instrumental entities. To foster theory development, Weber described work as an abstraction in which undifferentiated beings performed undifferentiated rational acts. These acts involve deferred gratification based on the calculation of rewards and the criterion of efficiency as a guide to action. He offered this paradigm so that social scientists could have the same kind of materials to work with as natural scientists. An atom is an atom; a worker is a worker; work is work. The resulting actions and interactions can be described by law-like theories similar to theories in physics, queen of the sciences.

Economists owe Weber a great debt. Whereas once they were tellers of dismal tales, now they have become men and women of science, honored with their own Nobel Prize and, even better, high status (and salaries) in the academic pecking order. Only one small problem exists. Their theory of work, while helpful, clearly is inadequate.

Doing what is in one's interest, according to economic theory, leads to results that are, when added to the similar actions of others, as good as possible for social welfare.[13] What does it mean, however, to act in a self-interested way? Or, what is it one is exchanging work for?

- One could work to attain more pleasure or happiness. Economists who take this approach usually speak of "preferences" as things to be achieved.

- A second way of looking at interests is in terms of whatever fulfills desires (whether leading to happiness or not) about one's life. Thus, I might work slavishly for eighteen hours a day, seven days a week, so that my miserable life fosters less miserable lives for my children. The only leisure available to me would be taken up with the consumption of sleep, which I am not likely to prefer, so the concept of "preference" is not used much in this kind of discussion.

- Even further removed from economist discourse is the idea of interested behavior being focused on what is known to foster the good. Some people somewhere probably do see their interests in this light.

Interests, and the purposes that serve them, can be characterized, then, as based on stable or transient preferences, life plans, or abstract principles. Work is the instrument to serve interests, but which interest? This question matters because the way people envision work is affected by the answer. If interests are preferences, then work is a much less serious and weighty endeavor than if interests are focused on life plans or principles. Common sense tells us that a person's interests are a mix of all three, with persons of virtue-based character focused less on preferences than persons of bad character. Whatever the character, however, some kind of reasoning calculus must be employed so that a person can decide on the kind and amount of work to engage in. A worker interested in more happiness will not be choosy about the type of work but will be concerned with the length of work—since long hours cut down on preference-fulfilling activities. A principled, life-plan-oriented worker probably will be more focused on type of work than hours.

It is not clear how people decide on work. They must somehow evaluate sets of preferences, fixing on those likely to advance happiness the most, and then they must compare the chosen preferences with plans and principles. Or do they do it in reverse, beginning with principles and ending with preferences? Novelists like Jane Austen and Henry James achieved great fame writing about people who begin with principles, but modern economists like Gary Becker have won prizes describing preference-focused individuals. No one is quite sure, moreover, how people evaluate preferences. Do they compare all available preferences with each other? Or do they incorporate all likely preferences that could occur in one's life? Suppose I work like a dog to earn enough to buy a big house, which gives me great happiness. But I must continue to work very hard for the rest of my life to earn the maintenance fees. It would have been rational of me to weigh my preference for a house—and hard work—against other current preferences requiring less work *and* against lifetime preferences and work to attain them. Perhaps I would not have chosen the hard work. Perhaps I would have. It is all quite confusing, and when we look at modern rational actor theories of labor, it gets downright unreal.

UNDIFFERENTIATED, PURPOSEFUL PIGEONS

Rational actor (or agency) theory is an area in economics which looks at organizations as bundles of assets owned by investors who are represented by agents called managers. These agents participate in the labor markets, where they negotiate with workers, each of whom sells his labor to the highest bidder. Managers as agents do not concern themselves with such things as "leadership" or "commitment." They focus instead on conducting exchange relationships with undifferentiated rational calculators of utility (note the influence of Max Weber here). How can workers be rational pursuers of their own individual goals yet be generally all the same? Labor economists certainly differentiate workers in terms of skill levels and roles.[14] Yet according to one economist, workers "behave similarly in the sense that they all maximize the same thing—utility or satisfaction. . . . They all derive that utility from the same 'basic pleasures' . . . and differ only in their ability to produce these 'pleasures'."[15] What is this set of pleasures? For Gary Becker, individuals pursue sensual pleasure, riches, reputation, friendship, power, status, benevolence, malevolence, knowledge, memory, imagination, hope, association, relief of pain, distinction, and excellence. His list is derived from the musings of Jeremy Bentham and Alfred Marshall, but Becker asserts, without evidence, that the set of pleasures is the result of sociobiological imperatives which emerge out of evolutionary natural selection processes. Thus this collection of interests and purposes is "best adapted to human society."

If all workers have the same set of pleasures/purposes, they are in an important sense undifferentiated. They can be evaluated by managers only in terms of their productivity through work of the pleasures. Undifferentiated goals thus force differentiation by ability and effort. Managing workers becomes the identification and compensation of those economic agents who are efficient in matching units of ability and work effort to units of pleasure to be attained. All people will know what they want, but only a select few will know best how to get it in the particular work environment described by a given manager. The manager must identify those few and negotiate an exchange with them. Selection becomes crucial in this economic theory of managing work, since each worker is assumed to offer only one unchanging level of effort for the job and the compensation. Once hired, he or she emits that level and no other. If it is the "right" one, all parties to the exchange will benefit. Workers, then, are undifferentiated in terms of goal set, and each worker is unchanging over time in level of motivation per unit of compensation.

Economists of the kind I have been describing and the managers who follow their ideas have stereotyped workers as rational economic actors and generalized about how to deal with them without feeling any compulsion to know them as individuals. Indeed, this version of economic theory encourages managers to develop an arm's-length relationship with workers so that independence of interest can be maintained and economic efficiency fostered. The idea is this: Managers already know what workers tend to want, so they do not need to get to know them (except for skills possessed and likely effort to be made). By not becoming more intimate with workers, managers are not likely to be influenced by worker interests to the detriment of owners' interests. Economic efficiency in a market exchange only occurs when each party is solely committed to its own interests and not to the interests of the other party. Some true believers assert that senior managers of, say, a plant in Ohio ought to be located in New York so that their arm's-length objectivity is not threatened by the non-arm's-length environment of camaraderie and community which often emerges in a workplace.[16]

In labor market and agency theories the wage a worker receives in exchange for labor is made up of (1) the return sought for the work, and (2) compensation for enduring violations of preferences for working conditions. The wage will help the worker attain a future state and accommodate himself to his current state. The key to an efficient match of owners and workers in the labor market is information. The owner must describe the work, and the worker provides information on characteristics which might be related to performance, things such as education, experience, and skills. The exchange act, then, is an important one and is treated with care by both parties. After hiring, however, economic theories of management for years were silent on the need for an ongoing relationship between owner's agents and workers. It is as if workers are presumed to be programmed to perform as initially mandated. This state of affairs could not go on, and behaviorist psychology soon became closely allied to economic theory in its preoccupation with conditioning people to engage in repeated instrumental actions.[17] Here is where response theories of work have been adopted by economists to make their own inadequate and unreal theories seem to function.

Management in terms of these economic and behaviorist perspectives, then, is a process of careful selection of workers through a market exchange process, followed by behavioral conditioning to reinforce and maintain the exchange agreement. The exchange and conditioning process, once institutionalized and formalized, becomes automatic, so that the role of manager as owner's agent can be maintained. Ideas of managers as leaders, communicators, patrons, teachers, or friends need not be entertained if workers are little more than purposeful pigeons.

Some observers have noted that these theories of work do not accommodate a number of realities. Hundreds of work operations in a single business require scores or even hundreds of wage rates, and a market pricing mechanism of exchange is inadequate as the sole description of the owner-worker-work relationship. In addition, the static nature of society and the lack of variance among workers, assumed by economists to facilitate deductive reasoning and mathematical approaches to economics, is unrealistic. Entrepreneurs, moreover, do not appear to set wages in accord with economic theory in many instances. Finally, these theories are mostly silent on income distribution to various strata in society, an issue which focuses on conflict, its resolution, and customs, things a market mechanism does not allow for in a world of rational calculators.[18] Clearly, the idea that work doesn't vary much because workers are undifferentiated, easily controlled purposeful pigeons doesn't hold up very well. It is more reasonable to believe that noneconomic, noninstrumental factors are associated with stable work behavior in addition to and at times in place of economic factors. But what are those factors?

THE EMERGENCE OF INSTRUMENTAL NORMS

As economists watched 20th-century American workplaces become more and more managed in terms of stimulus-response paradigms, they tried to incorporate causal mechanisms into their rational-actor theories. Their first attempt, noted above, involved a post–World War II reliance on explaining ongoing work activities which seemed unrelated to exchange as the result of programs of instrumental conditioning. Workers were still pigeons with purposes in this mode. However, by the 1980s behaviorism had faded in its influence when it became clear that it could not explain the thinking processes that occurred between the application of a stimulus and a response. Because these processes were the very things economists sought to describe to make their labor theories more credible, they had to look elsewhere or risk abandoning theory. Since an academic and his theory only are parted by death, new causal models which incorporated purposes had to be found. The idea of instrumental social norms began to emerge.

The 1963 version of *Webster's New Collegiate Dictionary* defines a norm as "a principle of right action binding upon the members of a group and serving to guide, control, or regulate proper or acceptable behavior." Although not always necessary or sufficient, a norm here definitely has a causal dimension to it. However, norms are the tools institutions use to build allegiance. Thus in marriage a husband exhibits commitment to the married state by obeying the rules against infidelity. When his wife does the same, a valuable stability emerges in the marriage. Moreover, society will treat partners better who adhere to the norms than those who do not. Clearly here norm adherence has some instrumental value in that compliance evokes an individual's desired outcome.[19] In labor theory, by turning responsive, norm-oriented work action into some kind of optimizing behavior, economists redefined what looked like a stimulus-response process into a purpose-laden, rational act. "To get along, go along" summarizes their expanded paradigm of work behavior.

Powerful social norms exist in our society to require people to seek work, to emit a certain amount of effort for a given task, to cooperate with other workers and managers, to accept and provide training, to fit oneself into a vertical structure of order taking and giving, and to reciprocate favors with favors. Earlier in the century the Harvard Circle saw norm rhetoric as an important way to move workers into appropriate work response modes.[20] Economists toward the end of the century tended to see workers as willingly choosing norm adherence because of the benefits offered from compliance. Notice the shift: from norms as behavioral propensities that cause work conduct to norms as behavioral choices that evoke gains to an individual.

Will norms save the labor market model for the 21st century? By turning both internal and external norms stimuli into choice options for utility-maximizing workers, economists retain their paradigm and move away from the model of a worker as an unthinking purposeful pigeon. But as their theories drift into the realm of the real world, "capture-the-norm" battles erupt that can be quite disruptive. While managers talk about norms of fairness in which pay is linked to performance, workers and their unions focus on raising pay levels in accord with norms of equality. Disputes over governing norms can turn negotiations into crusades in which neither party can exhibit flexibility without calling its ethics into question—and as I noted in Chapter 6, virtue ethics are likely to become quite a bit more prominent. Even worse, the aura of norms as tools of manipulation, either in service to management rhetoricians or calculating workers, drains them of legitimacy and power. Any 21st-century movement by economists to teach our young that social norms should be obeyed only when they are in one's self-interest will provoke strong resistance, as will cynical and hypo-critical corporate efforts to trigger desired work behavior with pious nor-mative harangues about "what our team expects of you" or "the American worker, he's up to the job." Neither economists nor organizational behav-iorists are going to save their models by relying on norms.[21]

NEW THEORIES OF WORK ARE NEEDED

Organizational behaviorists claim that an individual cannot hold two or more personal ideas that are inconsistent. This "cognitive dissonance" will cause the person to change one idea or belief to make it consistent with the other. In the workplace, if we believe that we are hard workers and poorly paid, we may resolve the dissonance by convincing ourselves that we enjoy the work or the social interactions. In this way we lower our estimate of the disutility of the job to bring it more in line with our pay. A clever manager will foster this kind of dissonance resolution with suitable rhetoric. Thus hospital administrators for years praised American nurses to the skies for the nobility of their profession and kept their costs low. It seems here that the model of work as a response to a cause-like stimulus is indeed effective in guiding managers' attempts to control workers. Yet economists who ar-gued that you can't fool all of the people all of the time also were right, since by the end of the 20th century nurses had rejected the model, organized themselves, and began pushing hard for more pay for a difficult and some-times dangerous job. Here the economic model of work as an instrumental input supporting a nurse's income maximization goal seemed to have tri-umphed. But that doesn't sound right either, given the deep commitments most nurses have and their adherence to professional norms in a manner that is not simply self-serving or responsive to rhetorical triggers. Being a nurse is simply, for some, a way of life. It is what one does, like making love, as part of living. Working is something more than a caused response or an instrumental act, and the two 20th-century models we have been discuss-ing have not dealt with this something adequately.

Hostility to the failures of the models are all about us. Richard Sennett's *The Corrosion of Character: The Personal Consequences of Work in the New Capi-talism* (2000) argues that economic approaches to managing workers stifle urges towards loyalty and trust and destroy character, while Lucy Kelloway of the *Financial Times* has made a career of poking holes in the "human resources" model's efforts to control workers by controlling the rhetoric they must endure. One fad worthy of scorn is the use of labeling. The use of terms like "worker," "staff," and "employee" are dropped in favor of "associate," "colleague," "team member," "partner," and "job owner" in an attempt to bring out behaviors that would not be evoked by the use of "worker."[22] Alarmed by economist zealots and managerial hypocrites, thoughtful people have been searching for new theories of work which augment or even replace economic and organizational behaviorist models. Work as an economic act is not going to go away in the 21st century, nor is work as, at times, a response to manipulated environments. But it is going to be something more. Work also is going to be seen as a process of ongoing, meaningful existence that is an end in itself. This idea is not new, but it will become much more prominent in this century in the United States and globally than it was in the last.

NOTES

1. F.W. Taylor, *The Principles of Scientific Management* (New York: W.W. Norton, 1967), 34. Taylor's articles, which make up the book, originally appeared in the 1890s. Marx's words are cited by Tibor Scitovsky, *The Joyless Society* (New York: Oxford University Press, 1992), 90.

2. Francis X. Clines, "Self-esteem and Friendship in a Factory on Death Row," *New York Times*, 12 January 1994, A1, A8.

3. P.B. Warr, "Work, Jobs, and Unemployment," *Bulletin of the British Psychological Society*, 1983, 36, 303. See also P.B. Warr, ed., *Work, Unemployment and Mental Health* (Oxford: Oxford University Press, 1987).

4. M.I. Finley, *The Ancient Economy* (Berkeley: University of California Press, 1985), 41. My comments and quotes here are from Finley, 75–76, 147.

5. P.D. Anthony, *The Ideology of Work* (London: Tavistock Publications, 1977), 74.

6. Ibid., 144.

7. This section is based on William G. Scott, *Chester I. Barnard and the Guardians of the Managerial State* (Lawrence: University Press of Kansas, 1992).

8. These quotations are from Barnard's *The Functions of the Executive* (Cambridge: Harvard University Press, 1938), 37, 40. Cited by Scott, ibid., 104–105. At times Barnard and his colleagues do speak of employees having purposes, interests, and goals, but their primary focus was on managing labor by managing stimuli to induce labor.

9. See Elton Mayo, *The Human Problem of an Industrial Civilization* (New York: Macmillan, 1946). For a critique see Reinhard Bendix, *Work and Authority in Industry: Ideologies of Management in the Course of Industrialization* (New York: Wiley, 1956), 308–319.

10. See Scott, op. cit., 112.

11. The list is from B.C. Forbes, *America's Fifty Foremost Business Leaders* (New York: Forbes Publishing Co., 1948).

12. Weber's ideas are presented in *The Protestant Ethic and the Spirit of Capitalism* (New York: Scribner Library, 1959) and *The Theory of Social and Economic Organization* (Glencoe, IL: Free Press, 1969).

13. I am drawing here on Derek Parfit, *Reasons and Persons* (Oxford: Clarendon Press, 1984).

14. See P. Hirsch and R. Friedman, "Collaboration or Paradigm Shift: Economics versus Behavioral Thinking about Policy," *Proceedings*, Academy of Management Meeting, 1986, and W.H. Form and J.A. Huber, "Occupational Power." In R. Dubin, ed., *Handbook of Work, Organization, and Society* (Chicago: Rand McNally, 1976), 751–806.

15. Gary Becker, *The Economic Approach to Human Behavior* (Chicago: University of Chicago Press, 1971), 145. The quote at the end of this paragraph also is from p. 145.

16. This argument is discussed by former Harvard Business School professor Amar Bhide, "What's Driving MBAs to Wall Street?" *New York Times*, 27 July 1986, Business Section, 3.

17. An excellent exposition of the marriage of economic and behaviorist theories is in Barry Schwartz, *The Battle for Human Nature* (New York: W.W. Norton, 1986).

18. See Joan Robinson, "The Second Crisis of Economic Theory," *American Economic Review*, 1972, 62, 1–18.

19. The best summary of the norms-as-causes-and-instruments discussion is Jon Elster, "Social Norms and Economic Theory," *Journal of Economic Perspectives*, 1989, 3 (4), 99–117. See also his *The Cement of Society* (Cambridge: Cambridge University Press, 1989).

20. See F.J. Roethlisberger and W.J. Dickson, *Management and the Worker* (Cambridge: Harvard University Press, 1939).

21. Failure will not come from want of trying. On pride in work as a trigger, see James N. Baron, "The Employment Relation as a Social Relation," *Journal of the Japanese and International Economy*, 1988, 2 (4), 492–525. On internalized norms see E.L. Deci, *Intrinsic Motivation* (New York: Plenum Press, 1975). The economists' position is debated in a series of papers on "The Interaction between Norms and Economic Incentives" (359–378) in Papers and Proceedings, *American Economic Review*, 1997, 87 (2). Efforts of economists to appropriate stimulus-response and similar research are summarized in Edward P. Lazear, "Labor Economics and the Psychology of Organizations," *Journal of Economic Perspectives*, 1991, 5 (2), 89–110.

22. For a sample of Kelloway's work, see her column for 17 January 2000, in the *Financial Times*, 8.

BIBLIOGRAPHY

Anthony, P.D. *The Ideology of Work*. London: Tavistock Publications, 1977.

Barnard, Chester I. *The Functions of the Executive*. Cambridge: Harvard University Press, 1938.

Baron, James N. "The Employment Relation as Social Relation." *Journal of the Japanese and International Economy*, 1988, 2(4), 492–525.

Becker, Gary. *The Economic Approach to Human Behavior*. Chicago: University of Chicago Press, 1971.

Bendix, Reinhard. *Work and Authority in Industry: Ideologies of Management in the Course of Industrialization*. New York: Wiley, 1956.

Bhide, Amar. "What's Driving MBAs to Wall Street." *New York Times*, 27 July 1986, B3.

Clines, Francis X. "Self-esteem and Friendship in a Factory on Death Row." *New York Times*, 12 January 1994, A1, A8.

Deci, E.L. *Intrinsic Motivation*. New York: Plenum Press, 1975.

Elster, Jon. *The Cement of Society*. Cambridge: Cambridge University Press, 1989.

———. "Social Norms and Economic Theory." *Journal of Economic Perspectives*, 1989, 3(4), 99–117.

Finley, M.I. *The Ancient Economy*. Berkeley, CA: University of California Press, 1985.

Forbes, B.C. *America's Fifty Foremost Business Leaders*. New York: Forbes Publishing Co., 1948.

Form, W.H., and J.A. Huber. "Occupational Power." In R. Dubin, ed., *Handbook of Work, Organization and Society*. Chicago: Rand McNally, 1976, 751–806.

Hirsch, P., and R. Friedman. "Collaboration or Paradigm Shift: Economics versus Behavioral Thinking About Policy." *Proceedings*, Academy of Management Meeting, 1986.

Lazear, Edward P. "Labor Economics and the Psychology of Organizations." *Journal of Economic Perspectives*, 1991, 5(2), 89–110.

Mayo, Elton. *The Human Problem of an Industrial Civilization*. New York: Macmillan, 1946.

Parfit, Derek. *Reasons and Persons*. Oxford: Clarendon Press, 1984.

Robinson, Joan. "The Second Crisis of Economic Theory." *American Economic Review*, 1972, 62, 1–18.

Roethlisberger, F.J., and W.J. Dickson. *Management and the Worker*. Cambridge: Harvard University Press, 1939.

Schwartz, Barry. *The Battle for Human Nature*. New York: W. W. Norton, 1986.

Scitovsky, Tibor. *The Joyless Society*. New York: Oxford University Press, 1992.

Scott, William G. *Chester I. Barnard and the Guardians of the Managerial State*. Lawrence: University Press of Kansas, 1992.

Taylor, Frederick W. *The Principles of Scientific Management*. New York: W. W. Norton, 1967.

Warr, P.B. "Work, Jobs, and Unemployment." *Bulletin of the British Psychological Society*, 1983, 36, 301–310.

———. ed. *Work, Unemployment and Mental Health*. Oxford: Oxford University Press, 1987.

Weber, Max. *The Protestant Ethic and the Spirit of Capitalism*. New York: Scribner's Library, 1959.

———. *The Theory of Social and Economic Organization*. Glencoe, IL: Free Press, 1969.

CHAPTER 9

WORK AND WORKERS IN THE 21ST CENTURY

In the 20th century we accepted the idea that employees are both instrumental and responsive in their approach to work, and in the 21st century we are moving toward a vision of toil as "the investment in something for its own sake, the commitment . . . to an activity that is its own reward . . ."[1] The roots of this new paradigm are to be found in the work of Karl Marx, but modern theorists and researchers have resurrected it. In this chapter I want to discuss the process idea of work and how it will challenge 21st-century global organizations to alter their ways of managing employees.

MARX AND WORK AS LIVING

Marx rested his grand theories on the assumption that work is a natural preoccupation of a human, one of the ways the self extends itself into the world as a matter of course. Working is thus living, and the results of work are objects embodying the skills and energies of the worker. Products, in a sense, are tied to the worker, as extended parts of his or her being. In another sense, they are necessary mirrors in which the worker sees himself. Without its products the self would have difficulty being embedded in reality and legitimizing its place.

the external aims [of work] become stripped of the semblance of merely external natural urgencies [to gain an income], and become posited as aims which the individual himself posits—hence as self-realization, objectification of the subject, hence real freedom, whose action is, precisely, labour. [2]

What Marx is so awkwardly trying to say here is that since the worker—when the world is correctly functioning—is to some extent also his work, work is an end in itself. It is neither a response to a stimulus nor an instrument used for the purpose of gain. It is simply the worker extended. Our dysfunctional society, however, supposedly has developed in ways that threaten this vision. The institution of private property has severed the links between worker, work, and product, since the capitalist, rather than the worker, owns the product before it is sold. The division of labor has fragmented work to the point where connectedness and the extended self are hard to envision. And the idea of labor as a commodity to be bought in exchange relations removes the self and makes work merely a midpoint between two negotiating selves.

The result is alienation, which to Marx is an attack on human essence. The self becomes thwarted in its extensions, disconnected, and finally diminished. Humanity is rendered less human. We can see here why Proudhon's model of work as a response to the dictates of justice (discussed in Chapter 4) so infuriated Marx. Nothing would be resolved by such a course. Workers would remain alienated, with any move toward resolution of the problem obscured behind a cloudy rhetoric of vague abstractions. The alienated worker, tied to unnatural visions of work as a response to opaque principles of justice or as an input to an exchange, would become numbed and impaired, unable to perceive and discriminate to the fullest. The process vision would decay. Notice that Marx does not view humans as social creatures responding to needs to belong or as calculating creatures with interests. They are really isolated beings for him, with powerful creative instincts. One wonders if he had read Shelley, who describes humankind after liberation:

> The loathsome mask has fallen, the man remains
> Sceptreless, free, uncircumscribed, but man
> Equal, unclassed, tribeless, and nationless,
> Exempt from awe, worship, degree, the king
> Over himself; just, gentle, wise. . . . [3]

The alienated worker would lose not only the chance for this golden world but also the possibility of even realizing that his nature demands nothing less.

The Romantic view of labor which Marx appropriated presented toil as a noninstrumental, nonresponsive process of creativity occurring in a series of timeless moments unconnected to a past or a future. The only connections would be spatial, with the worker's self extended into both the product and its use by another self. Thus work would fuse humankind together into a generalized

Man, one harmonious soul of many a soul,
Whose nature is its own divine control,
Where all things flow to all, as rivers to the sea;
Familiar acts are beautiful through love;
Labour, and pain, and grief, in life's green grove
Sport like tame beasts, none knew how gentle they could be.[4]

Through the freeing of humans, then, to follow their natures and enmesh themselves solely in processes of creative work, each individual would attain a state of ennobling isolation and yet be connected in a sacred bond with the rest of humanity. Any attempt to change or redefine the functioning of work would hinder human nature, degrade workers, and break solidarity.

A RETURN TO WORK AS AN END IN ITSELF

No modern theorists go quite as far as Marx and Shelley in their work process ideas or their hostility to capitalism, but several thinkers have called for a return to a vision of workers losing themselves in the timeless flow of challenging, creative toil as an end in itself. In *The True and Only Heaven, Progress and Its Critics* (1991) Christopher Lasch resurrected the old idea of work embedded in a culture based on a sense of limits, citing the writings of Thomas Carlyle, Ralph Waldo Emerson, and William James. Their vision involves "the habits of responsibility associated with property ownership; the self-forgetfulness that comes with immersion in some all-absorbing piece of work . . . the recognition that humans are not made for happiness. . . ."[5] Work here is pure process, the peaceful coexistence in timeless rituals of labor of the self-employed, free worker. Since life must end in death, no real happiness is possible, and an instrumental view of work is a delusion. The best course is to go with the flow.

In the modern era, Lasch claimed, "It was becoming harder and harder for people to find work that self-respecting men and women could throw themselves into with enthusiasm."[6] In effect, he argued that in the United States the imposed models of work as an economic input or as a response to some manipulation have pushed the process model into the background. The mechanisms responsible for this trend were the decline of religious institutions, which originally had advocated a theory of work as humble acceptance of rituals of toil, and the rise of the New Deal, which educated workers to see themselves as consumers and their work as solely instrumental. One of his villains is Rexford D. Tugwell, who characterized labor in *The Industrial Discipline and the Governmental Arts* (1933) as a wretched exercise of pain and suffering which could be relieved only by future technological advances. The achievement of those advances, however, required acceptance of current inputs of unpleasant work towards that end. Rhetoric about "the dignity of labor" would have to be abandoned since it hindered progress. Another villain is John Maynard Keynes in "Economic Possibilities for Our Grandchildren," who proclaimed, "We shall be able to rid ourselves of many of the pseudo-moral principles which have hag-ridden us for two hundred years, by which we have exalted some of the most distasteful of human qualities into the position of the highest virtues."[7]

Against these instrumentalists Lasch described a model of humanity in which people are moral agents, choosing to immerse themselves in work based on rituals rather than contracts, on social rather than economic relations, on tradition-enhanced present commitments rather than future-oriented expectations, on shared understandings and sentiments rather than competitive instincts, and on ties rather than interests. His view about the way individuals would approach work given the chance draws from a rich body of syndicalist and guild socialist thought critiquing the rise of huge corporations, their arm's-length, wage-based work relations between managers and workers, and their propensity to fragment coherent work processes through specialization and deskilling. They allegedly thwart immersion in work as craft and a sense of accomplishment and fulfillment from the work itself rather than the gains from work. Guild socialists reject modern social policies focused on creating tolerable working conditions, decent wages, and secure employment because they serve to legitimize an economic work vision rather than the more natural process vision, which emphasizes "time-honored work habits" and worker control over "the rhythm and design of production." Freed from the work-as-response model, Lasch notes, workers would have "the opportunity for invention and experimentation that made work interesting."[8]

One process theory which seems to be emerging today, based on the ideas of Marx in the 19th century; his admirers, Herbert Croly and Randolph Bourne, early in the 20th century; and Christopher Lasch and devotees of guild socialism at its end, runs something like this:

- Workers must have more control over work.
- The feelings of proprietorship which then develop will engender immersion in work processes.
- The result: "Labor might become an end in itself, something that satisfied the individual's need to regard himself as part of a common enterprise."[9]
- A worker freely immersed in work processes will follow his or her natural propensity to be creative.
- This creativity will foster the increased productivity which is the source of organizational and societal success.

Crucial to this model is a culture that downplays "unnatural" visions of work as purely instrumental or as a somewhat grudging response to some trigger or cue. The endless negotiating of the pure economic being is rejected, as is the values manipulation of Elton Mayo.

WORK AS LIVED EXPERIENCE

We have seen in Chapter 4 and here that 21st-century justice advocates will call for government policies and corporate actions that recognize employee ownership (of a sort) of their jobs, and they will support their arguments by citing Percy Bysshe Shelley, Karl Marx, Ralph Waldo Emerson, Henry David Thoreau, and other great European and American philosophers and social critics of the 19th century. Vivid scenarios will be offered of happy, creative workers immersed in their work processes as ends in themselves, with the wondrous by-product results of increased productivity, innovation, and economic growth. Claims will be made that *all* workers in the global labor force, not just Americans or Europeans, should be empowered to embed themselves in satisfying daily rituals of toil. And if economists and theorists manage to summon up the nerve to point out that employee ownership of companies rarely works and that the most empowered workers in the world, Germans, are the costliest, a new set of powerful arguments, based on 20th-century hermeneutic and interactionist philosophies will redefine work as a lived rather than a merely endured experience and the worker as a human in the process of becoming rather than merely being.

During the 20th century a profound set of new ideas began to emerge about what it meant to be human. In the 1930s the American philosopher G.H. Mead announced that it is human interactions that create our reality, give us morals, and mold our nature.[10] Theorists in sociology, drawing from Mead's work, by the 1960s were arguing that social reality is constructed through endless interactions, and organizational theorists soon were describing the workplace in terms of the importance of interactions, symbols, signs, corporate legends and myths, narratives, and rituals.[11] From the 1920s onward similar thinking had been occurring in Europe in the writings of Martin Heidegger, Jean-Paul Sartre, and Hans-George Gadamer under the name of hermeneutics and, in France, existentialism. Although these philosophers endlessly quibbled about "being" and "nothingness," their fundamental position involved a rejection of the earlier 19th-century views that humans are autonomous individuals characterized by an unchanging human nature common to all.[12] But the practical impact was the same. Whereas Shelley, Marx, and Emerson had sought the institutional empowerment of individuals to live out their lives in creative work and leisure processes that fulfilled the demands of their nature, American interactionists and European hermeneuticists claimed that human nature always was in a state of becoming and those humans should not be thwarted from developing the rituals, symbols, and interactions which engineered becoming. Both approaches envisioned work as lived, enriching experience.

Notice how different the Romantic and hermeneutic visions of the life of toil are from those of economists and workplace manipulators like Elton Mayo. Both of these latter groups see workers as beings, rather than becomings, who either manipulate the world as best they can to achieve their ends or are manipulated by it. Interactions and processes are trivial—mere transaction or throughput costs—compared to purposes or to triggers and cues that evoke work and the output of the work. Managing here is an exercise in manipulation and in communication to inform employees of what is desired and what will be paid for it. In contrast, the hermeneutic vision calls for management as the fostering of lived experiences, which require interacting, symbol-using, and history-making—anything, really, that enables the employee to say, "The work makes sense. It is meaningful for me to do this." Work of this kind need not be easy or clean or free of conflict. It is simply toil arranged so that a human being can recognize a human activity in it. Work is lived experience when the worker sees it as part of life in the way she sees leisure, birth, death, and sex as part of life.

The Romantic Marxists wanted to give workers control of work to fulfill the demands of their nature to be creative and productive. The interactionists and hermeneuticists want to make the workplace meaningful. They are united in wanting the processes of working to be the prime focus of managing and motivation rather than the stimuli prior to work or the rewards afterwards. These of course always will be necessary, but their overemphasis in the 20th century will be replaced in the 21st century by a growing realization that humans are most productive and innovative when they have a sense of control of the workplace and that their labor is a meaningful lived experience which in part is an end in itself. A workplace of this kind will encourage small talk, gossip, informal channels, storytelling, culture creating, symbolic interacting, account giving and seeking—all the things that create a history to be interpreted and a future to be expected in a meaningful world. Workers in America will demand a workplace like this because they are tiring of the old ways, and non-U.S. workers will want it because they know no other that makes sense. A global corporation will have to adapt to a common human nature. Managing employees then will be more than the exchange of value; it also will be the exchange of meaning. It will be more than the identification of cause-effect, stimulus response sets. Managing globally will involve extensive interacting, teaching, and persuasion.

EMPOWERED TO FLOW

Theorists of work as process have received support from social and cognitive psychology, especially in the research of Michaly Csikszentmihalyi on flow theory. He and his colleagues have found that, while people will describe their understanding of work in conventional instrumental terms, a penetrating analysis reveals a more complex reality. Employees often exhibit more positive feelings at work—even supposedly alienating assembly-line work—than they do during leisure. Later on, however, they usually report a greater preference for leisure than for work, reflecting a learned input model of work as a disutility.[13] What is it about some work that is so attractive?

It is "flow," involvement in the moment without attending to past or future. It occurs "when a person perceives that the environment contains high enough opportunities for action (or challenges) which are matched with the person's own capacities to act (or skills)."[14] Flow creates feelings of being "active, alert, concentrated, happy, satisfied, and creative—although not necessarily more cheerful or sociable." These feelings occur more frequently during certain kinds of work than they do during leisure. Managers may experience flow while problem-solving, secretaries while typing, and blue-collar workers when fixing equipment. Their work becomes a process rewarding in and of itself rather than instrumental or responsive. According to Csikszentmihalyi, such work is not a response to self-actualization needs as defined in Maslow's *Toward a Psychology of Being*, nor is it triggered by the intrinsic motivation described in E.L. Deci and R.M. Ryan's *Intrinsic Motivation of Self-determination in Human Behavior*. These models treat work as output. Rather, flow work is similar to the process of play, the activity characterized by J. Huizinga in *Homo Ludens: A Study of the Play Element in Culture*. Flow is not rooted in expectations or desires, since it can occur in unexpected and undesired work situations. As long as challenges match abilities and "focused concentration" is possible, flow can occur and be experienced as "doing something that is worth doing for its own sake." Flow results in an absence of self-consciousness and a reduced sense of time passing—the same conditions called for by Christopher Lasch.

Csikszentmihalyi's research suggests that workers experiencing flow are more satisfied and more motivated than are workers experiencing anxiety, apathy, and boredom. Moreover, the more frequently flow is experienced, the more motivated and satisfied workers are. Flow theory, then, responds to the model of human nature described by Marx and later called for by Christopher Lasch, in which workers have a process vision as the natural approach to toil. For these thinkers, modern economic and behavioral control models are a betrayal, and inffective to boot. What 21st-century employee management really requires, in their view, is the creation of a work environment conducive to flow. This is accomplished, first, by careful employee selection—much more careful than in today's approaches—so that workers' skills ideally match the tasks they face and, second, by empowering employees to control their immediate environment. We can see here the obvious problem that flow-evoking workplaces can and certainly will be constructed by organizations tuned in to new models of labor, but the great mass of establishments is not going to be able to do such careful matching and empowering. Nevertheless, other routes to developing work as process exist; especially those involving an enhanced sense of labor as meaningful ritual and lived experience.

NON-FLOW PROCESS: THE NEED FOR MEANINGFUL RITUALS

A ritual is a symbolic action. It means something more than its immediate purpose, and it is not just a response. Rather it is a meaningful act which is its own end. Such an action is called a "trope" (turn) by literary theorists—a departure from commonplace utilitarian or responsive behavior which is not merely artful or designed to call attention to itself. Without the actor consciously thinking about it, the act calls attention instead to complex sets of meanings which are difficult to express but still deeply important to the tribe, group, or organization. "We always do it that way" is the answer workers will give when queried about ritual work behavior. The worker makes salient those beliefs, attitudes, and values which are hard to explain, or people do not wish to explain. After all, talking about some things—such as the rituals of lovemaking—may ruin them. The same is true in the workplace. Holding a quality-control team meeting in a certain way, reviewing a design in a certain way, conducting a performance appraisal in a certain way, repairing a machine in a certain way: all can be ritual acts. These are examples of work as process, since most of the behaviors are neither instrumental nor responsive, but they are not flow experiences, since the abandonment of self within a challenge is not an issue, and little cognitive activity occurs.

Ritual work processes of this sort, while not consciously purposeful or responsive, nevertheless have a number of valuable functions within the organization:

- They foster and affirm tacit knowledge, such as organization or work group membership.

- They communicate implicitly without risk, something difficult to do with verbal communication.

- They legitimize conventions which function to reduce uncertainty in the organization by establishing predictability and consistency.

- They are a way of acting out tensions and unresolvable conflicts (ritualized performance appraisals are an example here).

- Most important, they make sense to workers as meaningful acts.

Work as a process of symbolic actions is crucial to an organization, yet it is constantly under attack from American managers. Their fears are twofold. First, ritual behavior can look like apathetic behavior, the kind of indifferent, going-through-the-motion work that is ruinous to a firm. While this concern is defensible, a reasonably sophisticated person ought to be able to tell the difference between a functional ritual and functionless apathy. Second, rituals are not easily controlled by managers. In the United States, where prevailing managerial wisdom downplays process and overemphasizes work as output, managers worry that their power, always shaky in American organizations, will be further weakened and they will feel at a loss to manipulate work responses or to negotiate with workers during a crisis, when dramatic changes in behavior are necessary. Karl Weick has mounted an eloquent defense of ritualized work processes, showing how they emerge out of the very nature of the organization and how they add value to its functioning. From an organizational perspective, he makes a case for a theory of work in which an organization has much to gain and little to lose when it allows the natural process inclinations of workers to express themselves in meaningful work rituals.[15] He points out that routinized work responses are inevitable in organizations characterized by specialization (commitment to one way), formalization (requirements for a way), and socialization (valuing of a way). Over time, organizations find that these responsive acts turn into ritual behaviors untied from stimuli, rules, or purposes. Employees just do them as a matter of course.

However, while the rituals do function to help maintain the organization in the ways noted above, they also may render it unable to adapt to new tasks in a rapidly evolving environment. A work ritual can be thought of as a "competency trap" which embeds knowledge and skills no longer relevant to a changed world. If this criticism is correct, then an organization over time should become more smoothly functioning as rituals develop and foster tacit knowledge, conventions, and tension release, yet it should be less able to adapt to external changes. However, evidence suggests a different model—the older an organization is, the more likely it is to survive.[16] What happens is that rituals of work serve, first, to influence the organization to avoid changes that can foster failures by disrupting organizational processes and, second, to form the basic components of new, adaptive rituals. An organization, then, which lets workers develop the sense-enhancing rituals to which they are naturally inclined, and which the very nature of the organization itself encourages, increases its probability of survival. It avoids foolish change and is prepared to adapt.

How can a group of workers spending part of their time in ritualized processes be adaptive? The answer comes from Tibor Scitovsky in *The Joyless Economy*. An activity continuously engaged in at an optimum level of arousal, such as a satisfying work ritual, provides comfort but not pleasure. Pleasure occurs only during *changes* in the level of arousal toward the optimum. He says, "One must be tired to enjoy resting, cold to appreciate a warm fire, and hungry in order to really enjoy a good meal."[17] Since individuals seek both comfort and pleasure in their lives, they invariably will be open to changes from their rituals. Indeed, they cannot experience the pleasures of change unless they are embedded in the comfort of rituals. "For the new and unexpected to be pleasantly stimulating, it must be sufficiently related to the familiar to be manageable and create a reasonable exception of its manageability." An organization that wants its employees to adapt, then, must first allow them to develop some ritualized work processes. To motivate workers to make the effort to adapt requires a delicate balancing act by managers between employee comfort and employee pleasure. If the time spent in comfortable work rituals is too short, employees will want more comfort and less change. The firm will not adapt—I believe that this is the state of affairs with many American firms, which downplay work as process. But if rituals come to dominate the workday, employees can fall into a passive, numbed acceptance, a kind of comfortable drug-like state to which they are addicted. Neither approach is appropriate. Although every organization is different, perhaps one-third of the workday should be a process of flow experiences and rituals.

The clever organization recognizes human nature and allows work rituals to emerge, since they foster smooth functioning and create a base for adaptive change. But they do even more. The new technology of the 21st century in fact demands a work environment in which flow and ritualized work processes are crucial. Shoshana Zuboff, in *In the Age of the Smart Machine*, describes the growth of jobs "that demand continual responsiveness to a flow of data."[18] Such work is difficult to envision if one sees work only as sets of discrete responses or as inputs to exchange relations. The process approach needed, in Zuboff's formulation, is called "acting with" rather than "acting on." "Acting with" consists of learning, coordinating, communicating—essentially it is embedded functioning within a web of complex human and systemic relationships. This work, a mix of flow and ritual experiences, is not quite automatic. It requires cognitive ability, but it is work exercised within processes of highly symbolic ritual acts.

Work in the new age of information requires "human skills in ways of thinking that are conceptual, inferential, procedural, and systemic." It will depend on process thinking rather than simply instrumental actions, on relating facts to assumptions rather than simply automatic responses to facts, and on rituals which open up access to expertise rather than simply negotiating to have expertise available. To visualize this kind of work, think of Bill Gates at Microsoft. His day is often a series of interactions with systems and texts that are both sets of challenging flow experiences and highly ritualistic behaviors at a keyboard. Of course his work also is responsive to stimuli and is instrumentally calculative, but it is more, and the model of work as output, input, *and* process, which his activities illustrate, ought to serve as the model for managers and employees in many organizations, even those where few computers are in sight.

THE ATTACK ON RITUAL AND PROCESS

A greater attentiveness to work as process clearly is in order in the 21st century. Emerging technologies will require it, organizations cannot easily change without it, and highly motivated workers need it. However, early researchers who wrestled with the idea in the 20th century pointed out cases where too much ritual is demeaning, while others have called for the thorough destruction of ritualized work.

Ely Chinoy raised the issue in *Automobile Workers and the American Dream*. He recognized that ritualized work on an assembly line, characterized by "a feeling of being pulled along by the inertia inherent in a particular activity," actually could be "pleasant and may therefore function as a relief from tedium."[19] The work became an end in itself and its own cause—and presumably functioned in the useful ways described above. However, he eventually concluded that rhythmic work of this sort is alienating. The assembly-line rituals, constrained by time and space, repetitive, and requiring no initiative and only surface mental attention, thwart human creative impulses. Chinoy's thoroughly Marxist approach essentially demanded that work be mostly a series of flow experiences. When it was not, he rejected the work entirely. His point that a whole day spent solely in ritualized work is alienating probably is correct, but my argument, based on Scitovsky, is that a part of the workday ought to be spent this way, not the whole day. Humans seem to thrive in this kind of process, and organizational coping may depend on it.

Chinoy, representing workers, showed sensitivity to actual practices. A number of management theorists, eager to serve corporate executives committed to a control view of work as a managed response, have been quite hostile to rituals. One such is Larry Hirschhorn, whose *The Workplace Within* poses an interesting critique. As he sees it, the pressures caused by risks and complexity foster anxieties in workers in large organizations. In response, workers erect social defenses such as scapegoating, devaluing or depersonalizing others, and narrow or fragmented thinking. Even worse, many employees hide from anxieties within rituals, "a procedure or practice that takes on a life of its own and is seemingly unconnected to rational understanding of experience."[20] A ritual "helps all group members depersonalize their relationship to their work" and is in fact "neurotic behavior," a discounting of the reality of other people and oneself. It denies the uniqueness of each situation, relieving the participant of thought. This is not the way to cope with anxiety. Instead of rituals, employees should reduce anxiety through job rotation, which triggers feelings of anxiety-reducing competence, and through self-esteem, triggered by a corporate culture stressing the production of valued goods and services in society.

Hirschhorn has a vision of work as output. The company "creates a climate in which employees view the organization as an instrument for achieving valued ends . . . Such organizations create developmental cultures because people are free to focus on the work they do, can achieve a greater sense of wholeness, and can restructure their relationships to their own internal objects." His point is that a culture of excellence makes people feel good about what they do. They do it and feel good about themselves.

Manipulated corporate culture, a work-triggering device, is here an alternative to processes and rituals of embeddedness. Leaders are here not sometimes masters of ceremonies. Rather they are mostly purveyors of the rhetoric of cultural values. For Larry Hischhorn, motivated work is never, ever associated with the opportunity for occasional immersion in work processes. It is always a response to managerial control.

Another attack on work rituals, but for a different reason, occurs in Charles Handy's influential book, *The Age of Unreason*.[21] Because of rapidly changing environments and the need for constant re-learning, ritual processes in large organizations must be abandoned. "We've always done it this way" no longer works, and routine is death. Instead, work should be solely an instrumental exchange, the endless bargaining for information to identify opportunities or solve problems. Handy argues for constant change and constant learning, and he implicitly makes a case for work as mostly an input, sometimes an output, but never a process.

What would an organization look like when it has somehow managed to eliminate meaningful, ritual-like work processes? Here is one scenario.

- As recommended by Hirschhorn, a strong organizational culture will have to be created and managed so that work responses can be better controlled. However, there is danger in this, as noted by James March and his colleagues.[22] A strong culture fosters reliable values and knowledge in organizations but not necessarily valid knowledge. Reliable values and knowledge are shared and understood in the same way within the organization, while valid knowledge is useful for successful prediction. ("It makes sense," the employee will say.) Reliable, valid knowledge is thus distributable and authentic. Merely reliable knowledge is not authentic. Corporate culture of the manipulated variety controls work by making it a response to widely distributed values and by triggering information transfers rather than supposedly thoughtless rituals. However, externally generated information that contradicts held cultural beliefs may be downplayed or ignored (something that ritualized work deals with simply by adding new rituals or incrementally changing old ones). Thus reliability is defended at the expense of validity. Since no organization can survive for long without attending to the real world, employees will begin to pay lip service to corporate values and the sets of beliefs attached to them while surreptitiously adhering to new belief structures. A good example of this occurs in a big accounting firm which does both auditing and consulting. Strong corporate culture requires that lip service be given to the image of "professionalism" requiring that auditors evaluate rather than advise clients or try to obtain advising business. In reality, auditors constantly seek to develop lucrative consulting work. The result: hypocrisy and cynicism, which are now pervasive in the industry, and a weakening of professional culture. For some accountants in these environments, the work does not make sense and is not meaningful.

- As an overreliance on corporate culture to control work leads to its breakdown, "undirected viewing" emerges as employees without meaningful routines or values to guide them flounder about, collecting vast, indigestible amounts of information from the environment. This randomness may work well in rapidly changing, turbulent situations. But in most cases the organization becomes less and less responsive. Anxiety reigns.[23]

- Turnover now occurs—indeed, in big accounting firms it is encouraged—and the "naïve and ignorant" are hired (Japanese call these young people "innocent eyes") because they are neither cynical nor burdened by anxiety.

- Rather then letting new people work in terms of exchange relations mixed with some ritualization and the development of meaningful values, the organization again tries to establish an overwhelming control culture, and the scenario plays itself out again.

Under the influence of modern work-control theorists like Larry Hirschhorn and Charles Handy, senior executives in many large firms have adopted "Routine is death" as their motto and mounted an all-out attack on work rituals. While this may pay off in some organizations facing threats to their survival, it is an extreme tactic and ignores the natural inclinations of humans for processes and rituals that are meaningful and make sense. Twenty-first century workers worldwide will demand a more settled, placid workplace, yet such an environment ought to be more productive and innovative than in the 20th century, since it accords more with human nature.

MANAGING THE INCREASE OF PROCESS

What is needed in 21st-century global managing is a downplaying somewhat of work as part of an exchange and an increase in the recognition that work to some extent is a process that individuals engage in as a meaningful, chosen end in itself. In *The Joyless Society* Scitovsky sought to extend economic theory to include this insight. He noted the propensity of all humans to embed themselves in group processes: "The power of precedent, custom, fashion, mass movements all testify to the great strength in man of the desire to imitate and conform to the behavior of the group he belongs to or wants to belong to." In his model a worker moving towards greater immersion in group processes and rituals should "tell jokes, spread gossip, bring news, make witty or erudite conversation, dress well . . ."[24] Managers fostering employee immersion should give them *opportunities for intra-group communicating* and for symbolically *asserting group membership with uniforms, slogans, catchphrases on buttons and so forth.*

A second task of managers to downplay work as instrumental and foster process is to *stress equality as well as equity in pay.* Equity here means a correlation between work input and compensation. Equality means that the range between the highest-paid and lowest-paid employees is kept somewhat more narrow than is the case currently. A low range fosters the connectedness among workers which is a prelude to process.[25]

Third, managers must *reduce emphasis on what an employee can gain for motivated work*. Motivation by monetary incentives alone plays only to the market model and influences workers to focus on outcomes and rewards rather than on the process. As Alfie Kohn puts it, "The more a manager stresses what an employee can earn for good work, the less interested that employee will be in the work itself."[26] This should not be an excuse for the abandonment of merit and performance-based pay. However, these alone are inadequate. They should be accompanied by opportunities for increased flow experience in work.

The fourth task, then, is to *increase flow experiences for workers*. As we saw earlier, these deeply meaningful experiences are characterized by a sense of timelessness in which the worker becomes totally engaged in comfortable but challenging rituals or problems so that she loses awareness of time passing and work becomes an end in itself. Flow can occur in virtually any job, although obviously it is more difficult to evoke in some than in others. Here are two ways to develop or maintain conditions wherein the focused concentration of flow is possible:

- *Allow "we-always-do-it-this-way" rituals to flourish a bit more*. American managers are often too quick to reorganize and restructure activities that may upset work processes, with the loss of efficiencies inherent in time-honored practices. Moreover, job enrichment and job rotation should be carefully considered before being instituted. Do they have flow benefits that exceed the cost of breaking up habits and processes?

- *Hire workers with skill in implicit communication*. This kind of person is sensitive to the connotations as well as to the denotations of messages. Thus he or she is able to extract more information from what is said *and* to recognize the informational value of what is unsaid. These people can engage in implicit contracting with employers, thus dramatically reducing actual negotiation time.[27] Such workers then will have more time available to seek out and engage in uninterrupted flow experiences. In addition, they will be good at developing the tacit knowledge and unspoken conventions that replace contracts and negotiations as the governors of behavior. Latent knowledge structures and embedded customs make it easy for workers, once they have been socialized in the organization, to immerse themselves in the flow work and functional rituals. What I am proposing is the development of corporate culture, but not through managerial rhetoric with a control goal in mind. Instead, culture will emerge through the hiring of workers with implicit communication skill, and it will be the kind of culture that fosters work as process rather than as a response to control.

WHAT MUST BE DONE?

Romantic poets were among the first to recognize that toil is a natural preoccupation of humans, an important process of ongoing living in the way that play or lovemaking is. Marxists and socialists echoed this view and called for worker control over labor so that worker preoccupations could not be thwarted by institutions. While the empowerment issue is still very much alive, the crucial focus on work and workers is that of the interactionists and hermeneuticists who emerged in U.S. and European philosophical circles in the 20th century. They emphasized a vision of work as meaningful lived experience in which the task of managers involved the creation of workplace environments so that an employee anywhere, anytime, always would be able to say, "My job makes sense to me. It is meaningful." This kind of thinking, however, did not have much influence on employee management practices, which stressed work as either the result of an exchange relation within the extended order model of capitalism or of some kind of stimulus controlled by management. While paid labor of course is associated with these issues, it clearly is a more complex human activity. Indeed, the growing recognition that humans are more than just purposeful pigeons inevitably will evoke pressures on corporations to broaden their human resource management practices. This is especially true since millions of workers in the developing world who are about to join the global industrial system have no lengthy experience of work as purely an instrumental or a responsive act. They will expect a more thoroughly human approach to managing people in the new century.

What 21st-century managers will be challenged to do, then, is to create work environments in which flow conditions are possible. This will require an increased emphasis on employee selection and training so that skills and tasks are better matched. In addition, as we will see in the following chapters, increased use of the Internet at work can be managed to create flow conditions. A second challenge will be to develop new attitudes towards work as a process of lived experience within meaningful, functional rituals. Here, too, employee selection will be important, with companies benefiting greatly by identifying prospective hires with good skills at implicit communication and contracting. These are the kinds of people with whom management need not be endlessly negotiating and who easily adapt themselves to embedded, useful routines. Changes along these lines will be needed, as well as better management of economic relations and less reliance on control and manipulation, to develop higher levels of employee satisfaction than now prevail. In the United States, 51 percent of employees were not completely satisfied with their jobs in a 1997 nationwide survey, a number that is up substantially from 1970s levels—and this was in a period of rising incomes and low unemployment.[28] Globally, almost 60 percent of workers are not fully satisfied with their work. The challenge is clear, and global corporations will have to meet it.

NOTES

1. Stanton Wheeler, "Double Lives." In Kai Erickson and Steven Vallas, eds., *The Nature of Work* (New Haven: Yale University Press, 1990), 143.

2. Karl Marx, *Grundrisse* (1857). From Jon Elster, ed., *Karl Marx, A Reader* (New York: Cambridge University Press, 1989), 59. A modern rendering of Marx is in Sharon Beder, *Selling the Work Ethic* (London: Zed, 2000).

3. Percy Bysshe Shelley, *Prometheus Unbound*, Act III, Scene IV, 11, 193–197. In Thomas Hutchinson, ed., *The Complete Poetical Works of Percy Bysshe Shelley* (London: Oxford University Press, 1961).

4. Ibid., IV, 11, 400–405.

5. Christopher Lasch, *The True and Only Heaven, Progress and Its Critics* (New York: W.W. Norton, 1991), 16.

6. Ibid., 33.

7. Cited in Lasch, op. cit., 74.

8. Lasch, op. cit., 211, 315.

9. Lasch, op. cit., 337.

10. G. H. Mead, *Mind, Self, and Society* (Chicago: University of Chicago Press, 1934).

11. One of the most influential early works of this kind in sociology is P.L. Berger and T. Luckmann, *The Social Construction of Reality* (New York: Doubleday, 1966). Organizational theories along these lines appear in Karl E. Weick, *The Social Psychology of Organizing* (Reading, MA: Addison-Wesley, 1979) and M.S. Feldman and J.G. March, "Information in Organizations as Signal and Symbol," *Administrative Science Quarterly*, 1981, 26, 171–186.

12. See R.J. Howard, *Three Faces of Hermeneutics* (Berkeley: University of California Press, 1982).

13. See Michaly and Isabella Csikszentmihalyi, eds., *Optimal Experience, Psychological Studies of Flow in Consciousness* (Cambridge: Cambridge University Press, 1988) and "Optimal Experience in Work and Leisure," *Journal of Personality and Social Psychology*, 1989, 56, 815–822.

14. Ibid., 816.

15. Karl Weick, "The Nontraditional Quality of Organizational Learning," *Organization Science*, 1991, 2, 116–124. The value of work rituals is a major focus of Thomas H. Davenport and John C. Beck, *The Attention Economy: Understanding the New Currency of Business* (Cambridge, MA: Harvard Business School Press, 2001).

16. See M. Hannan and J. Freeman, *Organizational Ecology* (Cambridge: Harvard University Press, 1989) and Richard R. Nelson and Sidney Winter, *An Evolutionary Theory of Economic Change* (Cambridge: Harvard University Press, 1982).

17. Tibor Scitovsky, *The Joyless Economy* (New York: Oxford University Press, 1992), 71. The second quote in this paragraph is on 57.

18. The quotes here and in the next paragraph are from Shoshana Zuboff, *In the Age of the Smart Machine* (New York: Basic Books, 1988), 296, 172.

19. Ely Chinoy, *Automobile Workers and the American Dream* (Urbana and Chicago: University of Illinois Press, 1992), 142. Similar issues were raised by W. Baldamus, *Efficiency and Effort* (London: Tavistock Publications, 1961).

20. Hirschhorn's remarks here and in the next paragraph are from *The Workplace Within, Psychodynamics of Organizational Life* (Cambridge: MIT Press, 1988), 67, 218.

21. Charles Handy, *The Age of Unreason* (Boston: Harvard Business School Press, 1989).

22. James G. March, Lee S. Sproul, and Michael Tamuz, "Learning from Samples of One or Fewer," *Organization Science*, 1991, 2, 1–13.

23. This bleak scenario is explored in R.L. Daft and K.E. Weick, "Toward a Model of Organizations as Interpretation Systems," *Academy of Management Review*, 1984, 9, 284–295, and James G. March, "Exploration and Exploitation in Organizational Learning," *Organization Science*, 1991, 2, 71–87.

24. Scitovsky, op. cit., 115, 121.

25. The importance of this and other measures of equality and fairness are discussed in Andrew E. Clark and Andrew J. Oswald, "Satisfaction and Comparison Income," *Journal of Public Economics*, 1996, 61, 359–381.

26. Alfie Kohn, "Why Incentive Plans Cannot Work," *Harvard Business Review*, 1993, September-October, 62.

27. The importance of hiring employees who are good at implicit contracting started to become evident to economists and labor theorists towards the end of the last century. See Paul Beaudry and John DiNardo, "The Effect of Implicit Contracts on the Movement of Wages Over the Business Cycle: Evidence from Micro Data," *Journal of Political Economy*, 1991, 99 (4), 665–689; Walter J. Wessels, "Contract Curve or Implicit Contract: Which Will a Union Choose," *Journal of Labor Research*, 1991, 12 (1), 73–90; and Debra L. Nelson, James C. Quick, and Janice R. Joplin, "Psychological Contracting and Newcomer Socialization: An Attachment Theory Foundation," *Journal of Social Behavior and Personality*, 1991, 6(7), 55–72.

28. The 1997 data was based on a survey of 19,000 workers in twenty-seven nations. See David Blancheflower and Andrew Oswald, International Social Survey Programme data, www.oswald.co.uk. Also see their working paper, "Well-being, Insecurity and the Decline of American Job Satisfaction" at the same URL. The effects of overly-controlling managers are described by Barbara Ehrenreich in *Nickel and Dimed: On (Not) Getting By in America* (New York: Metropolitan Books, 2001).

BIBLIOGRAPHY

Baldamus, W. *Efficiency and Effort*. London: Tavistock Publications, 1961.

Beaudry, Paul, and John DiNardo. "The Effect of Implicit Contracts on the Movement of Wages Over the Business Cycle: Evidence from Micro Data." *Journal of Political Economy*, 1991, 99(4), 665–689.

Beder, Sharon. *Selling the Work Ethic*. London: Zed, 2000.

Berger, P.L., and T. Luckmann. *The Social Construction of Reality*. New York: Doubleday, 1966.

Blancheflower, David, and Andrew Oswald. *International Social Survey Programme*, www.oswald.co.uk.

Chinoy, Ely. *Automobile Workers and the American Dream*. Urbana and Chicago: University of Illinois Press, 1992.

Clark, Andrew E., and Andrew J. Oswald. "Satisfaction and Comparison Income." *Journal of Public Economics*, 1996, 61, 359–381.

Csikszentmihalyi, Michaly, and Isabella Csikszentmihalyi. "Optimal Experience in Work and Leisure." *Journal of Personality and Social Psychology*, 1989, 56, 815–822.

———, eds. *Optimal Experience, Psychological Studies of Flow in Consciousness*. Cambridge: Cambridge University Press, 1988.

Daft, R.L., and Karl W. Weick. "Toward a Model of Organizations as Interpretation Systems." *Academy of Management Review*, 1984, 9, 284–295.

Davenport, Thomas H., and John C. Beck. *The Attention Economy: Understanding the New Currency of Business*. Cambridge: Harvard Business School Press, 2001.

Ehrenreich, Barbara. *Nickel and Dimed: On (Not) Getting By in America*. New York: Metropolitan Books, 2001.

Elster, Jon, ed. *Karl Marx, A Reader*. New York: Cambridge University Press, 1989.

Feldman, M.S., and James G. March. "Information in Organizations as Signal and Symbol." *Administrative Science Quarterly*, 1981, 26, 171–186.

Handy, Charles. *The Age of Unreason*. Boston: Harvard Business School Press, 1989.

Hannon, M., and J. Freeman. *Organizational Ecology*. Cambridge: Harvard University Press, 1989.

Hirschhorn, Larry. *The Workplace Within, Psychodynamics of Organizational Life*. Cambridge: MIT Press, 1988.

Howard, R.J. *Three Faces of Hermeneutics*. Berkeley: University of California Press, 1982.

Kohn, Alfie. "Why Incentive Plans Cannot Work." *Harvard Business Review*, 1993, September-October, 60–70.

Lasch, Christopher. *The True and Only Heaven, Progress and Its Critics*. New York: W.W. Norton, 1991.

March, James G. "Exploration and Exploitation in Organizational Learning." *Organization Science*, 1991, 2, 71–87.

Mead, George H. *Mind, Self, and Society*. Chicago: University of Chicago Press, 1934.

Nelson, Debra L., James C. Quick, and Janice R. Joplin. "Psychological Contracting and Newcomer Socialization: An Attachment Theory Foundation." *Journal of Social Behavior and Personality*, 1991, 6(7), 55–72.

Nelson, Richard R., and Sidney Winter. *An Evolutionary Theory of Economic Change*. Cambridge: Harvard University Press, 1982.

Scitovsky, Tibor. *The Joyless Economy*. New York: Oxford University Press, 1992.

Weick, Karl E. "The Nontraditional Quality of Organizational Learning." *Organization Science*, 1991, 2, 116–124.

———. *The Social Psychology of Organizing*. Reading: MA: Addison-Wesley, 1979.

Wessels, Walter J. "Contract Curve or Implicit Contract: Which Will a Union Choose?" *Journal of Labor Research*, 1991, 12(1), 73–90.

Wheeler, Stanton. "Double Lives." In Kai Erickson and Steven Vallas, eds., *The Nature of Work*. New Haven: Yale University Press, 1990, 140–150.

Zuboff, Shoshana. *In the Age of the Smart Machine*. New York: Basic Books, 1988.

CHAPTER 10

THE INTERNET: GLOBAL VILLAGE OR MASS SOCIETY?

During the last half of the 20th century, the use of network-oriented communication soared in such forms as electronic funds transfer, electronic data interchange, and financial data services. No one claimed that these tools for rapidly transferring information would change society as we know it. Then came the Internet, the World Wide Web, and a standard coding system (HTML). These differed from the older networks in being based on nonproprietary protocols (TCP/IP) rather than proprietary; being open to all users rather than closed to most; being able to accommodate data, text, audio, and video rather than just data and text; being interactive (called synchronous) rather than not (asynchronous); and being able to connect computers, telephones, mobile phones, televisions, cable systems, and electronic appliances (with the help of new systems known as Bluetooth, the Wireless Application Protocol, and others). Universal connectivity at low cost has encouraged millions of people and organizations to become users, and stable, widely agreed-on standards have encouraged investors to pour billions into system development in the hope of profits from the sales of products, network services, operating systems, hardware, and software applications. The Internet, including e-mail, allows inexpensive, easy communication of one to one, one to many, many to one, and many to many—an achievement unparalleled in human history. By the middle of this century, almost every person on the planet will have the opportunity to be in contact at low cost with every other person at any time and in any place.[1]

We have seen that as business becomes more globalized in the coming decades, it will have to deal with challenges to extended order ideas of market exchange as the basis for economic life. Calls will be heard in the United States and elsewhere for more just, orderly, and virtuous ways of conducting productive existence, ways which affirm and defend national, tribal, religious, and ethnic identities and which foster the idea of labor as a process of living a meaningful life rather than merely as a prelude to leisure. How will the explosive, worldwide development of the Internet affect these challenges? In this chapter I want to explore the Net's impact on society and the individual; in the next I will examine the Net's influence on business operations. My general conclusion is straightforward: The Internet, in its various forms, is going to have both positive and negative effects on individuals and businesses, and it is going to be a potent force in the hands of both those seeking justice, order, virtue, sovereignty, and life-affirming work as well as those focused on market exchange. It will be both a blessing and a curse, a community-enhancing and an alienating force, and a boon to business revenue at the same time as it threatens to raise costs. It will be a most ingenious paradox.

THE WEB AND THE WORLD

The global Internet includes e-mail, which I will discuss in the following chapter as a business activity, but most of our attention is drawn to the World Wide Web, a collection of about 800 million files, called pages, residing on about 60 million host servers used by 3.6 million sites. On average, then, each site has about 222 pages. While individuals who develop sites may have only a few pages, corporations often have thousands. Home Depot, for example, has about a million pages on its site. The development, management, and maintenance of pages and sites, which are easy to generate but hard to keep updated, will be a major economic activity in the coming decades. Currently this is not the case. Employment and spending on information and communications technology in the United States, for example, are modest as shares of totals. Close to 6 million are employed in these industries, which contribute about 8 percent to GDP. But only 26 percent of U.S. households were connected to the Internet in the late 1990s (it's probably over 40 percent now). When everyone eventually connects, employment and spending will rise. About 60 percent of discount stock commissions are generated by the Internet, as is 50 percent of software sales, but these are the exceptions rather than the rule. However, it is clear that books, financial services, greeting cards, cars, music, and travel services will continue to enjoy expanded sales on the Internet to the point at which distribution channels change drastically, forcing major changes in manufacturing. When an individual can order a highly customized version of a car directly from the manufacturer on the Net and expect delivery within a week, production systems will have to adjust accordingly, as will inventory management and the way employees are recruited, trained, motivated, evaluated, and compensated.

The Net is not a seamless, global, centralized economic system. Cross-border revenues for Amazon were about 26 percent of its total in the late 1990s, but only a few other companies were in that league. Because of regulatory and goods transportation difficulties, most Web companies have been moving to set up subsidiaries and targeted sites in major nations rather than, as the technology allows, to operate from one site in the home country. Although most sites are in English, non-English speakers prefer their own language, and this too is influencing decentralization. In many parts of the world, buyers will not engage in credit card sales unless they are confident that they can trust the seller. A local presence thus helps. Moreover, in China and Singapore one set of Chinese characters is used for text while a somewhat different set is used in Taiwan, Hong Kong, and most overseas Chinese communities. Chinese search engines, regardless of the characters used, make searches based on characters or phrases rather than words, and they tend to generate either too many or too few results.[2] Localized search engine sites, therefore, where results can be filtered in accord with local needs and presented in appropriate characters, probably will be the norm in Asia. For other reasons this also will be the case elsewhere. About 75 percent of Web pages are less than a year old, with 20 percent less than twelve days old, and users have found that most sites are not strongly linked to other sites.[3] This volatility and loose coupling makes it difficult for individuals to find information and hard for search engines to keep track unless they are actively involved in learning their territories, which in many cases will be geographic rather than topical.

For economic activities involving searches and retail sales, then, the Web will be more decentralized than its technology requires. For business-to-business selling and for noneconomic activities, sites aiming at a global audience probably will not have to be replicated, especially when the language problem is solved by both the spread of English and improved translation software. The great worldwide function of the Internet will be in the future what it already is now, the transfer of information through e-mail and Web site viewing. The question is, what will be the impact of this deluge of information?

Will we live in a better informed and connected, more engaged and participatory society—or in a society of lonely ex-couch potatoes glued to computer screens, whose human contacts are largely impersonal and whose political beliefs are easily manipulated, relying on the icons of a wired or wireless society?[4]

In other words, will we live in a Global Village or a mass society?

THE GLOBAL VILLAGE

In *Understanding Media: The Extensions of Man* (1964), Marshall McLuhan defined a shoe not as a foot covering but as an information-gathering extension of a person. A shoe accelerated and enlarged the set of human functions concerned with perceiving and understanding the world. More important than shoes, however, were the developing electronic media of the 20th century, which were forcing humans to redefine the nature of their existence. No longer could we be thought of as tool producers and utility maximizers, as classical economics would have it. Rather we were information processors shaped and guided by the data we gathered and the knowledge, opinions, and beliefs we formed. Moreover, since the way a new communications medium operated was so influential on how and what we processed, in effect "the medium is the message." And the overall message of the telephone, radio, television, and the computer is that we now live in a Global Village:

In the electric age, when our central nervous system is technologically extended to involve us in the whole of mankind and to incorporate the whole of mankind in us, we necessarily participate, in depth, in the consequences of our every action. It is no longer possible to adopt the aloof and dissociated role of the literate Westerner. . . . As electrically contracted, the globe is no more than a village.[5]

No village dweller can, as it were, sit back, paring his fingernails, while the hum and buzz of life passes by, alternatively amusing, depressing, or worthy of analysis to evoke a judgement, decision, or choice.

In a further elaboration of the village metaphor in *The Medium Is the Massage* (1967) McLuhan presciently described what we know as the Internet:

We now live in a global village . . . a simultaneous happening . . . Electric circuitry profoundly involves men with one another. Information pours upon us, instantaneously and continuously. As soon as information is acquired, it is very rapidly replaced by still newer information. An electronically-configured world has forced us to move from the habit of data classification to the mode of pattern recognition.[6]

At some point in the 21st century, when most of us are connected to the Web and e-mail most of the time through personal computers and mobile devices, any chance of rational, utility-maximizing objective thought will, in McLuhan's view, fade, to be replaced by aesthetic, emotional, subjective, all-encompassing involvement of the individual in the global community and it in him or her. If he is right, then the destruction of homo economicus will have been accomplished. Global Village dwellers instead will concern themselves with the things every villager cares about: order, in an environment where everyone is in close contact with everyone else; justice, since a village is focused on hum and buzz, not endlessly litigating fair treatment; and virtue, since villages are guided by practices, not laws.

In the Village evoked by the Internet what is global will be local and the local global. Traditions and cultural values of the few will be weakened in the face of the economic model of globalism but perhaps legitimized in the Village as they extend outward into everyone's awareness (for more on this, see below). Individual autonomy will be strengthened as the Net breaks down authoritarian social relations and empowers the formerly ignorant and uninformed. In a 1998 study, researchers found that 36 million Americans were using the Internet to get news at least once a week. What they were looking for was globally important information on health, finance, and science. Yet they had not reduced their perusal of local newspapers and television.[7] Software with names like Freenet, Gnutella, and Gnarly! enabled individuals to distribute and exchange information anonymously so that neither copyright lawyers nor state secret police could easily stop anyone from knowing about anything. Activists in NGOs could use the Internet to mobilize attacks on governments on behalf of localities and individuals with some chance of success in changing world public opinion and political processes. The Net-based Global Village perhaps will solve the economic, political, and social conflicts of the 20th century, which pitted individuals vs. community, local vs. not local, rational vs. irrational, and science vs. art. As the individual connects to everything, these dichotomies perhaps will be subsumed within one big global whole.

SOVEREIGNTY AND THE VILLAGE OF THE NET

The Global Village of the Internet model supports the idea of a shift from 20th-century homo economicus rooted in a world of transactions aimed at future well-being to 21st-century communal man embedded in orderly, just, and virtue-enhancing processes focused on living well in the present. But it does not appear to support the movement towards a stronger embeddedness of peoples in narrow national and cultural identities. One attempt to resolve the apparent conflict between the Village and the nation-state is that of Lee Kuan Yew, senior minister and former prime minister of Singapore. In a 1994 interview he worried about a nation and its corporations trying to "foist their system indiscriminately on societies in which it will not work."[8] It was America and its democratic-capitalist model Lee had in mind. In his view, Singapore and the societies of Asia have as their goal "a well-ordered society so that everybody can have maximum enjoyment of his freedoms. This freedom can only exist in an ordered state and not in a natural state of contention and anarchy." The threat Singapore allegedly faces is from the spread of an American culture emphasizing individual rights above the state's rights without in fact a corresponding emphasis on moral responsibility.

Westerners have abandoned an ethical basis for society, believing that all problems are solvable by a good government, which we in the East never believed possible.

For Lee, individual autonomy without moral gravitas results "in people urinating in public, in aggressive begging in the streets, in social break- down."

The cultures Lee wants to protect are those of Singapore, Korea, Greater China, Japan, and Vietnam, in which the family rather than the individual is the prime unit of society. It, rather than the government, holds major re- sponsibility for the individual, and family self-reliance is valued. Implicitly Lee argues for the family-centered business model common in Korean *chaebol* and among overseas Chinese in Asia in contrast to the corporate form. Individuals supposedly value "thrift, hard work, filial piety and loy- alty in the extended family," which can include a business. Thus employ- ees, rather than engaging in exchange relations with managers, receive paternal benevolence from bosses and owners and respond with childlike allegiance. The orderliness of this model is threatened by foreigners who value market exchange. Even worse, since the Asian Model is clearly the way toward long-term well-being, Western institutions are damaging to East Asia's long-run prospects.

Lee Kuan Yew recognized that an order-based society lacks a focus on the innovation, change, and experimentation needed for economic growth. His solution was a breathtakingly simple and innovative conceptualization of the Internet:

In a world where electronic communications are instantaneous, I do not see anyone lagging behind. Anything new that happens spreads quickly, whether it's super- conductivity or some new lifestyle.

Lee was predicting here that the Internet would become the culture-pro- tecting buffer insulating East Asian societies from foreign investment and expatriates. East Asians merely would need to monitor Western discourse on the Web to learn what was required for economic growth; they would not need to tolerate culture-damaging Western subsidiaries in their coun- tries. The learning fostered by these intruders now would be acquired at no cultural cost from the Internet and other communication media. In this clever formulation the forces of globalization would be made to defend na- tional identity, sovereignty, and order values. The Net would halt the growth in global capital flows, especially foreign direct investment, which characterized the late 20th century, and keep culture-threatening foreigners out of developing countries eager to protect their ways of life without halt- ing economic growth.

In addition to helping leaders protect culture, the Net might be useful in maintaining their power. In China, for example, government officials suffer from a dearth of accurate information on such things as deforestation practices in provinces, customs data, and commercial invoices for tax purposes. The Internet creates an information collection and sharing environment quite useful in enhancing governance, administration, and survival in power.[9] In fact, the Internet will make it easier for nations to collect information needed to enforce national laws and regulations which thwart the global thrust of e-commerce. Consider the case of the European Union. Currently Internet advertisers will find that Sweden bans television ads directed at children under twelve; presumably that law will be extended to the Internet. Italy bans tobacco ads. Germany bans lifetime guarantees. Finland bans speed as a feature in car ads. In the area of commercial law, France requires all contracts to be written in French, a problem for Web B2C and B2B sellers with English-language sites. In order to come even close to harmonizing country laws applicable to those trading on the Net, the EU is trying to standardize rules for legal recognition of electronic signatures, the online provision of services, cooling-off periods to protect consumers from hard-sell Web merchants, and privacy protection. While this agonizingly slow process plays itself out over the coming decades, each European nation will use the Internet to develop ever more stringent and comprehensive enforcement of its laws.

If we broaden the view, the problem gets even worse. One of the major Internet battles of the next decade or two among nations will be fought over the answer to the question, Is a product delivered electronically a good or a service? The United States says it is generally a good. The EU and Japan say it is a service. The issue surfaced in 1998 when the WTO adopted its Declaration on Global Electronic Commerce and invited countries to comment. The United States argued that Internet trade across borders should be regulated in much the same way that goods are, with no duties on electronic transmissions and reduced barriers for imported Internet "infrastructure" products. Companies should not be hindered from cross-border Internet sales of goods; auction services; monitoring, metering, and diagnostic services (so that a company in Chicago could use the Internet to control the heat in a building in Cologne for a fee); electronic authentication services; portal hosting; and sales of data.[10] The EU and Japan responded with complex submissions generally claiming that sales of electronic transmissions are services. Thus an Internet greeting card sold across a border would not be a good covered by the WTO agreements emerging out of the GATT Uruguay Round but a service covered by the General Agreement on Trade in Services (GATS). Although they didn't say so, the Europeans and Japanese clearly wanted to be able at some point to have to power to erect trade barriers against Internet products under the much less trade-liberalizing GATS than the WTO goods agreements. The GATS allows for extensive protectionism of the kind needed to give non-U.S. firms a chance to catch up in e-commerce to their American counterparts.

Attempts to use the Internet to protect national cultural values, entrenched political power, and local corporations suggest that the Global Village metaphor may not be as revealing as many people think and that sovereignty will remain a hot-button issue in the 21st century. Nevertheless, we are deluged by claims that the Internet will kill off the nation-state and its corporations:

The cyber-economy is a deathblow to the national corporate model, the protected market and the profligacy of national governments with captive taxpayers. In the new economy, there won't be any mother countries for successful corporations.[11]

Supposedly these companies will develop private, Internet-exchanged currencies to replace national money as a medium of exchange. As Michael Klein of Royal Dutch/Shell puts it, "Once the demand for privacy, security, and trust is met via encryption, regulation, and branding, we may see a new world of financial settlement."[12] Holders of e-money would have claims against electronic, real, and financial goods, services, and assets recognized as such by Netizens but not by national central banks.

The idea of Internet-driven stateless corporations using stateless money to serve stateless Global Villagers is intriguing and attractive, especially if the market model is (with Internet help) modified to accommodate a more just, ordered, and virtuous global community. But the sovereignty problem is not going to go away, and the Internet Global Village vs. the Internet nation-state controversy will recur constantly in the coming decades. Indeed, some thinkers believe that the Internet could evoke a resurgence of the manipulative tactics of national elites common in the 20th century and associated with the unpleasantness of mass society and the genuine horrors of totalitarianism.

DOES THE INTERNET FOSTER MASS SOCIETY?

After the fog of war had lifted in 1945 and the peoples of the world could look on the ruination that totalitarianism's battle with democracy had wrought, intellectuals in the West embarked on a program to identify those conditions that sustain liberal democratic institutions, those that destroy it, and, most important of all, how we can avoid drifting unthinkingly from one to the other. The most influential 19th-century work on these issues was Gustave LeBon's *The Crowd*, a chilling analysis of mob psychology, and in the mid-20th century it was William Kornhauser's *The Politics of Mass Society* (1959). Kornhauser, a professor of sociology at Berkeley, showed that modern democracies are highly vulnerable to mass movements that, if unchecked, can evoke totalitarian political systems such as fascism and communism. These could emerge from the development of mass society rooted in social conditions such as atomization and alienation. But fascism died out, communism fell with the Berlin Wall, and Americans turned out to be not all that anxious or atomized. Courses on mass society faded from the curriculum, and Kornhauser's critique was mostly forgotten. Then the Internet came along, and mass society began its comeback. Will the Internet create legions of mass men, to be followed by mass society, with the eventual reemergence of totalitarian barbarism? The answer is probably not, but that "probably" ought to make us step back and do some hard thinking.[13]

All discussions of mass society focus on the nature of elites and their status. These are the individuals who consider themselves, and are considered, socially superior because they help form and defend values and practices society considers important. In America one encounters political, religious, moral, educational, business, and entertainment elites. These last, people like Robert Redford and Barbra Streisand, often can move in and out of elite enclaves with ease, something a business elite, say, cannot do. Every kind of society has elites, and they are crucial to its maintenance. In the communal societies of the premodern era, elites were legitimized and selected by tradition, which also held nonelites in webs of kinship and culture. The result was a collection of seemingly unchanging, static societies in Europe and Asia. But under the pressures of urbanization, technology changes, and industrialization, Western traditions and authority structures were beginning to erode by the 17th century, and the power of elites began to decline. To hold on, they had to make themselves more accessible to nonelites, and this meant nonelite selection of elites and greater accountability. George Washington, an elite in the United States, is a key figure here in the transition from communalism to democratic pluralism.

Both medieval communalism and democratic pluralism have something in common. The nonelites, let's also call them the people, are difficult to mobilize. Think of the lord of the manor trying to get the peasants to work on the roads or the mayor of New York today trying to get the public to accept higher taxes for highway repairs. In both cases it's a hard sell. This is referred to as the nonavailability of nonelites. The people are difficult to manipulate. If the Internet made it easier for elites to pull and push the people in various directions, then a highly unstable mass society could come into being, with a real risk of further movement towards totalitarianism. In Kornhauser's theoretical formulation, increased availability of the people to elite manipulation first requires conditions of social atomization and alienation. It would work something like this:

- Somehow social atomization develops, a condition in which individuals are not directly related to one another in a variety of independent groups. As one sociologist likes to put it, bowling club memberships decline, along with PTA and church-related affiliations. Since these were the major sources of individuals' beliefs and values, people have to look elsewhere for something to help them make sense of the world, and they become easy prey for emotion-laden manipulations engineered by power-seeking elites with access to the mass media and, perhaps, the Internet.

- What makes the manipulation task easier is the tendency of atomized individuals to experience strong feelings of alienation and anxiety and to gravitate towards groups or movements promising escape from these tensions. Many Internet chat sites and forums exist to serve this function.

- Atomization, alienation, and insecure elites eager to hang on constitute the conditions for mass society, in which the people yearn to attach themselves to symbols, leaders, and movements offering belonging and connectedness. Social and political life becomes fragmented and unstable.

- If a dominant elite group emerges, secure in its ability to maintain the allegiance of the people to what Kornhauser calls the "pseudo-community" it has created, mass society quickly may turn into a totalitarianism of the Nazi or Stalinist variety, built on a violence-prone base of racial, historical, ideological, and nationalist emotions.

Is the Internet a technology and a communication medium that will foster the drift from pluralism to mass society to totalitarianism? A "yes" answer means that the Internet evokes atomization, alienation, and the emergence of large pseudo-communities dominated by manipulative elites.

Take atomization first. In a 1998 study, Carnegie-Mellon researchers found that increased Internet usage was associated with decreased family communication and a reduction in the size of non-Internet social circles. A few years later, a Stanford University study of over 4,000 individuals yielded similar results, with Internet usage associated with decreased attendance at social events and less time spent with family and friends.[14] However, research by the Pew Internet and American Life Project suggested that, with the exception of introverts, increased Internet e-mail usage tended to strengthen family ties and social networks.[15] It appears that Web surfing and chat room participation may foster some social atomization, while e-mailing actually reduces it. As for alienation, the Carnegie-Mellon research also found a correlation between Internet usage and greater feelings of loneliness and depression over time. The number of isolated, lonely Web surfers probably is not large, but if it grows in the coming decades, then conditions will be ripe for the emergence of manipulated pseudo-communities peopled by individuals desperate to belong to something and willing to express their allegiance in accord with their leaders' wishes. As Xerox scientist John Seely Brown says, "We replace 'I think, therefore I am' with 'we participate, therefore we are.' "[16]

WHAT WOULD IT LOOK LIKE?

What would an Internet-created mass society look like? As individuals by the millions surfed and surfed, social relations would atrophy. Lonely Netizens would gravitate towards sites and forums offering beliefs around which emotions could form and be electronically shared with others. Under the guidance of self-selected Webmasters, some groups, perhaps those evoking racial, socialist, environmental, gendered, religious, nationalist, or cultural feelings, would develop agendas for change and action plans. Individuals who have never seen each other and contributed nothing more than keyboard stroking and mouse clicks nevertheless would begin to see themselves as part of a community rather than what they really are: an audience willingly suspending disbelief before a site-staged melodrama. Some pseudo-communities would grow to the point where political and institutional leaders would have to take them into account, and as multiple groups of this kind competed for attention, institutional values and practices would shift this way and that until bewildered, confused, and resentful members began to fall away.

In our pluralist society some of these things already have occurred. Various Protestant sects, for example, have suffered occasional membership declines as they have responded this year to gay marriage advocates or that year to capitalism's foes. But church memberships generally have remained strong, and clearly pluralism is no threat to religions or other institutions. In an Internet-driven mass society, however, several things will happen that did not occur in the old regime. To begin with, the memberships of pseudo-communities could be global, huge, and therefore much more powerful than the local and small community groups with which institutional leaders formerly dealt. Moreover, the ordinary lonely Netizen who is not in a pseudo-community would soon find that the Web performed informational services faster, cheaper, and less intrusively than institutional representatives. Whereas once a minister counseled an individual enduring existential angst, now a bright and breezy site would offer the same help. The legitimacy of the church soon would be called into question as others performed its functions, and it would be easier prey for pseudo-community predators. Many current advocates, indeed, proclaim the Internet as a viable replacement for institutional leaders such as professors, journalists, priests, politicians, and even CEOs. As John Seely Brown noted in *The Social Life of Information*, "Infoenthusiasts insist . . . that such things as organizations and institutions are little more than relics of a discredited old regime."[17]

In this scenario, then, the Internet attracts millions of Web surfers who become isolated and depressed. If they consider turning again to institutions for social relationships to establish meaningful connectedness, they will reject that option since the Net already offers so many of the services the institutions offered and the institutions are falling apart as priests marry, professors get laid off, and local politicians are replaced by Net forums. Net Man now has emerged, untied to place, group, club, church, or party, and he is primed to jump about from pseudo-community to pseudo-community until he finds the site offering a chance for true commitment and the opportunity to move the world in grand and great ways.

At this point Net Man becomes Mass Man, and society will begin to shudder and convulse from the pressures of thousands of powerful pseudo-communities. Eventually a yearning for order will allow an elite to grab and hold power without having to answer to the masses, who think they have influence but in fact are simply what they always were in the Internet world: an isolated and powerless audience.

INFORMATION AND THE SALVATION OF THE INTERNET

Will the Internet drive the peoples of the world into a stateless Global Village or a series of national elite-dominated mass and perhaps totalitarian societies? In their extreme forms, neither model, Global Village or mass society, is very compelling. Each one asks too much of the Internet and exaggerates its likely influence. One senses that some kind of location in a middle ground is going to emerge. The question then is: Will the Internet push us more towards being communal Netizens or mass men and women? The answer depends on how information is used on the Net and controlled. And that raises the privacy issue. Most discussion today focuses on protecting the individual from corporate manipulation through privacy regulation. This is an important topic, but the debate needs to be broadened to include identification of ways the individual can be protected from elite Internet manipulation so that a drift into mass society becomes less likely compared to a gentle floating towards the Global Village.

Take information first. It supposedly is independent of the mind; it is an objective entity that, when perceived, reduces one's uncertainty about the way the world really is. Supposedly information is independent of its encoding and transmission. Supposedly information that tells us something we already know is not information, since it does not reduce uncertainty. And supposedly information's enemy is *noise*, the amount of data a receiver gets that was not sent by the expected source and the amount sent that was not received. These are the tenets of information theory, as formulated by Claude Shannon, Norbert Wiener, and others.[18] Now consider what is becoming more and more obvious about the Internet:

- Lies, fabrications, distortions, and exaggerations often get treated as information from the Internet because we ignore the source. I once had a student turn in a report on investment conditions in Iran which was unbelievably, outrageously positive. It turned out that his chief source, about which he was blissfully unconcerned, was the home page of the Government of Iran. When we do a search for information, we may get hundreds of sites listed and pay little attention to the sender of information we use.

- Data coming across the Internet often is encoded and transmitted context-free so that our ability to interpret and make sense of it is limited. This does not stop us, however, since humans have a habit of constructing interpretations when none is implied. Thus when we access a search-generated site that is nothing more than a table of seemingly useful data with no text, no source, and no sense of how the data is to be used, we will impose our own biases and preconceived notions of the material. In many cases, the Internet simply fosters our talking to ourselves and believing we have learned something about the way the world really is.

- If we know that a Ford exploded in Peoria and killed a child, we would not have learned anything by seeing the incident mentioned on a hundred sites or in fifty e-mails. Yet frequency of occurrence of a message can evoke a sense of frequency of occurrence of the event. Psychologists call this tendency the vividness effect: what is vividly experienced may be deemed to frequently occur. The Internet, then, may tell us something we already know in such a way that we form a new, erroneous understanding of an event. Fords don't usually explode, but many of us may conclude that they do.

- Finally, we get e-mails all the time that we think are from x but really are from y. Often we do not check the header to see who actually sent something or the header somehow makes us believe that the sender is x. Moreover, when we do get a message from x, it may be one of hundreds we receive. In our overloaded state we ignore it, although x will conclude that we did not. These kinds of noise can be devastating in their effects, as x forms expectations of us and we of x, based on e-mails. When neither of us is able to live up to these expectations, relationships will deteriorate. I have interviewed several hundred companies so far, and this was one of the major Internet worries of managers.

Information theory, then, is inadequate in helping us understand what goes on in Internet communication, yet there is no other well-developed theory available to guide us. It seems that in some cases, the more we use the Internet to acquire information—and this is its major use—the more we are prone to validating our own biases, believing that rare events frequently occur, and learning to distrust others who don't do what we expect of them. How often we do these things and how damaging they are is not known, but in the 21st century we are going to find out. In the meantime, perhaps the Internet world will develop in a more helpful manner. What is needed is better education in schools on the external nature of real information in contrast to internal biases; better search engines and intelligent agents that guide us towards understanding, not just acquisition of data; better e-mail protocols so that senders are more certainly known and less easily impersonated; and "positive closure" signals that tell both parties when an x message has been understood by a y receiver. These and other small steps are the nitty-gritty things needed to head off any drift into elite manipulation and mass society and to make the Village hum and buzz productively and happily.

THREE KINDS OF PRIVACY

The way we deal with information on the Internet has profound social consequences, but so does the Internet's use of information about us. To be free of observation is to have privacy, and the Internet's users have the ability to observe us as we surf and search in ways that are unobtrusive and for purposes that may be unacceptable or disagreeable. Three ways of thinking about privacy exist, all focused on defining the nature of information about oneself, and one of them, the wrong one, is dominating current discussions. Personal information associated with privacy is said to be an *asset* which we can sell on the Internet if we wish. If it is taken without compensation or solicited in inappropriate ways, an invasion of privacy is said to occur. But private-self information also can be thought of as a *reservoir of power*, the loss of which, by becoming not private, may be personally and socially destabilizing. A third approach sees private-self information as *part of one's well-being*, with a loss being a threat to well-being. These latter two ideas will become more noteworthy in the future.

The asset idea is dominating current discussions.[19] The goal of economic growth within the context of efficiently operating product and labor markets tolerates the mostly unrestricted collection and sharing of information about individuals. However, since private-self information supposedly is a person's asset or property, a person has the right to sell it and to some extent control its use or not sell it. The loss of unobserved seclusion, or privacy, is thus an issue for negotiation and exchange, with rules of the game designed to protect the interests of both parties and to evoke a well-functioning market environment. The issues of importance are who, government or industry, sets the rules and what the rules will be. Acquiring information without compensation probably will be bad—it all depends on how fair-use rules will be worked out—but if an Internet user is targeted to be observed for compensation and information collected, he or she should have the option to refuse the deal or to negotiate conditions, including first use of the information (called "first rights"), second use, and all subsequent uses. Debate on these issues is amazingly complex; one hears discussions of data-mining, profiling, disclosure, informed consent, cookies, click patterns, reasonable access to collected data about oneself, and security. Industry groups have a standard-setting body named the Platform for Privacy Preferences, consumers' groups have various organizations, the United States has Congress and the Federal Trade Commission, and the European Union has Internet privacy laws, called "directives."

However, if the trends away from the extended order market model and towards concerns about justice, order, and individual autonomy continue, the privacy debate will shift away from information as an asset or property and towards personal information as a reservoir of power or an ingredient in one's well-being.

Privacy theorists among legal scholars often point out that a person's public self, the image a person presents to the world, is constructed, containing things we want to exhibit and things we do not. Law protects the constructed public self and the hidden self from untruths and "false light"

statements, as well as from the coerced purchase of silence (blackmail) regarding truths.[20] It also extends property-rights law regarding unreasonable searches to intrusive surveillance. The goal of law here is the
maintenance of social order, since personal, private information constitutes
a reservoir of power, the loss of which is individually and socially
destabilizing. We all know things about ourselves that others do not—or do
not know well—and this gives us power in economic exchanges and social
encounters. If ice-cream makers do not know that I secretly yearn every
hour of the day for an ice-cream soda, they will not work tirelessly to tempt
me to consume the stuff. If politicians of the left are unaware that I harbor
deep guilt over the miserable plight of poor Americans, they will not bom-
bard me with pleas for votes to save the weak. The ignorance of the marketers and the politicians gives me the power to avoid annoyance or, if I
change my desire for privacy, to invite solicitation. Information here is not
an asset that yields me income; rather it is the basis for my autonomy, my
ability to have some control over my lot. Although I might yield some of my
autonomy at times, mostly I want to retain it, since a loss of autonomy
threatens the integrity of the self and can bring on a sense of anxiety. As I
noted above, an Internet world that evokes atomization, alienation, and
anxiety can be used to manipulate people into unstable and dangerous
mass societal conditions.

In the private-information-is-an-asset model, one ought to be free to sell
or give self data to another, subject to fair use and fair dealing (often called
"opt-in") rules. However, in the reservoir-of-power model, while autonomous individuals have the right to sell or give away private information,
society should make rules to ensure that people recognize that it is not a
trivial act. Here the opt-in rules would be extended to include a waiting period and perhaps a kind of electronic notarization of an agreement. The
idea is to signal to individuals that giving up private information is an act
that may have negative consequences for both the person and the society.

The third privacy model, in which private-self information is part of our
well-being, is even more restrictive in its Internet government implications,
suggesting that surveillance, whether agreed to or not, is damaging to
one's health. In *Beast and Man, The Roots of Human Nature* (1978), Mary
Midgley noted a phenomenon common to humans and other species: "the
distinct and primitive horror of being stared at."

Being stared at produces horror widely, not only in man, but in a great range of animal species. In most social creatures, a direct stare constitutes an open threat. . . . It
may well have something to do with the fact that predators naturally stare fixedly at
prospective prey before jumping on it. . . . Those stared at often feel as much attacked as if they had been actually abused or hit.[21]

Anyone with any sophistication about the Internet knows this feeling of being stared at, since our surfing easily can be monitored by employers, ser-

vice providers, and people or companies who have planted certain kinds of software or cookies on our computers. This monitoring is viewed in the well-being model as an assault, and as such it should be prohibited, regardless of opt-in, opt-out, fair use, or other rules.

In the 21st century, in my view, the Internet privacy debate is going to shift away from the economic model. Perhaps emphasis then will focus on power and autonomy issues out of concerns over a drift into mass society. In that case, market researchers will adapt to the constraints placed on them. But perhaps the debate will begin to include discussions of the fundamental nature of humans and their basic need to be free of the implied assaults that Internet surveillance, a form of staring even though indirect, implies. If so, we can expect strong prohibitions against monitoring and data-mining. Market research will all but cease on the Net, as will most e-commerce of the business-to-consumer kind.

THE INTERNET IN THE 21ST CENTURY

The Internet consists of World Wide Web sites; e-mail functionality, including asynchronous discussion forums; synchronous chat lines; and interactive entertainment and gaming environments.[22] It is used to search for and exchange information in work and nonwork settings and to facilitate retail and non-retail commerce. Related to this economic activity are business uses of Web sites for advertising, public relations, market research, and financial disclosure, with the creation of a forward-looking, technology-alert public image the major function of many corporate home pages.[23] But it is noneconomic activities that dominate the Internet, as some individuals build or strengthen communal or family ties with e-messaging and Web sites (my ninety-two-year-old mother has her own site). Others simply use their sites to celebrate themselves, to affirm or legitimize their existence. Geocities and AOL thrive on this function, which can be construed as associated with the development of individual autonomy or perhaps atomization and alienation. The future, then, could see the Internet fostering a Global Village of liberated individuals thriving in new and expanded communal settings or a mass society of frightened loners prone to manipulation by the rich, famous, and powerful.

- *A move towards the Global Village model will strengthen the ideological attacks on homo economicus and the market model.* This kind of Internet will compel us to see ourselves as part of a global community—as involved, participative, and caring rather than analytical, objective, and standoffish. We will focus on justice, order, and virtue right now—all village concerns—rather than individual utility maximization in the future.

- *The Internet's threat to the nation-state and its elites will foster defensive responses.* In its Village-enhancing mode, the Internet threatens political, religious, and economic authority networks associated with nation-states. But elites in these networks will respond by using the Internet to build, or as an excuse to build, barriers against foreign capital and expatriates in their countries. Moreover, they will use the Net to improve surveillance of their own peoples. The Global Village-nation-state conflict will recur throughout the century, with multinational corporations caught in the middle.

- *A drift in several countries towards mass society and totalitarianism could ensue.* As the Village-state battle heats up, threatened local elites desperate to hold on to power could begin using the Internet to manipulate isolated, alienated Netizens. Net-evoked racial or ideological passions, highly destabilizing, could foster a move towards totalitarianism in some countries. Japan is a candidate for this process. Its elites, who have failed the society's need for economic growth, increasingly will be under attack in the coming decades. They will use the Net to mobilize support for programs centered around ideas of racial purity and national greatness. Institutional leaders in religion, education, and business are quite weak in Japan and will be powerless to hinder developing mass movements.

- *Flawed information flows across the Net could support mass society tendencies.* The Internet will enable people to know more than they ever conceived possible. And the cost will be minimal. Will they become smarter or simply devalue knowledge? In most places today in the developed world water is everywhere, it is virtually free, and we do not care about it. A similar process on the Internet could be dangerous, especially given the other information problems discussed in this chapter. If we become overloaded with "useless" information lacking in credibility that we have difficulty interpreting, we will begin to substitute our own biases or those of a few Net manipulators for a truth and reality we find ever more elusive.

- *New views of privacy are likely to emerge, and these will check the dangerous tendencies of the Net.* The salvation of the Internet may lie in a shift of the privacy debate from a vision of private-self knowledge as not so much a commodity to be traded but as an element of well-being integral to personhood. While market research and e-commerce will be hurt by surveillance restrictions driven by this vision, the possibility of drifting towards manipulation and mass society will be reduced.

NOTES

1. See OECD, *The Economic and Social Impact of Electronic Commerce* (Paris: OECD, 1999) and OECD, *OECD Information Technology Outlook* (Paris: OECD, 2000). Most of the data cited here and below comes from these sources and refers to the OECD countries, where virtually all Internet activity currently occurs.

2. According to Connie Lee, "Language Barrier," *Wall Street Journal*, 22 November 1999, R62.

3. See John Markoff, "As Web Expands, Search Engines Puff to Keep Up," *New York Times*, 29 May 2000, C3, and Ian Austen, "Study Reveals Web as Loosely Woven," *New York Times*, 18 May 2000, D8.

    4. Norman H. Nie and Lutz Erbring, *Internet and Society, A Preliminary Report*. Palo Alto: Stanford Institute for the Quantitative Study of Society, 17 February 2000, 3.

    5. Marshall McLuhan, *Understanding Media: The Extensions of Man* (New York: Signet Books, 1964), 20.

    6. Marshall McLuhan, *The Medium Is the Massage* (New York: Bantam, 1967), 63.

    7. See the results of the Pew Research Center 1998 Poll at www.tvrundown.com/pew3.html.

    8. See "Culture as Destiny, A Conversation with Lee Kwan Yew," *Foreign Affairs*, 1994, 73 (2), 110. The other quotes in this section are on 111, 112, 113, 114, and 116.

    9. Sheila Melvin, "Beijing: the Nexus of China's Internet Riddle," *Asian Wall Street Journal*, 20–26 March 2000, 17. Ms. Melvin quotes the *People's Daily* on the Internet: "We cannot help but be amazed at its limitless space and boundless pleasure . . . The Internet's omni-directional, multi-elemental service truly lets people have the sense of being a god." The same godlike status may be available also to the people's rulers.

    10. The various documents are available on the WTO Web site at www.wto.org, including the "Work Programme on Electronic Commerce" and submissions by the United States, European Union, and Japan.

    11. David Roche, "Traditional Sectors Will Add Value to the Cyber-Economy," *Asian Wall Street Journal*, 10–16 April 2000, 16.

    12. Michael Klein, "Banks lose control of money," *Financial Times*, 14 January 2000, 11.

    13. My analysis here is based on William Kornhauser, *The Politics of Mass Society* (New York: Free Press, 1959) and James W. White's *The Sokagakkai and Mass Society* (Stanford: Stanford University Press, 1970). The Sokagakkai is a militant lay religious movement in Japan with growing political power and a taste for mass manipulation. Japan rather than the United States may be more likely to drift into a mass society in the coming decades.

    14. See R. Kraut, M. Patterson, V. Lundmark, S. Kiesler, T. Mukopadhyay, and W. Scherlis, "Internet Paradox: A Social Technology That Reduces Social Involvement and Psychological Well-Being," *American Psychologist*, 1998, 53 (9), 1017–1031. The second study was conducted by Lutz Erbring and Norman Nie for the Stanford Institute for the Quantitative Study of Society. See *Internet and Society, A Preliminary Report*. Palo Alto: SIQSS, 17 February 2000 (see note 4).

    15. The study results are discussed in Rebecca Fairley Raney, "Study Finds Internet of Social Benefit to Users," *New York Times*, 11 May 2000, D7. Also see Lisa Guernsey, "Cyberspace Isn't So Lonely After All," *New York Times*, 26 July 2001, D5.

    16. Interview with John Seely Brown, *Financial Times*, 19 January 2000, FT-IT Review, X. Mr. Brown is hopeful that Internet and related technology can be used to foster cooperation and improved work performance. However, some of his examples are disturbing, such as the office coffeepot sending an e-mail message to employees when a fresh pot is ready so that informal gatherings for coffee can be formally manipulated by management, or linking Web data on Xerox's share price to the office water fountain's volume.

17. John Seely Brown and Paul Duguid, *The Social Life of Information* (Boston: Harvard Business School Press, 2000), 16.

18. Robert B. Ash, *Information Theory* (New York: Dover Publications, 1990). See also Claude E. Shannon and Warren Weaver, *Mathematical Theory of Communication* (Champaign-Urbana: University of Illinois Press, 1963).

19. See Lawrence Lessig, *Code and Other Laws of Cyberspace* (Boulder, CO: Basic Books, 1999) and Andrew Shapiro, *The Control Revolution: How the Internet Is Putting Individuals in Charge and Changing the World We Know* (New York: Public Affairs, 1999).

20. See Chapter 25 of Richard Posner's *Overcoming Law* (Cambridge: Harvard University Press, 1995). Judge Posner reviews the literature briefly and argues the case for the economic, information-is-an-asset, model.

21. Mary Midgley, *Beast and Man, The Roots of Human Nature* (Ithaca: Cornell University Press, 1978), 10, 11–12.

22. One of the best discussions on the Internet and its functions is Patricia Wallace, *The Psychology of the Internet* (Cambridge: Cambridge University Press, 1999).

23. See Jeremiah J. Sullivan, "What Are the Functions of Corporate Home Pages?" *Journal of World Business*, 1999, 34 (2), 193–210. This function dominated United States, German, and Japanese home sites.

BIBLIOGRAPHY

Ash, Robert B. *Information Theory*. New York: Dover Publications, 1990.

Austen, Ian. "Study Reveals Web as Loosely Woven." *New York Times*, 18 May 2000, D8.

Brown, John Seely, and Paul Duguid. *The Social Life of Information*. Boston: Harvard Business School Press, 2000.

Erbring, Lutz, and Norman Nie. *Internet and Society, A Preliminary Report*. Palo Alto: SIQSS, 17 February 2000.

Guernsey, Lisa. "Cyberspace Isn't So Lonely After All." *New York Times*, 26 July 2001, D5.

Klein, Michael. "Banks lose control of money." *Financial Times*, 14 January 2000, 11.

Kornhauser, William. *The Politics of Mass Society*. New York: Free Press, 1959.

Kraut, R., M. Patterson, V. Lundmark, S. Kiesler, T. Mukopadhyay, and W. Scherlis. "Internet Paradox: A Social Technology That Reduces Social Involvement and Psychological Well-Being." *American Psychologist*, 1998, 53(9), 1017–1031.

Lee, Connie. "Language Barrier." *Wall Street Journal*, 22 November 1999, R62.

Lessig, Lawrence. *Code and Other Laws of Cyberspace*. Boulder, CO: Basic Books, 1999.

Markoff, John. "As Web Expands, Search Engines Puff to Keep Up." *New York Times*, 29 May 2000, C3.

McLuhan, Marshall. *The Medium Is the Massage*. New York: Bantam, 1967.

———. *Understanding Media: The Extensions of Man*. New York: Signet Books, 1964.

Melvin, Sheila. "Beijing: The Nexus of China's Internet Riddle." *Asian Wall Street Journal*, 20–26 March 2000, 17.

Midgley, Mary. *Beast and Man: The Roots of Human Nature*. Ithaca: Cornell University Press, 1978.

OECD. *The Economic and Social Impact of Electronic Commerce*. Paris: OECD, 1999.

OECD. *OECD Information Technology Outlook*. Paris: OECD, 2000.

Posner, Richard. *Overcoming Law*. Cambridge: Harvard University Press, 1995.

Raney, Rebecca Fairley. "Study Finds the Internet of Social Benefit to Users." *New York Times*, 11 May 2000, D7.

Roche, David. "Traditional Sectors Will Add Value to the Cyber-Economy." *Asian Wall Street Journal*, 10–16 April 2000, 16.

Shannon, Claude E., and Warren Weaver, *Mathematical Theory of Communication*. Champaign-Urbana: University of Illinois Press, 1963.

Shapiro, Andrew. *The Control Revolution: How the Internet Is Putting Individuals in Charge and Changing the World We Know*. New York: Public Affairs, 1999.

Sullivan, Jeremiah J. "What Are the Functions of Corporate Home Pages?" *Journal of World Business*, 1999, 34(2), 193–210.

Wallace, Patricia. *The Psychology of the Internet*. Cambridge: Cambridge University Press, 1999.

White, James W. *The Sokkagakkai and Mass Society*. Stanford: Stanford University Press, 1970.

Zakaria, Fareed. "Culture as Destiny: A Conversation with Lee Kwan Yew." *Foreign Affairs*, 1994, 73(2), 108–118.

CHAPTER 11

THE INTERNET AND E-COMMERCE: FROM MARKETS TO MARKETOIDS

In 1996, business done across the Internet worldwide generated $2.9 billion in revenue on 50,000 sites. By 2002 it was expected to be as much as $2 trillion. In 1996, about 14 million domain hosts managed Internet traffic, a number that grew to 72 million four years later. Web pages grew from 1.3 million to 1 billion. Time online monthly at search engines grew from under forty-five minutes per person to over two hours, and search engines grew from a few to over 3,000. In 2000, ten of the *Financial Times'* Global 500 firms were "pure play" Internet companies. Only three, America Online, Yahoo!, and CMGI (a holding company owning over sixty companies), had annual revenues over $100 million. Most were intermediaries, offering portal, search, and marketplace services, and most were United States-based. Outside of the United States, only Pacific Century Cyberworks in Hong Kong and Terra Networks in Spain made the Global 500. The Internet could be accessed from computers, wireless devices, and television sets, suitably equipped, in 2000, with Americans ahead in computers and the Europeans and Japanese ahead in wireless connecting. Wireless usage was expected to grow from 10 percent of the total to about 50 percent in 2005, according to some projections.[1]

At some point early in the 21st century, most developed-country individuals, groups, and organizations will have inexpensive, fast access to the following Internet menu:

Transaction Activity	Parties to the Transaction	Initiating Technology	Communication Medium
Business to consumer (B2C)	One to one	Computer-based	Voice only
Business to business (B2B)	Many to one	Wireless-based	Video and voice

| Consumer to consumer (C2C) | Many to many | TV-based | Text/forms/data |
| Consumer to business (C2B) | One to many | | Everything |

Anywhere, anytime, economic exchange will be possible, so that no individual need ever be outside the environs of a marketplace. In ancient Athens, Socrates' wife had to walk to the *agora*, the central shopping, administrative, and political area, to buy food for the great man's table. With the Internet menu she could do her marketing from the house and have the purchases delivered. Or she could do it down by the river while laundering Socrates' clothes. Or at the temple after sacrificing to Pallas Athene. While a wired Socrates railed against the namby-pamby chaos of the Global Village and sang the praises of the Internet's ability to empower the right sort of elites in his version of a mass society, he probably would have failed to notice that the buzz of truck and barter had come to pervade every space during every minute of the day and night. Once he did notice, he would have had to figure out if electronic commerce worked in service to the elite guardians he and his disciple, Plato, favored, or to the Village's poets, actors, rhetoricians, and storytellers he despised. It would be a tough call.

Electronic commerce consists of market exchange, services facilitating exchange, and pre- and post-sale services. The markets covered involve the sales of goods, services, real and financial assets, and labor. By 2000, U.S. B2C sales were about one percent of all retail sales. In the B2B category, only 32 percent of manufacturers were doing business online, but surveys suggested that 90 percent of them would be B2B-involved by 2003. Over 750 Net marketplaces served transactions needs.[2] It was clear that B2B transactions would dominate Internet commerce in the coming decades, especially if one included within-business intranets and extranets among linked firms.

What kind of Internet world are we living in? Is it a world of diminishing returns, where companies must add investment to capture Net customers until the return on investment per new customer goes below some hurdle rate and growth stops? Or is it a world of increasing returns and network effects, where the cost of each new customer is near zero and the greater the connectedness among customers, the more they are willing to pay? Is it a world of signals and symbols, where brand names and company logos summon up customer feelings of trust and loyalty, regardless of prices or network benefits? Is it a world of order in which firms customarily offer a certain product at a certain price as a matter of course? Is it a world of justice, where prices are deemed fair and customers spread out their buying to help all of an industry's Net firms? Is it a world of virtue ethics, in which Internet purchases are driven by what's right and good? Or is it a world of sovereign states in which national goals drive buying behavior? The questions follow a progression from a world of markets through a world of emotions and habits and end at a world of values revolving around ideas of order, justice, virtue, and sovereignty. These may be the worlds of the 21st century, and e-commerce will have to serve them all. They will range from market environments where truck and barter dominate to Global Village *marketoids* where values, customs, and communities turn what initially looks like economic exchange into something much more complex. No wonder Microsoft once asked, "Where do you want to go today?" It wasn't that Bill Gates was able and eager to take you there; rather it was that he genuinely had no clue and needed answers.

THE IMPACT OF THE INTERNET ON COMPANIES

After interviewing well over 100 firms engaged in global business, my colleagues and I concluded that four types of firms have emerged in response to the explosive development of the Internet.

- *Winners*. For these firms, the subject of most Internet hype stories in the business press, the Web and e-mail provide market growth opportunities, and employee resources are freed up through Internet usage to pursue these opportunities. Firm Web sites attract new clients, help to improve supply and distribution channel management, and foster better customer relationship management. Reliance on other Web sites reduces the need for internal experts and paid consultants by providing fast, easy, inexpensive access to information. E-mail and Web benefits also involve reductions in the cost of travel, paper, and postage and increases in employee autonomy. The daily ritual of messaging and surfing also evokes flow conditions that make for more satisfied and productive workers.

- *Defenders*. For all the rest of the firms in our research, the Internet was either a mixed blessing or a downright curse. Defender firms enjoyed operational improvements. External e-mail communication reduced fax and telephone costs, facilitated project and task management, allowed for real-time interacting in synchronous chat mode, and eliminated worries about communicating across many time zones. However, the opportunities for market growth through the firm's Web sites were outweighed by increased competition from new entrants in the industry who had found that a cleverly constructed site could develop a customer base at low cost, something that could not have been done previously. Easy entry in industries where this had not been the case in the pre-Internet era was forcing defender firms to use all of their Internet-freed-up employee resources to defend against competitive threats brought on by the Internet.

- *The Frustrated*. Here companies found growth opportunities globally through their sites that increased revenues, but profits either were stagnant or fell due to the cost of decreases in employee performance brought on by Internet usage. Time-wasting during fruitless or unnecessary Web-surfing reduced time available for other tasks. Salesmen, unsure of what their roles were in the Internet era, began to perform their old roles badly. Security worries required costly software fixes. The speed-up in information flows forced managers to make decisions more rapidly than they wished, and expensive mistakes were made. The biggest problem, however, was overload. As employees became deluged with two or three hundred messages a day, they were forced to prioritize, and in many cases clients were lost and deadlines missed. Misdirected or failed messaging also incurred costs.

- *Losers.* Not only did the Internet raise operating costs for some firms, it also inspired revenue declines as competition increased from new entrants. For them the Internet was a disaster. And the more they relied on e-mail, the worse things got. As messaging took the place of telephone and face-to-face communicating with clients, the employee's ability to "read" the customer declined, as did the ability to send and receive complex, subtle messages and messages sensitive to feelings, biases, and cultural values. This lack of personalization and complexity resulted in weakened or broken bonds with clients. Just as bad, e-mail technology encouraged the expansion of queries coming directly to managers without the filtering done in telephone mode. Whereas a caller typically had gone through a "press one, press two" routine, now a supplier, client, or government official easily could learn a manager's e-mail address and fire off an unmediated message.

In the coming decades firms will enjoy the growth opportunities offered by the Internet, and the challenges of increased competition will be dealt with. The big problem, however, is increased costs, especially those associated with declining employee productivity. The Frustrated and the Loser firms, which made up about 40 percent of the firms I studied, will have to learn how to manage such things as employee information-seeking surfing and messaging. Below I want to discuss the productivity problem and how it can be made at least a little bit less burdensome through the reemergence of the internal expert in corporations.

THE THREAT TO EMPLOYEE PRODUCTIVITY

The productivity-destroying habits of Web surfers in offices can be illustrated by a scenario. Assume a boss has assigned an employee, Jane Doe, to find out the copyright situation in Malaysia, where the U.S. company wants to sell a technical manual. What are the relevant laws protecting intellectual property? How rigorously are they enforced? What is the extent of illegal copying in Malaysia? What are the United States, the WTO, and other global players doing about any problems? Before the Web, Jane would have pored over books, magazines, and articles in a morning trip to the library. In the afternoon, she would have telephoned her legal department, Malaysian sources, and perhaps academic experts. After eight hours she would know a lot more and know what she did not know—a very good start. Now fast-forward a few years to a Web-enabled Jane. First, she accesses a search engine, say Google, and types in the terms "Malaysia and copyright." A list of 500 sites is returned, and she begins going through them. After two hours she gives up, realizing that the term "and" on the Internet is not the connector it purports to be. Lots of sites are on Malaysia and lots on copyright, but nothing on both. Next she turns to the Web version of ABI / INFORM, a database of recent articles on various topics. An hour spent at this produces nothing. Frustrated, she begins calling lawyer friends (her legal department no longer exists) in search of URL tips. She spends the rest of the day fruitlessly on this. The following day she telephones Asian friends, with similar results. Finally she contacts the professor who used to help her out from time to time. She discovers that he now charges a $1,000 fee. Within an hour she receives an e-mail from him detailing much of what she needs to know. A report is on her desk next day with everything else.

Jane Doe's performance in the Web era has deteriorated from that in the pre-Web era—and she cost her company money. What happened? To begin with, she put too much faith in the Internet and reduced her reliance on the telephone. Moreover, while using the Web, she expected too much of the search engines. How then did the professor succeed where Jane had failed? First, he had read a lot—that's what he mostly is paid to do—and had a rough knowledge of the answer to Jane's question. Jane is paid to talk and do, not to read and think, and no technology is going to overcome the shortcomings of role and task requirements for managers in a business organization. Second, the professor surfed the Web every day and assigned his students to do the same. He had amassed, within his specialty, a deep knowledge of data resources. He would have found the Malaysian copyright information in the "Country Commercial Guide—Malaysia" page buried deep within the National Trade Data Bank pay site, nestled within the U.S. Department of Commerce site. Without specific knowledge of this source, Jane would not have been able to find the information she needed. In the future the Janes of the world are going to have to come back to the telephone and the librarian as necessary complements to the Web. Moreover, they are going to have to rely more on internal experts who combine both topic knowledge with Web-search knowledge. This is a problem, since the Internet is calling the whole idea of expertise into question.

THE EXPERT HAS LEFT THE BUILDING

You are the CEO of your firm, which makes profits by mass-marketing branded products. Revenues are maximized by price-cutting rooted in rigorous cost control. Periods of declining revenues and profits are tied to cyclical downturns in the economy. This year, however, the economy is booming but profits are falling. You call in a marketing expert from your strategic planning office and ask for her advice, which you, enjoying success, have not sought before. She tells you that the firm should be selling high-priced, niche-market products if it wants to maximize profits. Forget about over-reliance on price-cutting and cost controls, she says, and focus on targeted marketing to luxury product buyers. Because she has a track record, has data, and talks a good game, you accept her recommendation, which turns out to be a correct one. This is expertise at work. A good expert has knowledge in the form of experience, analytical skills, and information research methods, and this knowledge transcends common sense and the common wisdom of the organization. She adds value by identifying problems unnoticed by others and solving them, observing meaningful trends not observed by nonexperts, recognizing appropriate and inappropriate goals, questioning and testing received wisdom, and persuading decision-makers to adopt her views and recommendations.[3]

Even before the Internet implicitly promised to eliminate the need for on-site experts, they were in trouble in organizations. Strategic-planning units did not earn their keep and have been in decline for a decade, while day-to-day complex decisions formerly made by experts now are made by expert systems. What really hurt expertise's good name, however, was the emergence of "hotshots," "nerds," and "cloud-walkers"—all foisted on corporations by academic-credentialing factories with little concern for the specific concerns of industries. Hotshots possess elaborate tools but no real sense of the significant problems to which those tools should be applied. Nerds work long and hard to solve nonproblems. Cloud-walkers solve problems perceived to be significant but which in fact do not serve organizational goal attainment. They are admired by some senior executives, highly paid, and contribute little.

"Every manager his own expert" is the slogan of the day, and companies have spent billions on databases, decision support and expert systems, and shared wisdom networks. The arrival of the Internet fit in perfectly with this trend.[4] A financial manager eager to use complex risk-management tools, for example, can log on to one of several Web sites, receive elaborate training on-line, and then be inserted into a Web marketplace for a variety of option and swap products. Similar services are available in law, accounting, information systems management, and so forth. Internet expertise will be more up-to-date than any internal source, so firms will begin to reduce the number of people in staff-expert positions. Indeed, the hiring of managers will begin to focus more not on what an individual knows in a specific domain but rather on ability to creatively use internal knowledge networks and the Internet. The systems analyst and the network manager, rather than the expert, will be the key staff functions of the 21st-century corporation.

Jane Doe, our manager involved in a time-wasting search for Malaysian copyright information, was helped by the Web, but only through purchasing the services of an intermediary. Her firm's CEO, unwilling to pay for more consultants, may hire analysts and networkers to build an internal wisdom-sharing process to serve Jane-type future needs, but he will not consider reestablishing a legal department. Assuming that the costs of networking are less than the costs of Jane's and others' inefficiency in a Web-enabled world, the company will appear to have followed a prudent course and solved the employee productivity decline problem. But see what happens with the disappearance of internal experts:

- Internal experts establish the context in which advice is given. This educational function helps decision-makers make sense of what they are doing and be better prepared for follow-up.

- Experts do not just inform. They also sell, and their rhetoric makes their advice credible and defensible. What Jane Doe gets from the Internet will be less credible and, more important, less defensible. If something goes wrong, "the Internet made me do it" will not serve as an appropriate justification for her actions in response to the copyright information. Next time, Jane will be more risk-averse, passing up opportunities she would not have passed up under the guidance of an internal expert.

In sum, then, the Internet can evoke declining employee performance in terms of wasted time; it also can foster overly conservative decisions in response to Web expertise only partially understood and not strongly defensible.

THE VIRTUAL ORGANIZATION

Today's received wisdom proclaims the emergence of the Internet-enabled virtual organization, which is smaller than its non-virtual predecessor, more centrally controlled, and focused on the integration of operations and customer-relationship management systems rather than discrete production and marketing functions. Many of the services formerly provided in-house will be purchased on the Web, and strategic alliances of suppliers and distributors will be bypassed or downplayed as Web spot markets crop up to match B2B and B2C buyers and sellers who would not have wanted in the past to spend the time and money finding each other. But just as the loss of internal expertise may hurt employee performance, the abandonment of face-to-face, personalized networks may come at a cost that sometimes outweighs benefits. Consider the Japanese or American *keiretsu*, networks designed to reduce the commercial, financial, and business risks of their members.[5] A network member firm always could count on financing being available from a friendly bank and payment on time from client firms committed to purchasing the firm's output. What the company lost in foregone opportunities for higher-priced sales, it made up for in lowered risks.

The Web-enabled virtual organization does not seek alliances to reduce risk; it trolls the Net looking for business opportunities. Transparent pricing destroys high-cost producers who must operate in faceless electronic spot markets. Japanese *keiretsu* networks—and their American counterparts—will be overwhelmed by a B2B e-commerce market expected to be $700 billion in 2003 in Japan and $1.7 trillion in the United States. As these alliances break up, the risks they controlled will increase. Low-cost, always-available financing from a bank requiring only a wink and a nod will disappear, as will committed buyers. Moreover, commercial risk, the risk that buyers do not pay, will increase as transactions become more impersonal. None of this will happen because these firms wish it to be so. Rather, the spread of e-commerce will force it on them. Suppliers secretly will begin to auction off components on the Web and find that they get higher prices than they did in the alliance. As manufacturers experience sourcing problems, they too will turn secretly to the Net, to purchase in an arm's-length transaction what they formerly obtained in the alliance's relationship-based market. Instability will creep in as orders are not fulfilled or buyers fail to pay, and the cozy, structured nature of some industries will fragment. Managers who have built their careers on the basis of socializing and face time will be pushed aside by skilled Web surfers and systems analysts.

But will the virtual organization really be smaller? True, it will use the Web to outsource more than it used to, and it won't need squadrons of mid-level managers and their staffs to maintain all those *keiretsu* relationships. Transaction costs in time and money should decline as it becomes easier and cheaper to search for, acquire, and analyze market information; establish contacts; and monitor them. But what about enforcement? Order fulfillment already is a problem in e-commerce, and it could get worse, as could commercial risks if buyer-strangers skip payments. Coping with these risks was only a modest problem in the physically connected world. In the electronically connected one, risk-management costs could rise even as Net-evoked opportunities increase. Currently it is fashionable to see the virtual organization as smaller.[6] But it might end up at about the same size as corporations are today.

It might even get bigger. If e-commerce fosters globalization of markets, firms will have to get larger to handle the new business and to reap economies of scale benefits. Moreover, only larger firms will be able to offer mass customization services to consumers. Low-end mass marketers always will be around to serve the poor, and high-end customizers will serve the well-to-do. But the middle class increasingly will see the Internet as a place where they can have it all. Engineers used to say, "You can have it good, fast, or cheap. Pick two." Now they cannot say that, given e-marketers' implied promises that they can interact with e-customers on a one-to-one basis and respond with rapid delivery of inexpensive, quality goods tailored to individual needs. Order fulfillment will require extensive production and warehousing systems located near urban markets; manufacturers tying themselves as much as possible to specific customers once considered part of a mass; community involvement as a way of learning needs; and expansion of quality control and customer services. Companies may expand the number of employees rather than cut them. The virtual organization with a mass customization, global focus may have to be bigger, not smaller.

THE STRANGE CASE OF E-MAIL

We saw earlier in this chapter that e-mail is not a benefit for all organizations. Messages get misdirected and employees become overloaded. But the problems just begin there. Most people are poor typists and thus keep their messages short. Any chance of subtlety is lost, complex issues are not handled well, and differences in cultural values are not treated with any sensitivity. It seems strange that e-mail is so pervasive. But e-mail is fast, cheap, convenient, and provides for instant record-keeping. It is not going to go away, but all the talk about paper disappearing is just that, talk. As John Seely Brown and others have noted, paper is basically immutable, immobile, and past-oriented, while e-mail is mutable, mobile, and focused on the present or the future.[7] Papers—reports, memos, letters, and forms—are documents, usually considered to be reliable and valid. That means they reduce our uncertainty about something of interest to us. E-mail generally has a pre-document quality to it. A message might possibly be useful; then again it might not. As it circulates, is commented on, and evokes a new message, a point may come when a written report is generated that has gravitas in the organization. The report is based on e-mail, but it has the weight of a document while the e-mail does not. A paperless organization would be one in which no one ever would have any faith in the information crossing his or her awareness, and no one would feel confident in his or her knowledge. Risks could not easily be assessed, so no one would make risky decisions. It appears that e-mail and paper need each other and work well together. E-mail alone would be a disaster.

Managers who have tried e-mail alone for negotiating soon recognize its limitations. In a face-to-face encounter, a party can express emotions to drive a point home or to exhibit commitment. The other party soon recognizes what can and cannot be accomplished. An emotion-laden e-mail message, however, is annoying. Moreover, whereas people can soften extreme statements in face-to-face, they cannot easily do it in e-mail. In business communication, few managers employ the various typographical symbols, called emoticons, used by chat line participants, and "IMHO" ("in my humble opinion") accomplishes nothing. Negatives expressed in e-mail seem to be overweighted. In fact, in many organizations e-mail is used more frequently to send routine negative rather than positive messages. Complaints and criticisms of a minor nature are reserved for e-mail, while "attaboys" and praise occur on the telephone or face to face. And since most e-mails are copied to others, a sense grows that the organization is not a friendly place.

A solution is at hand in the form of multimedia messaging centers. These already are being developed to handle customer relations, and they eventually will be developed to deal with internal communication in a company. The center is a single system uniting e-mail, the Web, fax, telephone, file transfer, wireless, and audio/video. Instant messaging will be available with switching. Thus an e-mail sent from one employee to another can be immediately answered with text, voice, audio/video, or a combination of these. Complex, sensitive communications and routine messages can be fitted to the appropriate media. Customers or potential customers accessing a company's home page will be able to contact sales employees and actually see them as they conduct their business. Purchasing people will be able to have personalized encounters with suppliers to augment EDI and B2B forms on text-based communication. All in all, the expansion of channels in e-mail should bring it into its own in organizations as the dominant communication tool. However, its pre-document quality will remain a problem, as will problems connected to overload and privacy issues.[8]

HOW GLOBAL WILL E-COMMERCE BE?

Here is the theory. The Internet is an open, standardized, inexpensive, and convenient system for transmitting information. If so, United States firms ought to be able to speed up product development as better market information is rapidly acquired and also procurement, as improvements in supplier relationships occur. Product cycles will get shorter and market turmoil should ensue, opening up niches for new entrants in an industry. These new firms will find that e-commerce will enable them to become instant competitors without bearing high start-up costs, and marginal costs approaching zero in Web transactions will foster growth. As United States markets become saturated, global expansion will occur until the Internet will have brought about the final, complete globalization of economic life on earth. In sum, the Internet will evoke national competition, market saturation, and global expansion.

The realism of the model will not be known for some time yet, until we learn the answers to a number of questions. Will first movers on the Net enjoy increasing returns and network effects so that competition and growth are stifled? If Amazon is already there and rapidly acquiring customers who would find non-Amazon environments less convenient and more expensive, then Amazon will dominate retail bookselling and deter United States competition. No impetus for globalization will occur. Will national regulations and trade barriers bar expansion? The European Union and Japan already are developing ways to hinder U.S. global services sales over the Internet. Are existing international and national channels of supply and distribution so embedded that Internet sellers cannot easily challenge them? Economists like to believe that supply and demand determines prices, but in placid, well-functioning markets custom, habit, and accidents of history often dictate how and what people will pay for goods. Anyone disagreeing with this statement need only spend a few months in Japan to have his eyes opened.

These structural problems suggest that the theory has problems, and things get worse if we simply list the kinds of products unlikely to be sold globally through Internet transactions:

- B2B products requiring special customization, e.g., prefabricated steel beams.
- Non-branded B2C products that require buyer perceptions of trustworthiness.
- Products that are highly regulated (drugs).
- Products whose shipping costs are a major component of the end-user price.
- Products requiring lots of post-sale service and support.
- B2C products sold on credit (credit sales are not used much outside the United States).

While some of these kinds of products sell across the Internet in the United States, their chances for global markets are slim. What this suggests is that when the Internet causes saturated U.S. markets for customized, heavy, non-branded, expensive, regulated, and high-maintenance products, their prices will fall towards opportunity costs since few chances will exist for global Internet sales. Products that are commodity-like, light, branded, cheap, unregulated, and low-maintenance will do well globally in a new Net world. Over the next few decades, then, globally successful companies may be those who are first movers or good at getting around structural impediments in national markets, but real success will be due to the ability to build a sense of worldwide trustworthiness among buyers in company reputation or brand name. None of the other attributes of global products is quite as manageable as trust.

THE CENTURY OF BRANDS AND NEW INSTITUTIONS

The 19th century was noted for the emergence of mass markets and commodity-like products. By the mid-20th century, however, producers had learned that what consumers bought was more than just the obvious use value of goods. In addition, they sought benefits from the relationship with the seller, the transaction process, and the reputation of the manufacturer. In other words, they wanted products that were easy to buy from pleasant, helpful sellers and manufacturers whose reputations suggested that the products were safe and reliable. Each product, then, was or ought to be really a bundle of product, relationship, process, and reputational information. The transmission of complex product messages about these things to consumers was out of the question, but it became clear from the success of modernist writers and poets in the literary realm that symbolic communication could be employed in the commercial world. A symbol is a sign of an object by virtue of a rule or habit of interpretation rather than similarity to the object. A dollar sign is a sign denoting monetary value, but as a symbol

serving as a corporate logo, it, after consumers get or are helped to get ac-
customed to it, suggests value, wealth, and perhaps power. It also could
suggest greed and selfishness, but clever and sustained advertising and
public relations would help to reduce this line of interpretation.

The remainder of the 20th century saw the commercial appropriation of
symbolism in the form of logos, company and brand names, tag lines, and
spokespersons. With symbols, large amounts of information about complex
products could be transmitted in a highly controlled way to potential consumers. The symbols (which I will generically call brands from now on)
would not themselves directly tell anything about the products, but they
would summon up habitual thoughts and feelings which sellers felt it would
be useful for buyers to have pursuant to a transaction. By the beginning of
this century, it had been clear for a decade that symbolic modes of selling
were perfect for a global market, and the race for worldwide branding was
on. The Internet, with the global reach of corporate Web sites, seemed ideal
both for the direct selling of products and for brand building. Direct selling
globally of B2C products, as we have seen, has its problems, but the Web is indeed suitable for developing global habits of interpretation.

What makes the Web so suitable is its ability to move potential consumers out of "lean-back mode" into "lean-forward mode." The passive recipients of print and television advertising are not prepared to fully engage in
the process of building interpretive habits that brand development requires. But when they actively choose to select a corporate Web site, they
are prepped, as it were, for the operation to begin. Moreover, Web sites can
be elaborately interactive, thus establishing a dialogue in which the seller
gently can lead the buyer towards a state in which appropriate modes of
thought are embedded. None of this is operant or instrumental conditioning; the site visitor has choice all along the way, is able to be fully aware of
what's going on, and continues because the interaction is pleasant, easy,
safe, and useful. Site operators often do much more than trumpet a product's attributes and try to sell it. They will provide education and training,
portals for searching out new information, membership in clubs or organizations relevant to the industry, surveys to learn preferences, help in evalu-
ating a product before purchase, and assurances of various kinds to build
trust. Trust, after all, is at the root of branding, since consumers must have
faith that their symbol-evoked interpretive habits are reliable and helpful.[9]

So important is branding becoming that warfare has broken out in the
Internet realm over the practice. "Cybersquatters" will register a brand
(e.g., Haggis Backpackers in Scotland) as a domain name (www.
haggisbackpackers.com) solely with the aim of selling it to the brand's
owner.[10] Others will engage in "passing off," the use of a domain name
which easily could be mistaken for the brand's. A version of this is
"typosquatting," in which a user's mistaken spelling (www.amazom.com)
of a URL takes her to a rival company's site. Probably illegal is "framing,"

where one site's brand-building content is appropriated by another site, which frames the content with its own advertising. "Metatagers" are routing devices that divert searchers using key words to other sites. For those seeking *Playboy* magazine, for example, some will be directed to the site of Terri Wells, a former Playmate of the Year. Finally, there are "reactive advertisements"; these occur when a search engine company is paid to exhibit company B's banner ad when a company A search occurs.

Successful brand building on or through the Internet establishes a relationship between seller and buyer that may become something more than the arm's-length information searching and transacting envisioned by the economic model. At some point consumers are likely to expect more from Amazon than just an electronic bookstore. It could become similar to a real neighborhood bookstore, where browsers come to chat with the salespeople or each other for the sake of present community, not future economic utility. No doubt Jeff Bezos would be delighted. "We'll sell more books," he might say. But Amazon's successful branding could turn it into a quasi-institution rather than an economic agent. An institution has obligations to society and accepts them as such; an economic agent is primarily committed to gain of some sort. An institution mediates between the needs of society and those of individuals and has non-arm's-length relationships with both. Simply put, it cares, and not just because caring defends the brand and evokes profits. The complexity of modern Internet branding moves the economic paradigm some ways down the road from transactions to trust to corporate obligations to dependence of consumers on the firm to the firm defining its mission in terms of clients having equality with shareholders. The brand is tied to the consumer and she to it in a way that is no longer purely economic. Markets become *marketoids*. This is the Global Village, 21st-century model I have been exploring, in which values of stability, justice, and virtue either destroy or enrich the 19th-20th-century market paradigm, depending on one's values. The Amazons, AOLs, and Yahoos will lead the way, but the Fords and General Electrics soon may follow.

THE INTERNET, "TIME WELL SPENT," AND FLOW

Thornton May of Cambridge Technology Partners in Great Britain sees the experience of consumers on the Internet as almost an end in itself. "The new economy is not based on financial considerations but on temporal ones," he notes. "Consumers will be looking for a return on time rather than investment, and the key satisfaction rating will be 'time well spent' rather than value for money."[11] As interactions to develop brands build marketoid communities, they will be helped along by sites offering consumers flow experiences of the kind some of them will demand from the evolving workplace. As we saw in an earlier chapter, these compelling experiences result in a highly pleasurable loss of self-consciousness when skills and challenges of an interaction are balanced. Employees emerge from a flow state pleasantly surprised that so much time has passed, and they may become more motivated and more loyal to their employers. Similar effects may occur if flow conditions can be evoked when consumers or B2B buyers visit corporate Web sites.[12]

In addition to work, flow experiences are known to occur during sports and hobby activities, as well as computer use. Individuals become completely involved in an activity to the point at which time seems to stand still and nothing else matters. Thoughts and perceptions not relevant to the interaction are screened out and become insignificant. The experience itself is intensely gratifying, as are feelings about it afterwards. Web surfing clearly fosters flow for many Internet users and it seems likely that eventually corporate site builders will figure out how to provide flow for visitors, the idea being that happy consumers become brand-loyal consumers. Upscale retailers like Bloomingdale's have done this for years, offering highly involving store shopping experiences to develop buyer allegiance. Geographic and space limitations, however, have restricted the number of people who could enjoy shopping flow. No such restrictions exist on the Internet.

Creating a high challenge/high skill flow environment is not easy. Site designers somehow must attract visitors with the right skills and then must challenge them appropriately. Failure results in visitor apathy (low skills/low challenge), boredom (high skills/low challenge), or anxiety (low skills/high challenge), none of which is likely to inspire brand loyalty. Vanderbilt University researchers have found that the right kind of site visitor is comfortable using the Web, good at performing searches, and sees herself as autonomous and in control during Web surfing. The site experience must be stimulating, challenging, and meaningful. Specific e-commerce activities associated with flow are ease of ordering, contacting, canceling, payment, returns, and delivery. Extensive online customer support also is connected to flow. What all of this suggests is that consumers gain the opportunity to experience flow by *not* having to be challenged by transaction tasks. If the transaction is smooth and effortless, flow conditions are possible. Flow itself is fostered by providing site visitors with what the researchers call "excitement" and challenges to action to achieve a goal.

Interesting online games and simulations on an e-commerce site may be the best way to create flow experiences and subsequent brand loyalty. If I am buying a car online, I would love to be inserted in a simulation where I play the role of a Ford executive making decisions all along the line from product development to site selling. Then I can compare my decisions to the car I had in mind when I visited the Ford site and learn how producers and purchasers often follow different paths, to the detriment of both. This kind of involving experience certainly would embed the Ford name in my consciousness when I think of a car purchase. A real-life attempt to create flow for a site's visitors is that of Madeforchina.com, a Beijing company that seeks to provide compelling experiences for Chinese youth on its own site, 51go.com, or on sites created for other companies. As young people click through games or dwell in chat rooms, their actions are recorded, providing information on their likes and dislikes that then is made available to Madeforchina.com's clients. This is not flow to build brand loyalty, but one can envision the company moving into this market quite soon.

THE EMERGENCE OF INTERNET MARKETOIDS AND PSEUDO-MARKETOIDS

When an individual can be connected to a transaction environment at any time in any place, the whole idea of a market is called into question. The world of buying and selling, concerned as it is with expectations of future gain, on many e-commerce Web sites mixes in with a world of immediate experiencing concerned with present time well spent. These mixed worlds are similar to those of the Athenian *agora*, where transacting, administrative, and leisure activities occurred simultaneously twenty-four hours a day. Yet *agora* is not quite right for a simile to describe e-commerce sites. Consider porno sites selling sex videos. A site operator often will have a mission statement, educational material, "community" service announcements, forums, and huge amounts of free material. We could say that all of this is merely a fake commodity community designed to attract and hold potential buyers coming in the electronic door, and no doubt most sites of this sort are like that. But not all. Some operators of legitimate non-porno sales sites see what they do as a way of life rather than just a means to a way of life. Their environments could be called *marketoids* rather than markets. They are like markets in that transacting goes on, but it is transacting as a part of an integrated whole where committed people and trusting people come together to form bonds (or pseudo-bonds, if you worry about mass society) based on benevolence and allegiance as well as utility-seeking.

In Internet e-commerce brand building often is community building, and flow-like experience sometimes is an end in itself. It is all quite weird, but it tells us a little about what 21st-century e-commerce will look like.

- *In B2C and even some B2B, marketoid environments will emerge.* These will be transaction environments in which transacting gradually becomes bonding, and brand building fosters buyer stakeholders with just as much clout as shareholders.

- *Successful companies will be big.* Talk about the virtual organization cannot hide the reality that only big firms can afford to develop and operate global marketoid sites and to cope with the increased competition evoked by easy entry into e-commerce.

- *Multimedia messaging centers and attentional user interfaces will become crucial for organizational functioning.* The problems created by lack of gravitas in e-mail and overload will have to be dealt with, and coordinated messaging and message rationing will emerge as major technologies.

- *Prices will stagnate for products that cannot be globalized through e-commerce.* As e-commerce increases U.S. competition, firms will have to sell globally. But customized, heavy, non-branded, expensive, regulated, and high-maintenance products cannot be sold easily to consumers over the Internet. Their U.S. prices will stagnate, a trend that will set off ferocious brand-building efforts—and perhaps the creation of sites that are pseudo-marketoids, markets posing as something more in imitation of real marketoids.

NOTES

1. Data in this section are from "FT-IT Review," *Financial Times*, 5 July 2000; Lisa Guernsey, "The Search Engine as Cyborg," *New York Times*, 29 June 2000, D1; Lorraine Harrington and Greg Reed, "Electronic commerce (finally) comes of age," *McKinsey Quarterly*, 1996, No. 2, 68–77; "Government and the Internet," *The Economist*, 24 June 2000; "FT 500," *Financial Times*, 4 May 2000.

2. U.S. Department of Commerce, *Digital Economy 2000*. Washington: Commerce Department, Economics and Statistics Administration, June 2000.

3. Jeremiah J. Sullivan, "Experts, Expert Systems, and Organizations." In Michael Masuch, ed., *Organization, Management, and Expert Systems* (Berlin: Walter de Gruyter, 1990), 1–33.

4. As one Internet guru puts it, "There is no reason to suppose that in the future, customer support, bill processing, accounting, or any of the traditional functions of corporations will need to be done within a particular corporation or geographic area." See "Starting Up in High Gear, An Interview with Venture Capitalist Vinod Khosla," *Harvard Business Review*, 2000, 78, July-August, 96.

5. Alexandra Nusbaum, "Web cuts out an entire order of middlemen," *Financial Times*, 5 January 2000, 14.

6. On firms becoming smaller, see Larry Downes and Chunka Mui, *Unleashing the Killer App: Digital Strategies for Market Dominance* (Boston: Harvard Business School Press, 1998).

7. John Seely Brown and Paul Duguid, *The Social Life of Information* (Boston: Harvard Business School Press, 2000), 197 ff.

8. Not to worry. Help is at hand in the form of Microsoft's Attentional User Interface, a product in development. In this software, a so-called notification manager monitors incoming data in e-mail, voice mail, Internet news stories, and instant messaging notes. It alerts the user when something worthy of her attention comes in, taking into account past user decisions and preferences, time of day, and the activity the user is thought to be engaged in. Alerts would occur on PC screens, cell phones, or pagers.

9. See Sandeep Dayal, Helene Landeberg, and Michael Zeisser, "Building digital brands," *McKinsey Quarterly*, 2000, No. 2 (www.mckinseyquarterly. com/newpub/).

10. The *Financial Times* regularly publishes reviews of e-commerce that are remarkably comprehensive and insightful. The examples here are taken from vari-

ous articles in their "FT-IT Review" series. Another valuable resource is the *Wall Street Journal*'s regular e-commerce inserts.

11. Quoted in Penelope Ody, "Search for the 'Total Experience'," *Financial Times*, 19 January 2000, FT-IT Review, II.

12. Flow research is summarized in Thomas P. Novak, Donna L. Hoffman, and Yiu-Fai Yung, "Measuring the Customer Experience in Online Environments: A Structural Modeling Approach," *Marketing Science*, forthcoming. What research there is focuses on surfing in general and flow. No work yet has been done on the site experience and flow.

BIBLIOGRAPHY

Brown, John Seely, and Paul Duguid. *The Social Life of Information*. Boston: Harvard Business School Press, 2000.

Dayal, Sandeep, Helene Landeberg, and Michael Zeisser. "Building Digital Brands." *McKinsey Quarterly*, 2000, No. 2, www.mckinsyquarterly.com/newpub/.

Department of Commerce. *Digital Economy 2000*. Washington: Commerce Dept., June 2000.

Downes, Larry, and Chunka Mui. *Unleashing the Killer App: Digital Strategies for Market Dominance*. Boston: Harvard Business School Press, 1998.

"FT-IT Review." *Financial Times*, 5 July 2000.

Guernsey, Lisa. "The Search Engine as Cyborg." *New York Times*, 29 June 2000, D1.

Harrington, Lorraine, and Greg Reed. "Electronic Commerce (Finally) Comes of Age." *McKinsey Quarterly*, 1996, No. 2, 68–77.

Novak, Thomas P., Donna L. Hoffman, and Yiu-Fai Yung. "Measuring the Customer Experience in Online Environments: A Structural Modeling Approach." *Marketing Science*, forthcoming.

Nusbaum, Alexander. "Web cuts out an entire order of middlemen." *Financial Times*, 5 January 2000, 14.

Ody, Penelope. "Search for the 'Total Experience.'" *Financial Times*, 19 January 2000, FT-IT Review, II.

Sullivan, Jeremiah J. "Experts, Expert Systems, and Organizations." In Michael Masuch, ed., *Organization, Management, and Expert Systems*. Berlin: Walter de Gruyter, 1990, 1–33.

CHAPTER 12

THE MULTINATIONALS: FACING UP TO THE CHALLENGES

During the 1990s globalization was threatened by banking and currency crises in Mexico, Asia, Russia and Brazil; the collapse of OECD efforts to develop a multinational agreement on investment; and the derailment of the WTO's trade liberalization efforts during the Battle of Seattle in 1999. Yet none of these events had more than a momentary effect on the mergers and acquisition activities which constitute the major share of cross-border, non-portfolio global capital flows. From 1990 to 1999 annual world foreign direct investment grew from about $200 billion to over $800 billion. Almost 75 percent of these flows consisted of European and American corporations buying and selling each other. Even so, in 1999 $198 billion was associated with developing countries, 500 percent more than in 1990. The globalization process is now well under way, and the engines pulling it along are the 53,000 multinational corporations, whose foreign revenues account for 7 percent of world gross domestic product.[1] These companies control 450,000 affiliates and subsidiaries, an average of nine each, suggesting that most MNCs are medium-sized firms that may have to get bigger to survive in an Internet-driven world of the kind described in Chapter 11. Their affiliates' revenues are growing faster than world trade, an indication that entrenching themselves in host-country markets is their goal rather than exporting back to the home country. Mostly they are American, European, and Japanese manufacturers seeking to get closer to foreign customers in an increasingly competitive world where deep knowledge of end-user needs spells out the difference between success and failure, but they also are expanding into service businesses such as distribution and marketing.

Except for the big oil companies, which are highly internationalized, American multinationals have tended to focus on American markets. Where 46 percent of Siemens' employees are foreigners, only 35 percent of General Electric's are. Forty-seven percent of Volkswagen's workers are outside of Germany, compared to General Motors' 34 percent. Even IBM still has about 50 percent of its staff in the United States. Most mid-sized U.S. multinationals, firms with about 500 employees each, three or four subsidiaries, and perhaps 30 percent of revenues from foreign trade and investment, have just started going global, and they still are feeling their way. An executive of an aerospace parts manufacturer once asked me for advice about setting up shop in Southeast Asia. "You had better get to know Kuala Lumpur," I replied. "Who's he?" the executive asked. This is ignorance with a vengeance. I call it the pride of ignorance, the faith in one's knowledge and beliefs to the point that what one does not know is deemed inconsequential. Most American managers in multinationals are not bumpkins of this sort, but even they are not prepared for the challenges they will face in the coming decades. As they go about their business learning the ways of the new world, their old world is about to change. And as it changes, the global order also will change.

THE EXTENDED ORDER VS. THE GLOBAL VILLAGE

In Chapter 3, I described Friedrich Hayek's revelation in *The Fatal Conceit* that the economic model does not emerge out of laws of nature. Market exchange behavior, he claimed, is unnatural, incoherent, and fabulously successful at improving human well-being. The extended order of the model is submitted to out of an almost embittered recognition of its benefits rather than some felt urge, genetically based, to truck and barter. Hayek's claims may be overblown, since humans at times do seem to pursue exchange as part of their nature. The real issue, then, is the extent to which truck and barter behavior dominates human nature. Hayek thinks very little, and a whole range of thinkers and activists agrees. But they then make the conclusion Hayek does not: if humans are predisposed to follow some other model, then that model should guide economic, social, and political life in the new, globalized world.

What would the non-extended order model look like? In *Politics*, Aristotle argued, "It is clearly better that property should be private; but the use of it common; and the special business of the legislator is to create in men this benevolent disposition."[2] Thus economic life was associated with virtuous behavior, a belief echoed in the writings of Thomas Aquinas and even John Maynard Keynes, who felt that the goal of ethics was to guide individuals to a life well lived, with economics providing the tools to achieve the good life. Like most economists, Keynes saw the price-auction market system as usually the best way to allocate goods most efficiently in periods of scarcity. But in the Middle Ages, Jewish thinkers like Moses Maimonides (1135–1204) in *Guide of the Perplexed* claimed that authorities' reason and creativity were better than markets at allocation, a belief echoed in the work of medieval Christian thinkers. By the 17th and 18th centuries the idea had emerged that individual selfishness acting within market exchanges led to prosperity. This model, prominently displayed in Bernard Mandeville's *Fable of the Bees* (the full version was published in 1733), arguing that "private vices" evoked "public benefits," broke Aristotle's linking of economics and virtue.

> The root of evil, avarice,
> That damned ill-natured baneful vice,
> Was slave to prodigality,
> That noble sin; whilst luxury
> Employed a million of the poor,
> And odious pride a million more:
> Envy itself, and vanity,
> Were ministers of industry;
> That darling folly, fickleness,
> In diet, furniture and dress,
> That strange ridiculous vice was made
> The very wheel that turned the trade.[3]

Eventually Adam Smith got around to publishing a counter theory in *The Theory of Moral Sentiments* (1759) and *Inquiry into the Nature and Causes of the Wealth of Nations* (1776). Instead of market benefits being based on avarice, pride, envy, vanity, and fickleness, they were rooted in "sympathy," a term suggesting empathetic fellow feeling, a sense of morality, and an idea of community. The invisible hand guiding the truck and barter which everyone now agreed was universal, whether natural or not, was ethical rather than immoral. Battle lines began to be drawn, and the two camps today are growing further apart. Defenders of the Smithian market model associate exchange with fellow feeling and call for freely functioning markets globally. Mandevillean positions are more complex. At one extreme, communists sought the eventual destruction of markets and fascists wanted to replace them with authority. At the other, extended order enthusiasts like Hayek said something like, "Hold your noses and vote for capitalism." After totalitarian models faded violently from the scene in the 20th century, the extended order, Mandevillean model began to be noticed, and what the justice, order, virtue, and sovereignty people saw they did not like. For them the Smithian paradigm did not describe the way the world really worked—the globe would be a lot nicer place if it did—and the extended order was too little a reward for enduring the 20th century's horrible wars against totalitarianism. A new way was needed, called the Third Way in Europe or the Asian Way in Asia. In Chapter 1, I called it the Global Village, since Internet-based communitarianism will play a leading role in the 21st century's attack on the extended order.

How do the two orders compare? Following Hayek, the Global Village supporter admits that markets and prosperity are linked, but she finds the unnaturalness of it all offensive and looks for a more appropriate social model in which markets are restrained in in favor of more lofty values and goals.

Claims of the 20th-Century Extended Order	Response of the 21st-Century Global Village
• Economic exchange should be based on arm's-length transactions of independent individuals acting purely in their own future self-interests within market environments.	• Exchange of this kind is hateful and unnatural. It must be modified by a commitment to justice, order, community, and virtue. Market environments are marketoids, in which individuals and firms are interdependent.
• Labor is an unpleasant activity to be endured out of an expectation of future gain.	• Labor can be in large part a process of ongoing pleasant experiences.
• Nature is to be exploited on behalf of shareholders and consumers.	• Nature is to be cherished on behalf of employees, the people, and the globe.
• Governments are or ought to be powerful advocates for the free flow of goods, people, services, capital, and technology.	• NGOs ought to be powerful advocates of managed flows on behalf of the people, nature, culture, victims, indigenous groups, and the gendered.
• Valued business behavior of individuals is that which evokes the greatest benefits for the greatest number.	• Valued business behavior is rooted in a courageous adherence to what is right and good.

MULTINATIONALS ARE CAUGHT IN THE MIDDLE

To some extent the extended order is enshrined in law; U.S. corporations usually must act in accord with shareholder profit demands. But they increasingly have been following a stakeholder model, a late 20th-century idea developed to account for criticisms of the extended order, in which the firm takes into account the needs of the public, employees, consumers, and the environment in setting its strategies. The next step beyond the stakeholder model is the Global Village, in which parties to exchange and production activities are much more interdependent. The multinationals based in the United States have resisted this move, thereby bringing down on themselves the wrath of advocates who award them extensive global power which they may or may not have, and then call for taking it away so no changes can occur. Prime Minister Mahathir of Malaysia, for example, sees the multinationals as threats to national sovereignty.

A situation of worldwide oligopoly seems to be emerging. If market forces are allowed free play, then oligopolies may end up as monopolies. I believe that the general consensus is that monopolies are unhealthy. Can it be possible that a corporation is not a monopoly in its country of domicile but a monopoly in the rest of the world? In such a case whose laws will apply? And if we restrain them, would we be accused of not subscribing to globalization and liberalization?[4]

More broadly focused and future-oriented are the members of Corporate Watch:

Instead of creating an integrated global village, these firms are weaving webs of production, consumption, and finance that bring economic benefits to, at most, a third of the world's people. Two-thirds of the world (the bottom 20 percent of the rich countries and the bottom 80 percent of the poor countries) are either left out, marginalized, or hurt by these webs of activity.[5]

According to Corporate Watchers, "The Top 200 [multinationals] are creating a global economic apartheid, not a global village. . . . This inequality, fueled by accelerated corporate concentration, deserves to be a central issue in the political debates of this period."

The thinking here is that the emergence of a Global Village inhabited by interdependent nations defending culturalist and peoples' interests cannot come into being because of the growing power of the multinationals. Even their stakeholder activities, undertaken as last-ditch efforts to shore up a threatened extended order, are received as merely part of a ploy to further entrench themselves. If multinationals build roads, set up schools, and improve labor standards in Malaysian export processing zones, Mr. Mahathir will accuse them of threatening his people's autonomy and NGO critics will see a power grab. "Do we really want a social-responsibility movement, where we have the corporations throw us some crumbs while they accumulate more power?" asked Russel Mokhaiber of the legal newsletter "Corporate Crime Reporter." "Or do we want to challenge the notion of the corporation. They shouldn't have the power that they have."[6] Of course, if the multinationals did not build the roads or schools or treat workers better than local markets required, they would be subjected to even more bitter criticism as outmoded defenders of a vile economic order whose time has come. No matter what they do, they cannot win, and when you don't win, you lose.

According to the Institute for Policy Studies' *Field Guide to the Global Economy*, "Debates rage around the world as to whether corporate-driven globalization helps or hinders the aspirations of the majority of people on earth."[7] As U.S. corporations invest abroad, they allegedly create a global labor pool in which American workers cannot compete with laborers who have weak labor rights and are paid exceptionally low wages. Multinational biotechnology firms supposedly are gaining control of the world's food supply and developing genetically engineered crops that could wipe out biodiversity. Corporations are accused of choosing production locations in nations where conservation and environmental protection laws are lax or not enforced, and thereby depleting fishing stocks, exhausting timber resources, and destroying the land with open-pit mines. They then are said to use threats of further capital flow abroad to force easing of environmental rules in the United States. As multinationals globalize they are accused of fostering increased inequality in the world and within countries, with the top getting richer and the bottom poorer (for more on this, see below). According to the *Field Guide*, U.S. companies' efforts to minimize their tax obligations are a sign that they now have little national loyalty, and their support for free-trade policies helps to "widen the gap between rich and poor, . . . increase social tensions in countries, and poison the ground for democratic development."[8] The international lending policies of the large banks allegedly bring on financial crises, which the handmaidens of the multinationals, the IMF and the World Bank, then must try to clean up by further immiserating the poor.

U.S. labor unions have led this attack on globalization and the multinationals, but they have plenty of support. In 1999 in Mexico City, Pope John Paul II said, "If globalization is ruled merely by the laws of the market applied to suit the powerful, the consequences cannot but be negative." In San Antonio, Texas, a few years earlier, the Benedictine Sisters filed a shareholder resolution with Alcoa, requesting that the company pay its Mexican employees adequate wages. Similar actions regularly are undertaken by the Interfaith Center for Corporate Responsibility, an association of 250 religious groups. Multinational labor practices are a concern of the American Friends Service Committee and the Rugmark Foundation in America, and the Clean Clothes Campaign in Europe. Environmental issues are raised by the Blue Angel program in Germany and by Greenpeace. One group, Equal Exchange in Massachusetts, tries to set up global channels of distribution that bypass multinationals, while the Center for a New American Dream educates people to simplify their lifestyles so they will be less in thrall to multinational consumerism. The Center of Concern promotes "just" international finance, while Jubilee 2000 wants to cancel poor-country debt. Multinational Monitor does exposés of global corporations, the Polaris Institute works "to counter corporate rule," and the Program on Corporations, Law and Democracy "challenges the excessive power of corporations."[9] Multinationals in the 21st century are not going to have an easy time of it. Although their detractors today are fragmented and somewhat at cross-purposes with each other, they are beginning to coalesce around the Global Village paradigm and will use the Internet to spread their messages and strengthen relationships.

MULTINATIONALS ARE CREATING HOMO ECONOMICI

The hostility, even downright hatred, towards multinational enterprises occurs in spite of or perhaps because of their generally benign impact on societies. They tend to pay higher-than-average wages, create jobs faster than their local competitors, foster innovation through R&D spending, improve employees' skills through training, and earn lots of hard currency through increased exporting.[10] But the greater their success, the more they allegedly undermine local communities and traditional ways of living, alter in unhappy ways the distribution of income and wealth, generate insecurity, degrade the environment, and "create human individuals of a particular sort: homo economicus, or egoistic, maximizing man," according to Michael Prowse.[11] This last criticism is more fundamental than the rest and alerts us to what is really going on: a growing battle between defenders of the extended order and those Global Villagers, like Mr. Prowse, who are aghast at "the spread of western materialistic values."

There are many hues of capitalism, depending on the degree to which market values are subordinated to broader social goals and interests. By default the world is now opting for a version of capitalism in which the profit motive is largely unrestrained. To be blunt, it is choosing an American flavor of capitalism.

For the Michael Prowses of the world the problem of multinationals extending the Americanist extended order must be dealt with, and they would like to see a "World Social Organization to represent the interests of the victims of market competition or to promote globally effective welfare policies" and a "World Environmental Organization to ensure that policies favored by global business do not have deleterious ecological consequences."[12]

Critics fear that the armies of homo economicus are on the march, and the multinationals are carrying their banners. Regardless of the good they foster, then, they must be countered. In 1990 roughly 5,000 nongovernmental international organizations existed. By 1999 there were over 25,000 of them.[13] This "NGO-swarm" flits about, but it can be mobilized and focused quickly through e-mail and the Web. About 1,500 domestic and international NGOs supported the 1999 Seattle demonstrations that halted the WTO meeting. I recall seeing people on the streets carrying signs such as "Gays and Lesbians Against Free Trade" and "Raging Grannies." In April 2000 thousands of protestors, including people from the National Queer Commission and the Social Justice Center of South Central Kansas, converged on Washington, DC, to express their feelings about the World Bank, the IMF, China joining the WTO, and a number of other issues. What united them was more than a desire to gang up on reigning NGOs like the IMF or to stop multinational expansion. As one protestor told a journalist, "all these separate issues . . . all have the same root—capitalism, corporate greed."[14] They want to change the model, and attacks on the extended order's shock troops are the way to do it. By 2000 polls suggested that Americans generally felt that U.S. trade policy favored multinationals over working Americans and that protestors deserved sympathy.[15] It was becoming clear that globalization was not the only cause for concern. It was also globalization in accord with the old economic model paradigm. In April 2000, the Starbucks Corporation, ever alert to change, began selling "Fair Trade Certified Coffee." Other multinationals soon would have to develop similar accommodating policies, it seemed.

THE BATTLE OVER INEQUALITY

Protestors and Global Villagers cannot run around yelling, "The corporations are all making homo economici of you and must be stopped." No one would listen. Instead, they fix on hot-button issues, and one of them is growing inequality between haves and have-nots. The argument takes many forms, but generally it goes something like this:

- Instead of globalization being a benign process of expanded communal relations, it currently is characterized by multinational corporations expanding capital and consumer markets globally through trade and investment.

- The extended order's market model of globalization is displacing local and culture-bound ways of distribution and investment.

- This disruption is fragmenting tightly-knit societies into hierarchies of winners and losers. The resulting growth of inequality hinders educational development and is associated with destabilizing corruption and social unrest.

- Educational decline, corruption, and unrest are associated with a decline in real well-being, in contrast to mere economic well-being.

According to Steven Bezruchka, whose views are typical of the anti-multinationals group, globalization carried out by large corporations is threatening world health.[16] The big companies are fostering pollution, their genetically modified foods are harming people, they flood the world each year with over a trillion cancer-causing cigarettes, and they exploit child laborers. If we step back from these alleged "facts," however, we supposedly can see a model emerging in which global capital's expansion is fostering a general decline in the well-being of peoples as inequality grows. Both within countries and between them, the rich get richer and the poor get poorer. According to Mr. Bezruchka, "Within poor countries, more people have been displaced from their subsistence economics than have been able to find jobs in the manufacturing sectors in overcrowded cities." In poor countries, a well-to-do elite profits from this shift, and income inequality grows. But inequality also grows in rich countries as low-skilled workers are replaced by developing-country labor.[17]

Inequality does seem to foster lower education levels and more social unrest.[18] But this is not to say that the Global Villagers' model is valid. For that to be so, increased trade and investment—mostly done by multinationals—would have to foster increased inequality. As trade as a percent of GDP increases, however, average incomes in a country increase and inequality begins to decrease somewhat as average per capita income for the poor keeps pace. In fact, as trade and investment-inspired economic growth occurs, productivity increases, as does per capita income in a country. It appears that the onward march of the extended order is the best thing that could happen to the world's poor. A 2000 study by the A.T. Kearney company showed that rapidly globalizing countries had economic growth rates 30 to 50 percent higher than nations less open to multinational investment and trade, and greater improvements in infant mortality rates, life expectancy, literacy, and government spending on social programs.[19] As globalization has increased, the number of people earning less than $2 per day in inflation-adjusted purchasing-power terms fell from 1.3 billion in 1980 to 727 million in 1990.

Why then do the Global Village advocates make the argument, as Mobilization for Global Justice puts it, that corporations are working hard "to create today's unjust, destructive global economic order" that is attacking "human and ecological dignity."?[20] For one thing, world inequality may be on the rise. While this probably is due more to the rich getting richer than the poor poorer, it still is worrisome. Moreover, as the A.T. Kearney study found, when multinationals show up in greater numbers, air pollution and bribery seem to increase. Using corruption measures developed by Transparency International, a widely respected organization that monitors corporate behavior, the study found that from 1980 to 1990 corruption increased 70 percent in the rapidly globalizing economies but only 11 percent in the slow movers. One could argue, as we earlier have seen John Gray do in *False Dawn: The Delusions of Global Capitalism* (2000), that the extended order is a threat to liberal civilization and decency in the world. The more capitalism's economic model expands, the greater the occurrences in nations of decay, fragmentation, and social collapse. This extreme view, based on an anticapitalist ideology and selective use of data, nevertheless has a certain resonance. Recall that Hayek's basic theme was "Hold your nose and vote for capitalism." In refusing to hold their noses anymore, Professor Gray and the other Villagers are saying that globalization in the 21st century ought to be of quite a different variety than globalization in the 20th. They are not against globalization but rather the centrality of the economic model and corporations to its development.

Notice that economic model defenders and Villagers talk past each other in debates. Set aside inequality and instability discussions, say the extended order people, and focus on the real increases in material well-being that increased multinationals' activity has brought about. Villagers loudly proclaim that real well-being is a life well lived in an ordered, just, sovereign, and virtuous society and that globalization led by the big corporations is threatening that. The inequality their actions supposedly evoke is unjust and fragments national identities, while the corruption they engender is immoral and triggers social unrest and disorder.

CORRUPTION AND THE MULTINATIONALS

Just what is the connection between corruption and the multinationals? Corruption, the abuse of public office by officials for private gain, destabilizes societies by eroding public confidence in institutions and fosters contempt for the law. Although it comes in many forms, such as fraud, embezzlement, nepotism, and extortion, bribery is its most noteworthy characteristic and is most associated with the actions of multinational foreign investors.[21] Sometimes brown paper bags full of cash are exchanged so that "licenses" may be obtained. Perhaps "consulting" firms owned by a minister are hired to perform trivial work. In Indonesia the practice is to loan a public official funds so that he can invest in a project with a multinational partner. Naturally the loan will never be paid off. As corruption in all its varieties becomes pervasive, the social fabric begins to fray. Citizens try desperately to avoid paying taxes that they know will be stolen. Worthy antipoverty and education programs go unfunded. The failure of bribed inspectors to do their jobs leads to building collapses. If A.T. Kearney is right and increases in multinationals' trade and investment do foster corruption and instability in a country here and there, then the Global Villagers will be able to add the corruption argument to the inequality argument in their anti-multinationals rhetoric.

No one paid much attention to the effects of corruption until the mid-1990s, when Transparency International (TI) began publishing its Corruption Perceptions Index for a list of 99 countries (as of 1999). Based on surveys of business people, the general public, and country analysts, its data are now widely used by banks in assessing the risks of cross-border loans, and its press releases receive wide public attention. In 1999 TI added a second data set, the Bribe Payers Index, to identify countries whose private citizens and corporations are most likely to be bribe payers abroad. The cleanest countries were Sweden, Australia, Canada, and Austria—the United States ranked ninth. The dirtiest among leading trading nations were China, South Korea, Taiwan, and Italy. Most bribery occurs in the public works, construction, and defense sectors.[22] Although TI data suggest that corporations in the United States and Europe are rather upright and honest most of the time in their international dealings, the blatant corruption-supporting behavior of many Asian multinationals provides all the evidence critics need to give at least some credibility to their claims that multinationals are fostering instability and disorder in the world. The fact that foreign bribing is illegal for American managers, some of whom have gone to jail for their sins, has not deterred anti-multinational activists in the least, who eagerly smear U.S. corporations for the activities of Korean and Italian firms.

COUNTRY RISK, BUSINESS RISK, AND GLOBAL RISK

If the world's peoples come to believe that globalizing multinationals are behind the growth in inequality and corruption-induced social decay, these firms will be less and less welcome in nations targeted for investment. Currently this is not the case, since critics of the economic model have not yet made a coordinated argument of the kind described in this book. But when the justice, order, sovereignty, and virtue advocates come together to make common cause, perhaps after some severe economic downturn evokes a "we've-got-to-do-something" mind-set, country risks will increase for multinational foreign investors, who might respond by reducing their business risks. The globalization movement as an extension of the economic model then could come to a quick stop and perhaps turn into something else. This to some extent is the scenario hinted at by Robert Kaplan in *The Coming Anarchy*:

corporations will be free for a few decades to leave behind the social and environmental wreckage they create. . . . Ultimately, as technological innovations continue to accelerate and the world's middle classes come closer together, corporations may well become more responsible to the cohering global community and less amoral in the course of their evolution toward new political and cultural forms.[23]

Risk is the probability of loss, and every corporate manager knows that there is no free lunch; every gain comes at the expense of increased risk. And sometimes risk turns into reality. The trick is to assess the risks a firm faces so that they are neither too small nor too large. Small risks are associated with small profits, while large risks presage big gains until the occasional catastrophic loss. In international economic activities it is best to categorize risks as those associated with market peril (business risk) and nonmarket peril (country risk). Business risks involve potential losses from increased competition, cost-control problems, loss of buyer interest in the firm's products or prices, and similar events. These are the dangers inherent in doing business, regardless of the setting. Country risk refers to possible losses due to political, macroeconomic, social, and physical conditions in a specific country. Perhaps the government destroys the company's investment by expropriating its assets or regulating it to death. Or the central bank floods the economy with money, setting off destabilizing inflation.

Rioting, earthquakes, and other social and physical upheavals may occur, ruining any chance of success.

Multinationals doing business in a country assess their overall level of risk and then take steps to reduce it, manage it, or avoid it. If business risk is high but country risk low, a company might conclude that an investment is worth continuing if the return on the investment is adequate. The same would be true if business risk is low but country risk high. However, one of the ways of describing globalization, as I noted in Chapter 1, is the increase in worldwide competition. Business risks, in other words, are rising everywhere. If country risk also is high, a multinational is likely to stay out of that environment unless return on investment is exceptionally high, in the range of 30 to 50 percent annually, or, as in China, future prospects are bright. If country risks rise everywhere, globalization will most likely stop. This is a real possibility if Global Villagers ever manage to coalesce and mount a sustained, country-by-country attack on multinationals. In an age of anywhere, anytime communication, this is a very real possibility.

What can multinationals that want to continue expanding do about these dangers? For one thing, they can begin to assess *global risk* as well as specific business and country risks for each market. Global risk is the probability of loss due to worldwide hostility to the extended order's economic model in general and multinational corporations in particular. It can be estimated as the probability in a period of a coordinated coalition emerging among justice, order, virtue, and national identity advocates multiplied by the probability of the world's peoples buying into their anti-model message. Over the next few decades the probability of a coalition emerging seems high, so the key to assessing global risk is the extent to which the extended order begins to lose its cachet. It survived in the 20th century by its defenders simply pointing out the horrors of totalitarian alternatives. That rhetoric is no longer viable. What will be needed to manage global risk is a massive, coordinated global effort by multinationals to convince people that the benefits of the extended order are greater than the occasionally unjust, disorderly, immoral, and culture-threatening acts perpetrated in its name.

Such an effort only could come about with the support of a major political force, namely the president of the United States. He or she will have to become a globe-trotter in defense of the market model. Since there are no electoral votes in Brazil, the likelihood of this occurring is small. Indeed, at some point in the century an antimarket U.S. president seems inevitable. The antimarket, Village model's attack on multinationals then would gain a powerful supporter. Thus, given all the possible scenarios, global risk is primed to increase. The U.S. president either will not provide the leadership needed to spearhead a worldwide defense of the extended order or will actively work against it.

If global risk increases, corporations will have several options. They may go it alone without political support and mount global campaigns of the "markets:-you-can't-do-without-them" sort. On the face of it this approach seems doomed to failure. Or they one-by-one in each country will try to reduce country risks by making themselves valued and indispensible corporate citizens, vividly attentive to a wide variety of stakeholder needs. This seems to be the current program. However, in the long term corporate focus will shift to the reduction of business risk due to the increased competition associated with globalization. The multinationals will not retreat from globalizing, but they will undertake efforts to reduce competition. We can expect an increase in cross-border mergers and acquisition and strategic alliances, as well as more blatant anticompetitive practices such as price-fixing, market allocation schemes, and licensor-licensee noncompetition agreements. While most countries have laws against these things, enforcement is spotty on the national level and quite difficult when violations involve cross-border conspiracies hatched on a global scale.[24] A final option will be to persuade governments to actively manage the business risks of large corporations in the home markets so that they can endure higher risks as they globalize. The disastrous practices of the Japanese government over the last fifty years may be replicated in a number of European and developing nations over the next fifty.

MANAGING THE SPREAD IN JAPAN

For decades after the Pacific War, Japanese government policies drove a number of initiatives designed to ensure that economic growth occurred. To create a huge fund of savings for investment in new machinery, land tax regulations were developed to keep land off the market (punitive taxes would be levied if anyone dared to sell his or her land). With growing housing demand and a static supply, land prices rose to the point where families had to save heavily if they were to have any hope of purchasing a house and the land on which it rested. This factor, plus high education costs and low social security, drove Japanese savings up. Then the Bank of Japan and the government managed corporate loan rates so that they were low. This often required money supply growth of 15 percent annually, but inflation was avoided by administrative guidance on pricing and export promotion to foster increased volumes, economies of scale, and productivity rises which matched money growth with output growth. These moves to push unit costs down occurred in tandem with policies to keep prices high. Cartels were tolerated in some industries, and regulations made entry into other industries difficult. Various anticompetitive practices pushed prices to world-high levels and held them there. The result was a constant spread between unit costs and revenues in large firms which, while not high, could be relied on. Managers were not afraid to seek increased financing, nor were banks worried about making loans. The result was low business risk and bank-financed domestic growth that went on for years.

The system which maintained the riskless spread depended on docile consumers without access to foreign goods or even information about foreign prices. It also required careful government manipulation of land values, social welfare practices, money supply, subsidies, trade and foreign investment barriers, and competition policies so that the spread always was positive. Negative spread—unit costs above unit revenues—would foster a sense of risk in corporate executives, and Japanese managers, like all managers, do not respond well to risk. Things started to fall apart in the mid-1970s, when rising inflation stalled export growth and soaring oil prices pushed costs up. Industrial production fell dramatically, and the spread went negative. What turned things around by the late 1970s was inflation and high interest rates in the United States, which pushed the dollar up, and a collective decision by Americans to reduce savings. They used the increased purchasing power of a high dollar to buy Japanese cars and electronic products.

This episode signaled to the government serious problems the economy would experience if the U.S. consumption engine sputtered and the dollar resumed its downward trend. Japan's elites decided that a strategy of low business risk at home supporting export-funded growth was too chancy, and they determined to push very reluctant Japanese corporations into foreign direct investment, especially in the United States, since Japanese companies in America would benefit from any trade barriers that went up there and might even become exporters to the rest of the world if the dollar's fall of the 1970s resumed in the 1980s (which it did in 1986). The money supply was increased, and firms were encouraged to invest their yen in equity and land, which then could be used as collateral to fund global investing. Everything worked as planned for a time, and exporting even increased as U.S. subsidiaries owned by Japanese firms purchased home-produced components for their assembly operations. But globalism coupled with communication improvements had unforeseen effects.

As Japan's corporate giants expanded, television coverage followed them abroad, and Japanese began to observe the lifestyles of Americans and Europeans with jaw-dropping amazement. As one friend of mine put it, "I knew that Americans lived better than we did, but seeing that Italians also lived better was too much to take." The Japanese consumer thus began a slow boil which finally spilled over in the 1990s when she threw up her hands, proclaimed "Enough!" and refused to buy until prices came down. It took many years for rage at high prices—one pillar of the spread—to express itself, but when it came, it terrified the corporations. Even worse, the 1980s birth of globalization and the waning of the Cold War awakened Americans to the consequences of Japanese trade barriers. Endless U.S. pressure ensued, and, as barriers began to come down, competition heated up in Japan and the era of stable high prices and low business risk began to come to an end.

Not only did the revenue side of the spread come under threat from Japanese consumers and U.S. competition, but the cost side began to crumble as lifetime employees of the 1960s became high-salaried 1990s middle managers and young Japanese abandoned their docility and started demanding higher wages. The rising yen also raised U.S. importers' costs when expressed in dollars, and Japanese exporters who could not cut prices started to experience losses. Throughout most of the 1990s, the spread was near zero or even negative, and business confidence in the system crumbled. The banks became reluctant to lend. Companies lacked financing from banks—and with no profits, a moribund equity market, and a small bond market—they floundered. The government desperately toyed with the old remedies: manipulation of interest rates (to the lowest levels recorded in 300 years), various nontariff trade barriers, tolerance of anticompetitive practices, and so forth, but it soon became clear that the old system was dead. From now on, Japanese corporations will have to look after the spread on their own, and they are ill prepared to do this. Their globalizing has been based on government efforts to keep business risk in Japan low so that they could take on more business and country risk outside of Japan. Those efforts have collapsed, and Japan's multinationals and their bankers now find themselves facing higher overall risk than they would have taken on without government's risk-management efforts. Some big failures of banks and corporations have occurred, and more failures are on the way.

In spite of the Japanese experience, however, other governments will feel compelled to follow a similar path when the pressures of global competition increase, as they almost certainly will. Tolerance for anticompetitive practices, currently in decline, may begin growing again, and Japanese-style policies to increase the spread by pushing up prices and to reduce home-market business risk will emerge. When high-priced domestic products are undercut by imports, nontariff trade barriers, which a weakened WTO will be unable to control, will rise. Export-promotion policies, already quite prominent in Europe and the United States, will become major elements of political agendas. The ideas may take hold that risky globalization is crucial for a country's economic strength and that its corporations will pull back from global efforts unless governments reduce their risks at home. All of these things look very much like a replay of 17th- and 18th-century European mercantilism, and one hopes that a 21st-century Adam Smith will emerge to put a stop to it. But the passionate, towering intellects of this century are as likely as not going to be Global Village advocates who will misinterpret government risk-reduction policies in service to multinational success and economic strength as moves towards more ordered, just, and communal societies. After all, support of this kind from the well-meaning and good-intentioned allowed Japan to pursue its follies for fifty years.

THE ROLES OF THE MULTINATIONAL WILL CHANGE

Multinational enterprises mostly take the corporate form as extended across borders. But what is a corporation? In Japan corporations are sometimes called "fate-sharing" institutions, collections of managers and employees who have thrown in their lot with one another to achieve a better standard of living than each could achieve alone. Some American economists take a similar collectivist view, but instead of emphasizing bonds of affiliation and allegiance as the unifying elements of the organization, as the Japanese do, they see contractual obligations as the defining feature of the corporation. This kind of talk infuriates critics, who point out that one of the earliest multinational corporations, the British East India Company, operated with sovereign-like powers during its existence from 1600 to 1858. It often minted its own currency, maintained its own army, and exercised legal jurisdiction within the regions where it did business. Its failures also brought on the Indian Mutiny, in which thousands perished. To speak of the East India Company as a set of contracts and exchange relations is unseemly and obtuse, two unfortunate characteristics of 20th-century economic thinking about industrial organizations. Yet how can one speak of it? It wasn't really a sovereign state, nor was it a community of fate-sharers (freebooters would be a better term). This muddle over the nature of the multinational corporation continues to this day.

Legal theorists and economists currently tend to see the multinational as a device for raising and mobilizing capital to develop worldwide production, distribution, and marketing systems. One element of what we call globalization is the progressive rationalization, coordination, and integration of these systems. Governments have tended to recognize the value of corporations and have protected them by treating them as "natural entities," a legal term meaning that corporations to some extent enjoy the same rights that individuals have, especially property rights and the right to enter into contracts and engage in exchange. In a sense they are imaginary individuals whose function is to accumulate real profit.

In the 20th century these imaginary individuals were thought to be guided by either the Mandevillean, extended order economic model in which great greed leads inexorably to greater well-being in society or by Adam Smith's model, sometimes called the stakeholder paradigm, in which fellow feeling and a moral sense constrain and channel self-interest. But as we have seen in this book, a new, communitarian model of economic life is rapidly coming into existence, in which both real and imaginary individuals will be guided by values associated with order, justice, virtue, and identity.

- *Multinationals will be asked to adhere to and support an expanded model of growth in societal well-being.* Economic growth over the last 200 years has been defined as an increase in the total value of goods and services produced in a society, with the optimal growth condition that in which no feasible growth-model alternative makes everyone better off than the existing one. This Pareto optimality condition is exceedingly difficult to specify concretely, so economists tend to see anything that fosters GNP increases as good and anything that doesn't as bad.[25] GNP increases in countries are associated with higher savings and investment, better education, improved health, and generally higher living standards for lots of people. The inability of experts to say whether or not these conditions are Pareto optimal opens the door to arguments from those whom I have been calling Global Villagers. They claim, first, that GNP growth produces too many losers—it's not Pareto optimal—and, second, that real well-being, a broader concept not addressed by economists, is often hurt by the global activities of multinational corporations. Economic well-being growth involves an increase in "utility," meaning more pleasure or less pain associated with generally better material conditions. Real well-being growth focuses on an individual's heightening sense of coherence in a just, ordered, moral existence. Economists emphasize aggregates, Villagers individuals. The one speaks of utility, the other coherence. In the emerging Village paradigm, multinationals will be asked, "What have you done to make individuals experience a more meaningful, coherent existence? How has your corporate strategy in a society increased the likelihood that a randomly chosen individual can say that her life makes more sense than it did before?" Answering that the company has offered higher-quality goods at lower prices will be deemed not so much a wrong answer as a woefully inadequate one.

- *Multinationals will begin to emphasize obligations as well as interests.* In the economic model, rational corporate executives have an interest in maximizing (subject to various constraints) shareholder gains. In the 20th century pressure from corporate critics could be treated as a constraint. The 21st century probably will see a powerful communitarian model emerge which forces multinationals to do well what the British East India Company did badly: act more as an institution with obligations than as an imaginary individual with interests. Societal obligations will move from constraints to goals existing side by side with profit goals. The hypocrisy underlying 20th-century corporate public-service pronouncements will drain away, leaving in the current century what could very well be a genuine sincerity.

- *Multinationals will try to manage global risk, which is likely to increase.* The shift towards greater multinational commitment to real well-being and societal obligations will be a decades-long process, involving massive, global-wide protests against corporate goals and actions and attacks on the theoretical and ideological bases for the economic model. Corporations initially will try to manage the global risks through equally massive public-relations campaigns and the mobilization of political support. As these efforts peter out, they will seek to reduce business risks as a counter to growing global risk. The occurrence of anticompetitive practices will increase, as will a home country's subsidies and protection for its national champions. The uproar from all of these risk-management practices may hasten the movement towards the Global Village model of expanded "marketoids" rather than merely an extended market order, involving goals of coherence and obligation rather than utility and interests.

NOTES

1. Data on multinationals are collected by the United Nations and are published annually in UNCTAD's *World Investment Report*.

2. Aristotle, *Politics*, Stephen Everson, ed. (Cambridge: Cambridge University Press, 1988), 1263a25–41. Quoted in Mark Perlman and Charles R. McCann, Jr., *The Pillars of Economic Understanding, Ideas and Traditions* (Ann Arbor: University of Michigan Press, 1998), 15. Comments on other thinkers in this paragraph are based on Perlman and McCann, 15, 19, 20.

3. This is from the poetry part of the *Fable of the Bees*, called "The Grumbling Hive: Or, Knaves Turned Honest," lines 177–188. In L.I. Bredvold, A.D. McKillop, and L. Whitney, eds., *Eighteenth Century Poetry and Prose* (New York: Ronald Press, 1956), 333.

4. Speech to UNCTAD-X, 12 February 2000 in Bangkok, Thailand, as reported by C. Raghavan, Third World Network, www.globalpolicy.org/socecon/un/unctad6.htm.

5. Sarah Anderson and John Cavanagh, "Top 200: The Rise of Global Corporate Power," Corporate Watch, www.globalpolicy.org/socecon/tns/top200.htm, no date. Also see Richard J. Barnet and John Cavanaugh, *Global Dreams: Imperial Conditions and the New World Order* (New York: Simon and Schuster, 1994).

6. Quoted in Laurent Belsie, "Rise of the Corporate Nation-State," *Christian Science Monitor*, 10 April 2000, www.globalpolicy.org/socecon/bwi-wto/wban/bigbus.htm.

7. Sarah Anderson and John Cavanaugh, *Field Guide to the Global Economy* (New York: New Press, 200), 2. Some NGOs hostile to multinationals are associated with the big labor unions. The AFL-CIO supports the Institute for Policy Studies, which seems to be linked to Corporate Watch, the Alliance for Responsible Trade, and the Economic Policy Institute. On the pro-multinational side, one finds associations such as the U.S. Chamber of Commerce, Business Roundtable, the National Foreign Trade Council, and the U.S. Council for International Business. Prominent pro-business NGOs are the Cato Institute, Heritage Foundation, the American Enterprise Institute, and the Institute for International Economics. See also Amory Starr, *Naming the Enemy, Anti-corporate Movements Confront Globalization* (London: Zed, 2000).

8. *Field Guide*, op. cit., 62.

9. See the *Field Guide*, op. cit., 92, 103, 106, 108, 134, 140, 141.

10. See OECD, *Guidelines for Multinational Enterprises*, June 2000, www.oecd.org/daf/investment/guidelines and "Foreign Friends," *The Economist*, 8 January 2000, 71, 74.

11. Michael Prowse, "Why Capitalism Needs to be Policed," *Financial Times*, 8 April/9 April 2000, XXVIII. The quotes below also are on this page.

12. One can see why criticism of the OECD's late-1990s proposal to create a worldwide accord on rules governing multinationals had such a hostile tone to it. The critics wanted their own NGOs to be created to counter OECD, WTO, and

IMF support for the extended order. The WSO and WEO would work to halt the spread of the homo economicus model.

13. See "The Non-governmental Order," *The Economist*, 11 December 1999, 20.

14. The quote appeared in the *New York Times*, 14 April 2000, A11.

15. "Seattle Comes to Washington," *The Economist*, 15 April 2000, 25–26.

16. Steven Bezruchka, "Is Globalization Dangerous to Our Health?" *Western Journal of Medicine*, 2000, 172 (May), 332–334.

17. Support for these claims is found in D. Braun, *The Rich Get Richer: The Rise of Income Inequality in the United States and the World* (Chicago: Nelson-Hall, 1997) and H. Beyer, P. Rojas, and R. Vergara, "Trade Liberalization and Wage Inequality," *Journal of Development Economics*, 1999, 59, 103–123.

18. See Roberto Perotti, "Growth, Income Distribution, and Democracy: What the Data Say," *Journal of Economic Growth*, 1996, 1 (June), 149–187. Also important are Klaus Deininger and Lyn Squire, "A New Data Set Measuring Income Inequality," *World Bank Economic Review*, 1996, 10 (September) www. Worldbank.org/research/journals/wber, and David Dollar and Aart Kraay, "Growth is Good for the Poor," World Bank, 2000, March, unpublished.

19. A.T. Kearney, "A.T. Kearney in the News," www.atkearney.com/ATK/NewsReleases/detail/1,1078,1205,00.html, 2000, April.

20. Mobilization for Global Justice, www.a16.org.

21. See the OECD's *No Longer Business as Usual: Fighting Bribery and Corruption* (Paris: OECD, 2000). Although the OECD likes to talk of the "demand side" (the bribe receiver) and the "supply side" (the briber), it is mostly silent on the role of multinational corporations in fostering corruption. It has promulgated the Convention on Combating Bribery of Foreign Public Officials in International Business Transactions, but the effectiveness of this agreement remains to be seen.

22. For a summary of the research, see *OECD Observer*, 2000, April, No. 220.

23. Robert D. Kaplan, *The Coming Anarchy* (New York: Random House, 2000), 81–82.

24. For example, German exporters have been known to form cartels in an industry to increase their market power outside of Germany. Also, rumors have circulated for years that European and Japanese steel producers have secret agreements allocating various geographic areas to each country's companies. The European Union has become more active in investigating cross-border anticompetitive practices, as has the United States. See Richard Schaffer, Beverley Earle, and Filiberto Aguste, *International Business Law and Its Environment* (Minneapolis/St. Paul: West Publishing Co., 2000).

25. The issue of welfare economics and the problems with Pareto optimality are summarized in Allan M. Feldsman, "Welfare Economics." In John Eatwell et al., eds., *The New Palgrave, The World of Economics* (New York: W.W. Norton, 1991), 713–726. For an attempt to turn Adam Smith into a Global Villager, see Emma Rothschild, *Economic Sentiments: Adam Smith, Condorcet, and the Enlightenment* (Cambridge: Harvard University Press, 2001).

BIBLIOGRAPHY

Anderson, Sarah, and John Cavanaugh. *Field Guide to the Global Economy*. New York: New Press, 2000.

————. "Top 200: The Rise of Global Corporate Power." Corporate Watch, www.globalpolicy.org/socecon/tns/top200.htm, no date.

Belsie, Laurent. "Rise of the Corporate Nation-State." *Christian Science Monitor*, 10 April 2000, www.globalpolicy.org/socecon/bwi-wto/wban/bigbus.htm.

Beyer, H., P. Rojas, and R. Vergara. "Trade Liberalization and Wage Inequality." *Journal of Developmental Economics*, 1999, 59, 103–123.

Bezruchka, Steven. "Is Globalization Dangerous to Our Health?" *Western Journal of Medicine*, 2000, 172 (May), 332–334.

Braun, D. *The Rich Get Richer: The Rise of Income Inequality in the United States and the World*. Chicago: Nelson-Hall, 1997.

Deininger, Klaus, and Lyn Squire. "A New Data Set Measuring Income Inequality." *World Bank Economic Review*, 1996, 10 (September), www.Worldbank.org/research/journals/wber.

Dollar, David, and Aart Kraay. "Growth Is Good for the Poor." World Bank, Working Paper, March 2000.

Feldsman, Allan M. "Welfare Economics." In John Eatwell et al., eds., *The World of Economics*. New York: W. W. Norton, 1991, 713–726.

Kaplan, Robert D. *The Coming Anarchy*. New York: Random House, 2000.

OECD. *Guidelines for Multinational Enterprises*. Paris: OECD, 2000.

OECD. *No Longer Business as Usual: Fighting Bribery and Corruption*. Paris: OECD, 2000.

Perlman, Mark, and Charles R. McCann, Jr. *The Pillars of Economic Understanding, Ideas and Traditions*. Ann Arbor: University of Michigan Press, 1998.

Perotti, Roberto. "Growth, Income Distribution, and Democracy: What the Data Say." *Journal of Economic Growth*, 1996, 1 (June), 149–187.

Prowse, Michael. "Why Capitalism Needs to be Policed." *Financial Times*, 8 April/9 April 2000, XXVIII.

Rothschild, Emma. *Economic Sentiments: Adam Smith, Condorcet, and the Enlightenment*. Cambridge: Harvard University Press, 2001.

Schaffer, Richard, Beverley Earle, and Filiberto Augusti. *International Business Law and Its Environment*. Minneapolis/St. Paul: West Publishing Co., 2000.

Starr, Amory. *Naming the Enemy, Anti-corporate Movements Confront Globalization*. London: Zed, 2000.

UNCTAD. *World Investment Report*. New York: United Nations, 2001.

CHAPTER 13

GLOBALIZATION IN THE 21ST CENTURY

Globalization, the rapid expansion and integration of business activities across borders in response to dramatic technology and government policy changes in the latter part of the 20th century, has fostered equally dramatic changes in the goals and strategies of corporations in the United States and elsewhere. Yet all parties recognize that we only are at the beginning of what appears to be a transitional period from something we were to something we will be. In the late 20th century we were believers in what Freidrich Hayek called the *extended order*, that body of traditions and learned values constituting the epistemology of the socioeconomic paradigm. The paradigm told multinational corporations what they could and could not do and legitimized their global push. The model is a good one in that it has fostered wondrous increases in well-being in the West and now in the East. However, it is a bad one in that its defenders must preach the beauties of tough competition, consumerist individualism, and utilitarian ethics. However valuable these are—and they are valuable—they are hard to stomach.

By the end of the century voices, and even shouts on the streets, were being heard that things were wrong. Some claimed that the paradigm was unjust; others claimed that it led to instability. It was seen as a threat to individual autonomy and collective identity. It required people to rely on calculation rather than character in their dealings with each other. It was ruining the earth. Most of the criticism was disorganized, even anarchic, but it was coalescing around the four themes of justice, order, virtue, and sovereignty/identity. Helped by the Internet, it seemed likely to evolve into a new, broadened socioeconomic paradigm, the Global Village. What would

American and global life be like in the 21st century? Whatever happened would be driven by the paradigms that interpreted the world for us, provided values and norms, and told us how to behave. Would it be the extended order writ large over the map of the world? Or would it be a global version of an idealized village?

LOOKING BACKWARD TO SEE THE FUTURE

Americans looking forward to the 21st century and wondering what would become of them could part the curtain somewhat by turning around and looking backward to the social and literary agendas of thoughtful people in 1900. These hopes and plans still resonate, and what they called for then are what current advocates of change still call for. The economic model that guides the business operations of our corporations must accommodate a more assertive, autonomous individual secure in his or her national, cultural, spiritual, ethnic, and indeed global identities. Companies must foster environments where a person of character is focused on virtue rather than the display of "pep," where values of justice and healthy stability constrain desires for gain and growth, and where work is treated as a meaningful process rather than merely as an instrument designed to pry leisure and its goods loose from the world. What is new is that now all these things are being sought on a global scale instead of a national one.

Writers of 1900 explored themes of illusion and betrayal as they saw—or thought they saw—America turning into an urban, industrialized society that reeked of excess, chaos, and unnaturalness and turned individuals into consumers of things rather than people consumed by virtue. They yearned for a world of coherence instead of fragmentation where individuals were value-driven as much as interest-driven. It would be a world where each American asserted her identity as a person in thrall to a character-laden self and not a cause, ideology, movement, party, or passion. This theme of the rooted yet autonomous individual enriched social thought throughout the 20th century and is now crossing over borders as American globalization progresses into the 21st.

The most prominent advocate today of the autonomous individual is Amartya Sen, whose *Development as Freedom* (2000) calls for a change in the way we define societal growth. In addition to changes in GNP that improve well-being, Sen stresses the need to expand our perspective to include increased opportunities for individuals to exercise "reasoned agency."[1] In a truly developed nation, individuals have, first, enhanced opportunities to exercise their capabilities and choices. Second, they have an identity, which they have chosen, that provides the basis for self-respect and guides decisions. Third, they have happiness rooted in the satisfaction of desires for material goods and leisure. In Sen's model, identity and happiness may exchange ranks from time to time, but individual autonomy always comes first. We can see here a new socioeconomic paradigm coming into being, in which the economic model and the business system, both in the United States and worldwide, become more inclusive. Indeed, Sen describes markets not solely as instrumental states of affairs where exchanges occur to the material benefit of society but also as intrinsically satisfying environments for individuals to exercise their agencies. This idea of labor and goods markets as in part processes of meaningful experiencing is very much in keeping with the emerging Global Village themes I have been exploring in this book.

In addition to their focus on individual autonomy and identity, American thinkers of 1900 expressed a willingness to support the business system only so long as it acted in accord with the Puritan Compromise and the cosmic optimism of the American people. The latter required delivery of progressive increases in well-being, an obligation which was and is being met by the nation's corporations and enterprises. Adhering to the Puritan Compromise, however, was another matter. It demanded that business foster virtues of diligence, thrift, prudence, and honesty and follow the dictates of justice requiring fair dealing. While much was achieved during the 20th century, much was left undone, and business at century's end found itself feeling vulnerable to attacks not only on its behavior but on the economic model itself. In the new century, corporations that had learned from 1900 would want to focus, in America and globally, more on individuals as both utility and autonomy seekers and on business itself as value and virtue-driven as well as interest-driven.

FROM THE DESERTED VILLAGE TO THE GLOBAL VILLAGE

According to Karl Polanyi in *The Great Transformation* (1944), the market society as we know it, wherein market functioning drives social behavior, only appeared in the 19th century. Before that, production and distribution were governed by norms of reciprocity and affiliation rather than economic exchanges rooted in self-interest. Pre-19th century peoples supposedly produced food, goods, and services in response to social values which required such behavior and in fear of social ostracism if they did not. They existed not in horizontal buyer-seller relations but in vertical social systems in which elites enjoyed allegiance from those below and bestowed benevolence in the form of distribution of goods and food. While Polanyi's model clearly was overstated—markets and exchange have been around for a long time—he hinted at an idealized world with which earlier thinkers and poets were much taken. Poet Oliver Goldsmith's worldview is explained in *The Deserted Village* (1770):

A time there was, ere England's griefs began,
When every rood of ground maintained its man;
For him light labor spread her wholesome store,
Just gave what life required but gave no more. . . .
Ye friends to truth, ye statesmen, who survey
The rich man's joys increase, the poor's decay,
Tis yours to judge how wide the limits stand
Between a splendid and an happy land. . . .
Around the world each needful product flies,
For all the luxuries the world supplies;
While thus the land, adorned for pleasure all,
In barren splendor feebly waits the fall.

Goldsmith bemoaned the fading of the old order, in which a highly structured, static agricultural system provided a "happy" rather than a "splendid" land. This demi-paradise, in his view, was rapidly decaying, in part because of the globalization of production as goods from "around the world" drove local producers out of business.

Whatever reality there was to the village model of society did indeed begin to fade in the 19th century, replaced by what Hayek called the extended order. Even if individuals are genetically primed for village tribalism and its intricate webs of norms and allegiances that regulate production and distribution, Hayek argued that people will opt for a splendid, rich life in place of a happy, poor life if they can get it, and they have realized that they can get it by adhering to learned values associated with competitive behavior, defense of property rights, accumulation and investment of capital, and the ever-expanding nature of business across borders. This model of the economic paradigm as learned and institutionalized was based on the 18th-century writing of Bernard Mandeville and contrasted sharply with that of Adam Smith, who argued that individuals naturally incline towards market exchange behavior modified by fellow feeling and virtuous inclinations. John Maynard Keynes later added an influential elaboration to the Smithian model by noting that humans also have a natural propensity for risk-taking, guided by a tendency towards passionate optimism. The naturalism of Smith and Keynes allowed for government interventions to keep human tendencies from drifting off into inefficiencies or excesses. Since nothing could change human nature, a bit of government prodding would not be of any harm.

The Smith-Keynes model was influential in the mid-20th century, but by century's end the extended order seemed to have triumphed. Government manipulation was considered an unnecessary complication to what was already a highly elaborate system, and leaders in developing nations begged for help in learning the ins and outs of the capitalist way, which clearly had evoked improvements in living standards. However, the extended order's great flaw was that it prospered only because of its consequences, not its inherent attractiveness. A number of critics pointed out that a "hold-your-nose-and-vote-for-capitalism" model was an inadequate base on which to build the emerging 21st-century global society. One of these, John Gray, argued that we must view the market economy "not as a state of natural liberty produced by deregulation, but as a subtle and complex institution, which needs recurrent reform if it is to be kept in good repair."[2] Here he stood Hayek's model on its head, claiming that *because* the extended order was learned and embedded in society's institutions, government had a right to regulate its unpleasantnesses so that security, justice, democracy, and other desirables would soften its unattractive elements.

Moreover, Donald McCloskey in *The Rhetoric of Economics* (1985) and other influential writings noted that the processes of market exchange—the truck and barter among buyers and sellers—should be thought of as an ongoing series of conversations in a communal existence, laden with emotion and persuasion, values and interests, calculations and affiliations, and future-oriented and custom-driven behavior. This kind of existence is very much like that of a village—at least a well-functioning village—where trust and character rather than expectations of gain dominate economic encounters. By the early 21st century, then, the values of Goldsmith's deserted village had staged a comeback in the guise of the new Global Village as attacks on the extended order multiplied.

JUSTICE, ORDER, VIRTUE, AND IDENTITY IN THE GLOBAL VILLAGE

American corporations now find themselves pressured by both past trends and future expectations. Out of the American past comes a yearning for individual autonomy and some sense that a spiritual or at least a loftier existence is possible beyond the grubbiness of getting and spending. These yearnings are behind a revival of the Puritan Compromise, which provides legitimacy to the economic system only as long as businesses foster moral and ethical behavior. Out of the European past, this time from the Romantic movement of the 18th and 19th centuries, comes a communitarian impetus based on a highly idealized vision of village life that calls for economic relations to be much more embedded in webs of affiliation guided by deeply felt concerns for justice, stability, and national and cultural identity. These yearnings and movements are putting severe pressure on the extended order model and very likely will evoke some kinds of changes in the way people of the West define economic life and seek to extend it globally.

One change the corporations can expect is a greater emphasis on the allocation of resources based on democratically determined rules of fairness, rather than merely exchange, so that each gets her due. *Justice* advocates like Ralph Nader and the leaders of thousands of NGOs are using the Internet to demand that economic outcomes should be "just" for small farmers, female workers, those dislocated by global trade, indigenous peoples, the gendered, the disabled, and just about anyone who even remotely fits the description of "victim." They see the current mode of globalization as too much beholden to government and corporate cabals and want to inject more popular sovereignty into the process. In the name of justice, NGO leaders will seek to expand the concept of private property as the right to dispose of assets, but a right constrained by justice concerns. Thus a legal person, who is the possessor of private property, may be redefined to include abstractions like the ecosystem, a race, or a class, and NGOs will demand compensation from MNCs for unjust infringements on those "persons'" property rights. They also will claim that workers in a country "own" their jobs and that justice dictates that another country's workers cannot take jobs away in the course of global trade expansions.

Corporations should also expect more frequent critiques of the supposed chaos of capitalism and calls for a more stable world. This yearning for *order* is associated in different ways with European Third Position advocates, Asian Way enthusiasts, and radical environmentalists. The Third Position also is referred to as welfare capitalism, corporatism, social democracy, and the social market economy. Its supporters seek controls on disorderly competition and labor markets, more inclusive models of corporate governance, a reduction in the claims a company can make on worker autonomy, and a focus on employee job tenure and high wages supported by extensive skills training financed by high taxes. Since the rigidities of this system are likely to put a damper on innovation, corporate profit strategies may be forced to focus more on efficiency gains rather than new product development.

The Asian Way, guided again in the coming decades by a resurgence of Japanese ideas as soon as Japan emerges from its current economic malaise, will emphasize benevolent paternalism and the immersion of employees within corporate modes of supposedly communal and highly stable existence. No-layoff practices will make labor a fixed cost, leaving little flexibility to companies during downturns. They then will turn to the government, seeking and getting support for schemes to keep prices high through regulatory practices and limits on enforcement of competition laws. As in the past, a rhetoric centered on the theme of "orderly markets" will attempt to persuade the public that American-style models are destabilizing and asocial.

The final group of order enthusiasists will be the Steady-State Way advocates among radical environmentalists. For them globalization and economic growth constitute threats to the natural order. A global citizen must be brought into being to support the ecosystem's rights over individual or country rights, and "ecological commerce" must be supported. This will involve proposals for heavy taxes to penalize nonconserving companies and to support NGOs advocating the precautionary principle (in the absence of data on dangers, doing nothing is better than doing something) of risk management.

In the more just, stable world called for by critics of the extended order, a *virtue ethics* will be proclaimed for multinational corporations. This will not require dramatic changes, at least in lip service, in most societies, but the utilitarian ethics that burdened American business during the 20th century will come under strong attack. As I noted earlier, Americans are beginning to reassert the demand of the Puritan Compromise that the business system develop and reward individual character and moral depth, and they will be joined to some extent by Europeans, Asians, and others uncomfortable with the current American practice of defining what is right and good as the result of a benefits-minus-costs calculation. Moreover, a return to virtue ethics in the United States—the ethics of the Founders—may solve the problem Americans will face as they globalize: a communitarian, ordered world of Global Villagers has no place in it for individualist autonomy-seekers endlessly calculating costs and benefits and launching "greater good" decisions that leave a good deal of destabilizing, community-threatening "lesser good" wreckage in their wakes. Americans committed to virtuous business practices stressing individual prudence, courage, dignity, diligence, and a respect for what most people can agree on as the right and good will not be thought of (as they are now) as valued but troublesome members of the global polity, no matter how much they talk of autonomy and freedom.

As globalization evokes concerns and programs focused on justice, order, and virtue, multinationals also will have to deal with a resurgence of claims for recognition, attention, and influence by various *identity and sovereignty-seeking* groups and nations. Capitalism's expansion will be seen as involving a power grab by corporations supported by institutions like the WTO and the IMF and the advocacy of free-trade ideologues. It will be countered by way-of-life defenders and nationalists who will call for trade and capital flow barriers for noneconomic reasons centered on establishing and defending lofty concepts of identity rather than merely economic interests. MNCs may have to either become stateless entities or, more likely, take on local identities in much the same way IBM Japan has. IBM is thought of as thoroughly Japanese in Japan. Global coordination and rationalization strategies may be hindered as companies focus less on producing globally standardized products and more on responding carefully to local demands. The 21st century multinational may end up being what it in fact mostly is now, a loose grouping of semi-independent, country-based affiliates rather than the tightly controlled network of subsidiaries envisioned by writers who proclaim the coming dominance of the "transnational" or "global" corporation.

MANAGING EMPLOYEES IN A NEW PARADIGM

As external challenges to multinational corporations and the economic paradigm supporting them grow more prominent and troublesome in the 21st century, internal changes are likely in the way employees and employers conceive of work in both the United States and abroad. Humans approach toil as part of living in a sensible way, and most people throughout history have treated labor as they treated love: an ongoing process of existing in a meaningful relationship with others. Yet in the 20th century this process view of work ran afoul of both economic theory, in which work is solely an instrumental act focused on future leisure or happiness, and management theory, in which work is neither a process nor an input but instead is a response—an output—to manipulated controls, stimuli, and rhetoric. Neither economic nor management theory offered much in the way of satisfying explanations or useful predictions—not so much because they were wrong but rather incomplete—and something more will be needed in the coming decades to legitimize the global employee management practices of multinationals.[3] In a globalized world, culture and paradigm-bound labor theories will have to be augmented by more encompassing theories, theories that take broad human propensities into account. As global companies are compelled to attend to increased demands by employees for individual autonomy and recognition of cultural and national identity, they also must construct workplaces more in accord with human nature.

Humans everywhere will accept compensated work environments where economic incentives are clear and acceptable and controlling stimuli reduce uncertainty as to what must be done and when. In other words, workers are not hostile to economists' and managers' approaches to evoking work. Indeed, these models have not held back people of the West from achieving rapid gains in material well-being. But Western workers never have exhibited the satisfaction levels one would have expected over the previous century, and the reason is that prevailing models have not incorporated the process view of work as ongoing lived experience in a communal setting. Human nature cries out for social and business institutions that recognize all of the elements of the worker-work relationship. Western workers are ready for an expanded model, and non-Western workers in a globalized world will expect nothing less, since they do not have long experience in work settings that are purely instrumental or purely controlling.

Managing employees successfully throughout the world will result in workers not just saying, "The work pays well" and "The boss makes it clear what is to be done and why." In addition, they will want to say, "The work makes sense to me and my coworkers." Work incentives and stimuli to evoke motivated effort will be needed, as they are now, in the globalized workplace, but greater emphasis will have to be placed on process issues. In many jobs employees will expect creative and challenging tasks fostering "flow" conditions in which workers experience a highly pleasurable sense of timelessness. Where possible, moreover, the frantic emphasis on change, so common today, will become muted, giving way to timeless rituals of toil and social engagement in the workplace. For both highly skilled and unskilled workers, then, the successful 21st century workplace, be it in New Jersey or Bali, will be—or ought to be—a more stable, ordered place in which people will feel secure in their individual and social identities yet comfortable in their employer's manifest recognition of their common humanity and its concerns.

A VIGOROUS PUSH FROM THE INTERNET

The spread of the Internet will enhance the pressure on MNCs to approach globalization as not just the spread of the extended order but as a new socioeconomic paradigm coming into being and affecting both external and internal exchange relations.

The Internet may support the idea that globalization can evoke a Global Village in which individuals are seen not simply as producers or consumers but as information processors, living in the present more than in the past or the future and connected as never before to the world and the world to them. In such a world, awash in data, our interest in objective, stand-back calculation will fade, replaced by immersion in all-encompassing, ongoing engagement processes. Life in the Internet age will become more like it was in the 18th-century village before it became deserted. *Pace* Goldsmith, an environment of this kind can be fractious, so an interest in order and stability will characterize the Global Village. Since fair-dealing norms obeyed by people of character are more efficient for exchange than legal rules enforced by litigation, the emphasis on justice and virtue ethics will increase. Since the Internet will link everyone to everyone else, a sense of membership in the global community will develop without a person having to give up his or her sense of local identity. Finally, the Internet-enabled workplace will satisfy worker needs for processes of flow and ritual. All in all, the Internet is likely to be a powerful tool in the hands of NGOs and other advocates offering various elements of the new paradigm.

However, instead of the Internet evoking a Global Village organized around norms of justice, order, virtue, and identity, it could foster the atomization, alienation, and manipulation characteristic of a mass society well on its way to barbarous totalitarianism. This is unlikely as long as information and privacy issues are dealt with in a more sensible way than at present. In our extended order world, information is an asset to be bought and sold, including information about oneself. As the Global Village paradigm takes hold, this narrow view may change, with private information more and more defined as part of one's well-being, like an arm or a leg, and not tradable. If an autonomy-enhancing view of this kind becomes pervasive, mass societal manipulations will be less possible—but so will that element of e-commerce which depends on Web-based consumer research.

The Internet-Village model could alter our idea of what commerce is. In the economic paradigm, a market really is more a set of principles rather than a place, stressing exchange among buyers and sellers in arm's-length relationships. In e-commerce, however, Web sites are more like market *places*, which I have called *marketoids*, where customs, values, and communities driven by ideas of order, justice, virtue, and identity influence exchange. It is still exchange, but less arm's-length, less interest-driven, more norm-driven.[4] Successful e-commerce B2C companies probably will be big and will focus on global sales of branded products. Part of brand building will involve providing Web sites that are flow-inducing, pleasant and easy to navigate, and useful. That means they must be challenging as well as entertaining and functional. Also, corporations will try to build an Internet relationship with site visitors based as much on trust as expected gain. This practice, already well under way, will push global firms towards taking on institutional as well as economic functions. The goal of a business institution will be not simply to generate profits for shareholders. In addition, it will be to act as an intermediary, transmitting the individual's needs and concerns to society, society's to the individual, and in the process fostering a legitimized social order. The merchant in the Global Village will be more and more like the merchant in a real village: a community builder, an advisor and interpreter, a listener, and occasionally a broker—all in addition to being a salesman. Companies will take on this expanded role for two reasons. First, the developing Village paradigm will demand changes in ideology and practice and, second, stringent privacy protections will restrict market research activities, pushing firms more towards information-rich trust relationships.

HOW WILL MULTINATIONALS RESPOND?

Multinational corporations today are the spear carriers of the extended order. How will they respond to the external and internal challenges of a changing economic paradigm in which concerns of justice, order, virtue, and identity grow and become salient and pressing in a Web-enabled world? The market model will be both constrained and expanded by values, NGO and national agendas, and a broadened view of work. The stakeholder model, currently in vogue, is a middle point on the path to a new model in which, as we saw above, corporations reduce their arm's-length relationships with clients and employees and take on institution-like obligations, obligations that in the coming decades may be codified by global rule-making (or at least rule-proposing) bodies such as the proposed World Social Organization and the World Environmental Organization (discussed in Chapter 12).

Corporations in global business must begin to assess global risk rather than just country-by-country and business risks. As the disparate elements of the Global Village paradigm come together and coalesce—if they co-alesce—a need will arise to decide on how to respond and to assess the costs (or benefits) of not doing so. Global risk is the probability of losses due to worldwide hostility to the extended order economic model and to MNCs. It equals (1) the probability of coordinated coalitions emerging, times (2) the probability of the world's peoples accepting the Village coalition's agenda.

I argued in the last chapter that the probability of (1) is going to be high in the coming decades, so (2) deserves the most attention. If corporations try to influence people to continue to accept the harsh functionings of extended order capitalism for the sake of its manifest benefits in terms of growth in material well-being, they are likely to fail. This failure does not guarantee that humanity then will opt for a new economic ideology—that remains to be seen, since the public may decide to opt for the old ways in spite of a distaste for global corporations. However, business executives will follow the dictates of risk-management protocols: If one element of risk seems about to increase, try to reduce risk in some other element. Global corporations, sensing that global risk is primed to grow, with potentially damaging constraints about to be placed on them, probably will act to reduce business risks by efforts to reduce competition. This would involve dramatic increases in cross-border mergers, acquisitions, and strategic alliances as well as efforts to convince home-country governments to increase their tolerance for anticompetitive practices such as price-fixing and market allocation schemes and to erect trade and investment barriers against foreign competition. Twentieth-century Japanese governments did this for decades; to help Japan's corporations cope with increasing risks abroad, they acted to reduce their risks at home. As 21st-century governments see their corporations seemingly endangered by growing global support for a new ideology of markets and business, they may want to help those companies reduce their risks at home. Thus the greater the probability of Global Village ideology taking hold, the more we may see atrophy in country competition environments.

HOW WILL ECONOMISTS RESPOND?

The capitalist model that has benefited us so greatly is not based on any laws of nature. The extended order is a human construction, and what humans have built up they can tear down. Humans do seem to have a propensity to truck and barter, but they don't have any compelling genetic imperative telling them to do it in accord with the dictates of current economic theory and policy, no matter how beneficial those theories and policies are. The "hold-your-nose-and-vote-for-capitalism" model today is seemingly triumphant, but a global economic downturn quickly would call it into question. Socialist and Marxist alternatives failed in the 20th century because they were both unworkable and occasionally inhuman. The emerging Village paradigm simply takes the existing capitalist model, which works most of the time, and embeds it in a more broadly conceived humanistic environment. Corporations must develop new ways of thinking about themselves in this model and must face new challenges in their relationships with customers and employees, but truck and barter will continue as markets turn into marketoids and market places.

How are economists dealing with these impending developments? This is important, since their ideology provides the protocols for multinational corporations. If ideology changes, companies will change; if it doesn't, they won't. Modern economic theory began in the 18th century with Mandeville's *Fable of the Bees*, which argued that humans are consumed by vices of desire, which drives economic growth in a society. The utility-maximizing human calculator later was called homo economicus and became a key element in the philosophical underpinnings of microeconomic theory. While some economists like to refer to homo economicus as a "stylized fact"—an abstraction useful in forming mathematical models of great rigor—many take it as a given that humans are, at times, indeed driven by "vast forces of greed" and "self-interest seeking with guile."[5] One group of thinkers sees these propensities as genetically inspired, but, following Hayek's idea of the extended order, others view them as learned responses. As I have argued in this book, this latter view currently is prominent, and developing peoples of the world are reported to be eager to learn ways and attitudes suitable to the capitalist.

The nature and behavior of homo economicus has been at the center of most economic theorizing, be it classical, neoclassical, Marxist, Austrian, Keynesian, monetarist, or Bayesian, but most of the theories one encounters are discussed in an environment which Donald McCloskey calls one of "deaf isolation."

Economists are deaf to history or philosophy; most of them yawn at geography or psychology; they do not take seriously anthropology or sociology . . . the suggestion that the study of literature or communication or even the nonliterary arts might also speak to them would be regarded by many economists as lunacy.[6]

The economists' constrained, crabbed way of looking at the world influences their students who go on to be executives of multinational corporations. Which of the following models is most likely to be the rationale for global strategizing of a typical multicultural corporation?

	Model A	**Model B**
Underlying Theory	Humans are everywhere the same; all consumers	Humans are shaped by culture, values, and inter-

	are rational seekers of happiness and pleasure.	ests in complex ways.
Goal of the Firm	Learn important commonalties among humans.	Learn important differences among humans.
Actions	Standardize the basic nature of products and sevices and aggressively inform consumers of their attributes.	Customize products and services for each society.

Elements of truth about humanity infuse both models, but most globally-focused managers lean towards Model A. Practically speaking, it's the most efficient approach, but equally important, it's the model taught to them by their professors. It isn't really wrong; it's just inadequate.

Fortunately change is in the air, and theories are broadening to the point where economics may incorporate the Village paradigm rather than the other way around. Labor economics is transforming itself from a narrow instrumental focus to one concerned with the decisions of families and households. Growth theories now incorporate historical trends, and much empirical research examines social interactions and the process of exchange.[7] In other words, homo economicus is fading and real people with pasts, friends, and loved ones are emerging. Economists are looking into preferences driven by conformism, jealousy, and various emotions rather than by calculations of expected gains. They soon will want to do more research on status, gender roles, justice, and culture—some of the issues that concern Global Villagers. Key here will be the growing realization, confirmed by recent research, that individuals who value communitarianism and believe that others do too will eagerly support and engage in collective action, even when it is not in their self-interests to do so.[8] If the Global Village paradigm elements coalesce in the coming decades, then, a new economic model may be in place to legitimize it. This will make the task of multinational executives easier, since their ideology will have developed in ways that help them understand and in part accept the changes.

TWENTY-FIRST CENTURY BUSINESS IN THE GLOBAL VILLAGE

Instead of arm's-length relations with customers and employees, the 21st-century enterprise—if the Village model develops in the way described above—will find itself in a more interdependent world of global marketoids as well as markets. In this world brands are as much bonds of affiliation as market signals, and work is as much a process as an instrument. Managing is as much leadership by people concerned with justice, virtue, and character as calculations of costs and benefits. Governance is as much responsiveness to the demands of the environment, the culture, and NGOs as to governments, stockholders, and clients. The increase of well-being is as much due to the productivity of workers content in a stable, connected, global yet local communalism as to harsh competitiveness. This is the optimistic view, whereby a return to 18th-century thinking occurs and Adam Smith's ideas about sympathy and fellow feeling join a renewed interest in Oliver Goldsmith's village society—now allegedly possible on a global scale thanks to the Internet and other technology breakthroughs. A pessimistic view presents a different story. Here the liberating flows of goods, services, people, knowledge, and money are constrained in the names of sovereignty, identity, and order. Here the integration of man and nature is considered laughably impossible, and new messiahs call for most humans (except, of course, indigenous peoples) to be moved onto enclaves to protect the earth from their depredations and restore humanity in nature (the U.S. Pacific Northwest is home to many of these individuals, who busy themselves with drawing maps of the enclaves and occasional attacks on power lines). Here justice advocates seek the abolition of the U.S. Congress and state legislatures, with replacement by local communes reporting to a national Commune that is a member of a Global Commune. Here multinational patriarchy gives way to participative corporate governance structures dominated by NGO representatives of the victims, tribes, and ecosystems. Here the Internet, instead of pushing us towards a Global Village, fosters atomization, alienation, mass society, and the birth of new Hitlers (one joke has Adolph Hitler emerging from hiding after all these years to tell his followers, "This time, no more Mister Nice Guy!").

The last time globalization began to take hold, in the middle decades of the 19th century as steam transport and cables united the world, Ralph Waldo Emerson considered the society that "the young American" would inhabit. In an address to the Mercantile Library Association of Boston in 1844, he described the new order of what we today call international and global business:

Meantime Trade has begun to appear: Trade, a plant which grows whenever there is peace. . . . And as quickly as men go to foreign parts, in ships or caravans, a new order of things springs up. . . . This displaces physical strength, and installs computation, combination, information, science in its room. . . . Trade goes to make the governments insignificant, and to bring every kind of faculty of every individual that can in any manner serve any person, "on sale." . . . This is the good and the evil of trade, that it would put everything into market: talent, beauty, virtue, and man himself.[9]

For Emerson the new global order of business mostly would be good, but the tyranny of markets would commodify everything, and governments would step in and make things worse.

In the century ahead he predicted further developments:

but Trade is also but for a time, and must give way to something broader and better, whose signs are already dawning in the sky.

The "sequel of trade" would see better education, the rise of unions, work for the poor, better access to food through chemical fertilizers ("artificial guano"), and the privatization of government functions by "private adventurers." He also refers to these last as "joint stock companies." Implicitly Emerson was arguing that the key to a better world was the development of large corporations in America. They would fund the educating, do the fertilizing, get along with the unions, and keep government at bay. To shift to current terminology, he envisioned multinationals, first, as both the cause and the cure for the ailments of globalization and, second, later on as the engines for carrying us into a less mercantile, broader existence. This is the world of humanism, where individuals cultivate and celebrate their being in a coherent, stable, universal order. It is a world of human flourishing, resting securely and confidently on a global economic system without in fact being dominated by it. It is the idealized world of Venice in the Renaissance, Goldsmith's village before it became deserted, and the Global Village.

WHAT IF THE EXTENDED ORDER CONTINUES?

Of course, neither the optimistic nor pessimistic views of the new paradigm may come to pass, and we may continue to hold our noses and vote for capitalism. This is a world of free flows of goods, services, capital, and knowledge. As for people, managers will come and go across borders but ordinary workers will not. One of the unstated ideas behind current versions of the extended order is that multinational corporations foster all of the flows of goods and capital so that individuals mostly will stay put. Governments tend to like this arrangement, and this is one reason why they lately have been bestowing a good deal of favor on transnational corporations. These companies create jobs, pay taxes, and bring technology into a country. In doing so they relieve governments from the duties of paying unemployment insurance, reducing spending to match weak revenues, and funding research and development.

We thus ought to see globalization driven by multinationals as a way of evoking order by reducing instability associated with mass migrations. Since most U.S. corporations for one reason or another tend to be, with some lapses, free of corrupt practices and treat their workers fairly, we ought to see them as fostering virtue and justice. And since these companies approach people as individuals yet are exquisitely sensitive to community and culture issues, we ought to associate the U.S.-led march of global capitalism with autonomy and identity. All of the things the Village model advocates want—order, justice, virtue, and identity—already are coming along quite nicely. Emerson suggested that a world of *commerce* would evolve into a *commerce plus* world, and it's happening. We all should be giving three rousing cheers for the extended order.

We do hear those cheers from some people all of the time, and most of us are willing to cheer some of the time. But no swelling Mormon Tabernacle Choir-like majority is belting out a hymn of praise to the world that economists envisioned, governments brought into being, and multinationals keep going. The economists are said to be too narrow, the governments too untrustworthy, and the corporations too selfish. How then can the current version of globalization continue if support for its basic ideology is so weak and its manifest benefits so ignored? Clearly it cannot, and either globalization will come to a halt or a new version will come into being. Across the plains and oceans, electronic smoke signals are being sent out, summoning the tribes, the victims, the gendered, and whoever else might conceivably have a grudge against the extended order. Each of them sees the threat from the approaching global cavalry in a different way, but they know that they must find some common meeting place to marshal a response. Perhaps a village can be set up along some new Little Big Horn, where they will put the matter to a test and await their fate. It is the fate of all of us that is at stake in the coming decades.

NOTES

1. Amartya Sen, *Development as Freedom* (New York: Alfred A. Knopf, 2000).

2. John Gray, *False Dawn, The Delusions of Global Capitalism.* (New York: New Press, 1998), 94. A more balanced but similar discussion is in Charles E. Lindblom, *The Market System* (New Haven: Yale University Press, 2001).

3. In a typical research paper, only 30 to 50 percent of variance in motivated work behavior is explained by economic incentive and control-oriented variables. Clearly the modern workplace is a more complex environment than that described by economics and business professors. For a sampling of the research, see Robert Dubin, R. Alan Hedley, and Thomas C. Taveggia, "Attachment to Work," in Robert Dubin, ed., *Handbook of Work, Organization, and Society* (Chicago: Rand McNally, 1976), 281–342; Kai Erickson and Steven Vallas, eds., *The Nature of Work* (New Haven: Yale University Press, 1990); F.J. Landy and W. Becker, "Adaptive Motivation Theory," *Annual Report to Office of Naval Research* (University Park, PA: Department of Psychology, 1982); H. Lebenstein, *Beyond Economic Man* (Cambridge: Harvard University Press, 1980); Meaning of Work International Research Team, *The Meaning of Work* (London: Academic Press, 1987).

4. An e-commerce Web site fits the definition of a market place in a community as a locale where wares are on view, sellers are numerous, onlookers may enter freely, and the organization of the participants rather than abstract principles determines the market functioning. See Polly Hill, "Market Places." In John Eatwell et al., eds., *The New Palgrave, The World of Economics* (New York: Norton, 1991), 419–423. Market places occupy a middle ground between the abstractions of economists and the nonmarket allocation systems described by Karl Polanyi in *The*

Great Transformation as pervasive until only recently. They involve economic exchange but clearly are norm-driven and often not arm's-length.

5. These terms are used by Kenneth Arrow, "Discrimination in the Labour Market." In J.E. King, ed., *Readings in Labour Economics* (Oxford: Oxford University Press, 1980) and Oliver Williamson, *The Economic Institutions of Capitalism* (New York: Free Press, 1985). See Ernst Fehr and Simon Gachter, "Fairness and Retaliation: The Economics of Reciprocity," *Journal of Economic Perspectives*, 2000, 14 (3), 159–181.

6. Donald McCloskey, *Knowledge and Persuasion in Economics* (Cambridge: Cambridge University Press, 1994), 28.

7. For a summary of developments see Charles F. Manski, "Economic Analysis of Social Interactions," *Journal of Economic Perspectives*, 2000, 14 (3), 115–136 and Joseph Henrich et al., "In Search of Homo Economicus: Behavioral Experiments in 15 Small-Scale Societies," *AEA Papers and Proceedings*, 2001, 91, 73–78.

8. The research is summarized in Elinor Ostrom, "Collective Action and the Evolution of Social Norms," *Journal of Economic Perspectives*, 2000, 14 (3), 137–138. The *Journal*, now the most dynamic publication of the American Economic Association, devoted much of its space in the 1990s to discipline-changing articles like Ostrom's and those cited above.

9. Ralph Waldo Emerson, "The Young American." Speech delivered to the Mercantile Library Association, Boston, 7 February 1844. Available at www.jjnet. com/emerson/youngam.htm.

BIBLIOGRAPHY

Dubin, Robert, R. Alan Hedley, and Thomas C. Taveggia. "Attachment to Work." In Robert Dubin, ed., *Handbook of Work, Organization, and Society*. Chicago: Rand McNally, 1976, 281–342.

Erickson, Kai, and Steven Vallas, eds. *The Nature of Work*. New Haven: Yale University Press, 1990.

Fehr, Ernst, and Simon Gachter. "Fairness and Retaliation: The Economics of Reciprocity." *Journal of Economic Perspectives*, 2000, 14(3), 159–181.

Gray, John. *False Dawn, The Delusions of Global Capitalism*. New York: New Press, 1998.

Henrich, Joseph and Robert Boyd, Samuel Bowles, Colin Camerer, Ernst Fehr, Herbert Gintis, and Richard McElreath. "In Search of Homo Economicus: Behavioral Experiments in 15 Small-Scale Societies." *AEA Papers and Proceedings*, 2001, 91, 73–78.

Hill, Polly. "Market Places." In John Eatwell et al., *The New Palgrave, The World of Economics*. New York: Norton, 419–423.

King, J.E., ed. *Readings in Labour Economics*. Oxford: Oxford University Press, 1980.

Landy, F. J., and W. Becker. "Adaptive Motivation Theory." *Annual Report to Office of Naval Research*. University Park, PA: Department of Psychology, 1982.

Lebenstein, Harvey. *Beyond Economic Man*. Cambridge: Harvard University Press, 1980.

Lendblom, Charles E. *The Market System*. New Haven: Yale University Press, 2001.

Manski, Charles F. "Economic Analysis of Social Interactions." *Journal of Economic Perspectives*, 2000, 14(3), 115–136.

McCloskey, Donald. *Knowledge and Persuasion in Economics*. Cambridge: Cambridge University Press, 1994.

Meaning of Work International Research Team. *The Meaning of Work*. London: Academic Press, 1987.

Ostrom, Elinor. "Collective Action and the Evolution of Social Norms." *Journal of Economic Perspectives*, 2000, 14(3), 137–148.

Sen, Amartya. *Development as Freedom*. New York: Alfred A. Knopf, 2000.

Williamson, Oliver. *The Economic Institutions of Capitalism*. New York: Free Press, 1985.

INDEX

About the Author

JEREMIAH J. SULLIVAN is Professor of International Business at the University of Washington in Seattle. He has been a visiting professor at New York University's Stern School of Business and at Doshisha University in Japan. He has consulted for both the U.S. Department of Commerce and the Ministry of Foreign Trade in the People's Republic of China. Among his six books are *Invasion of the Salarymen: The Japanese Business Presence in America* (Praeger) and *Exploring International Business Environments*. In addition to his research in management and international business, which has resulted in more than 50 scholarly articles, he has published articles on folklore, culture, comparative literature, and human nature.